For my RV friend Roger

Thanks for all your Bandito
hospitality & friendship -

Saddle up and ride
with Casey and me -

Rusty Richards

Praise for Rusty Richards and

Casey Tibbs – Born to Ride

Rusty Richards captures the legend of Casey Tibbs as only a close friend and fellow horseman could. The character, the sense of humor, the talent to ride a bucking horse as no other man ever has...it's all here, the story of a unique westerner, told by another.
Duncan Hunter, former U.S. Congressman

Casey Tibbs was to rodeo what Babe Ruth was to baseball, a true legend. The story of the flamboyant, dangerous and exciting lifestyle of the great saddle bronc rider and all-around champion of the world, could only be told by Casey's long time friend, Rusty Richards.
Jack Roddy, World Champion Steer Wrestler, Pro Rodeo Hall of Fame, National Cowboy Hall of Fame

This is truly a "must read" written by a great artist about a cowboy who revolutionized rodeo and the way it is viewed by the rest of the world.
John Miller, Two-Time PRCA World Champion Team Roper

Casey Tibbs touched a lot of people. Some might say he was a good guy, but the truth is, he was larger than life. Each one of us who knew him has our own Casey story. We drop his name in conversation and it's like rubbing rodeo's greatest touchstone. That Rusty Richards has a way with words, is like saying Casey Tibbs could ride a bronc. It's appropriate that Casey's biography has been written by a cowboy who is his equal.
Baxter Black, Cowboy, Poet, and Humorist

This book will bring back treasured memories to those of us who knew Casey personally and introduce those who never met him to the most colorful character I've ever met. Welcome to the world of Casey Tibbs, true friend, world-class practical joker, and above all, a cowboy.
Charlie Daniels, Musician and Singer

Casey was a prankster, great cowboy, rodeo ambassador, and master storyteller. But the stories about Casey are legendary. And now, master storyteller Rusty Richards makes Casey's exploits and personality come to life.

Red Steagall, Singer/Songwriter, Actor, and Television and Radio Personality

Rusty Richards' cowboy credentials are unquestionable, and his biography of Casey Tibbs stands to be the definitive work on one of rodeo's legends. More than that, it's a cracking good read, told with dash, humor, and authenticity.

Whether you're a rodeo fan or just fond of a cowboy tale well told, this is a book you'll want to throw a loop around. Climb aboard, hunker down, grab your slack, and let 'er buck. I guarantee you'll enjoy the ride!

J.R. Sanders, Historian and Western Author

Congratulations to Casey's longtime friend, cowboy, music man, author Rusty Richards for a job well done. *Born to Ride* is a superbly crafted, richly textured, amazing story of a true American icon, rodeo's original superstar, Casey Tibbs. Casey grew up tough during tough times and lived life to its absolute fullest – this book is a wonderful testament and journey through that life. Enjoy the ride, I sure did.

Don't pick up this astonishing book until your chores are done...I guarantee you won't be able to put it down.

Larry Mahan, Six-Time All-Around World Rodeo Champion

Over the years I have read many books about cowboys, but this book about Casey Tibbs is at the top of the list! I just wanted to tell you that I've been reading this book, and it's the best damn book about a cowboy, by a cowboy, that I have ever read, and if you aren't a cowboy by the time you finish reading it, then there was never any hope for ya!

Harry Carey Jr., Actor and Author of Company of Heroes, Life as an Actor in the John Ford Stock Company

From roundups to winning awards and insight into the very heart and soul of Casey Tibbs, this book has it all. I am honored that now I have a knowledge of a great American Legend that I will not soon forget.

For all who love a slice of the true west, a big bite of rodeo history, and just a downright great story about one exceptional man, you will love this book. Very well done. Recommended.
Shirley Johnson/Senior Reviewer MidWest Book Review

Casey Tibbs was not only one of rodeo's greatest athletes, showmen, and champion, but he was also a wonderful story-teller…. Now his life story has been told by his friend, Rusty Richards, a master story-teller himself! Congratulations, Rusty. Great book!
Bob Tallman: Seven-time Recipient of the ProRodeo Cowboy's Association "Announcer of the Year Award" and Member of the ProRodeo Hall of Fame

Having been in the publishing business for over 40 years, I truly admire the talents of Rusty Richards within this book. He has told the story of a great cowboy, Casey Tibbs, in a way only a true friend and cowboy could do. I knew Casey Tibbs very well, his sense of humor kept me on edge...
Bob Feist, T.V. Announcer for the NFR , PBR, and Steer Roping Finals, Publisher of Ropers Sports News, Producer of Bob Feist Invitational Team Roping Classic

Casey not only doubled me in the movies, he was the Godfather of my granddaughter, Carly, and a dear friend. Like so many others I admired his great cowboy skills, but I was never more proud of him than for the battles he fought near the end of his life!

Brace yourself, Rusty Richards' book, *Casey Tibbs - Born to Ride,* tells this great story beautifully. I see a terrific movie coming!
Buck Taylor, Actor, Artist, Friend, and Member of the Cowboy Hall of Fame

I have always loved Rusty Richards' songs because he is a superb storyteller. This book is like his songs: it tells a wonderful story about the life of a fascinating man, Casey Tibbs. I couldn't put it down.

Cheryl Rogers-Barnett, Entrepreneur and Author (Daughter of
Roy Rogers and Dale Evans)

The author draws you in with his skill, weaving the threads together of this great American cowboy story. Casey Tibbs was the last of a rare breed. I knew many of the charactaers in this book and was present for many of the moments. The author's writing brings them all back to life for me. I laughed and cried all over again for a great American cowboy…Casey Tibbs.

Steve Ford, Actor and Motivational Speaker (Son of former President
Gerald Ford and Betty Ford)

Casey Tibbs

Born to Ride

Rusty Richards

MOONLIGHT MESA
ASSOCIATES

CASEY TIBBS – BORN TO RIDE

Published by:

Moonlight Mesa Associates, Inc.
18620 Moonlight Mesa Rd.
Wickenburg, Arizona 85390

www.moonlightmesaassociates.com
orders@moonlightmesaassociates.com

ISBN 978-0-9774593-9-1

LCCN: 2010929399

Cover photo by David Kovar, Hollywood photographer to the stars.
Photo from Casey Tibbs' personal photo collection.

This book is dedicated to Casey's mother Florence Tibbs, my mother Ann Richards, my wife Amy Richards, and all the mothers, wives, and sweethearts of cowboys everywhere. God bless them all for their support, love, and understanding.

CONTENTS

The Champ
Acknowledgements
Introduction

Out of the Ashes - 1
Born to Ride - 11
Bustin' Loose - 23
Dances with Champions - 39
From Logs to Concrete Canyons - 55
The Best Damn Bronc Rider in the World! - 67
High Rollin' - 81
Growing Popularity - 87
The Devil Made Him Do It! - 93
Father of the National Finals Rodeo - 105
World's Fair - 117
Fiasco in a Far-Off Land - 131
The Twain Marry - 137
Success in the Far East & America's Most Beloved Rooster - 143
A New Direction - 153
More Loves and Tours - 165
A New Career - 175
Alcohol Related - 187
Love Lost…And Found - 199
His Own Counsel - 207
A World of Friends - 215
Trail Rides and More - 221
Good News…And Bad News - 227
Hell, I *Was* Good! – 241

THE CHAMP*

Palm up, he lifted the rein up high
Like a gift he was giving to God
And the gate swung wide as a mute "Outside,"
From his hat brim tipped the nod.

Within the bronc, like boiling sin
All systems launched the plan
Inspired by rage and turbo charged
To rid themselves of man.

But sparkling rowels rose near the mane
As pommel and chaps squeaked rosin
Rough locked, the Champ endured the wait
That the mark out rule was causin'.

But power and speed were building
As the roar of the crowd was heard
And spur clad boots reached deep in the bows
Like the feet of a diving bird.

No thought of failure mars the plan
In the mind of a bronc born to buck,
But a champion rides with a plan that resides
In his mind, that is far more than luck.

A duck to the left or a kick at the flank
As cleverness conquered power
His free hand stretched back in a teaspoon sign
As if he was picking a flower.

With a rhythm and timing like a poem that's rhyming
It was beauty and grace to the whistle,
As shedding fur balls drifted in pairs
Like the down of a flowering thistle.

Ignoring the pickup, he landed
And doubled the bronc by the rein,
Loosened the flank and unsaddled him
And stood in the thistle flower rain.

A flick of an eyelash moment,
Separating the future and past
Captured the great Casey Tibbs in his prime
And forever in bronze it's been cast.

"Ride Cowboy, Ride," is carved inside the heart
As it was in the heart of our friend
Who was Cowboy, Legend, and Showman,
And a Champion, right to the end!

Rusty Richards, 1992

*Reprinted courtesy of Saddleback Publishing

ACKNOWLEDGEMENTS

I wish to express a very special thank you to my wife, Amy. It was her idea for me to write this book, and her help and encouragement has been endless. She was somehow able to read my not-so-great handwriting and type the manuscript up. She was a great sounding board and listened critically to what I had written. She believed in my ability to write and kept me going in so many ways. Her help in putting the various stories in chronological order, as well as keeping track of names and photos, was invaluable. She spent hours on the phone taking care of the many details. Thank you, Amy. You are the best.

I must thank Becky Coffield of Moonlight Mesa Associates for her enthusiasm, belief in the value of this book, her support and ruthless editing. I must also thank Vin Libassi for the beautiful cover design.

I also wish to thank the many folks who took time to share with me their memories, or who gave their kind advice in other areas of this book. I also wish to express my deepest apologies to any of you kind folks whose names we may have omitted. We have tried our best to include everyone, but this book is twenty years in the making, and over that period of time, I am sure we have not done everyone justice.

Gil Aguirre, Eddy Akridge, Noureen Baer, C.R. Baucher, Charlie Beals, Buck Bean, Milos (Sharkey) Begovich, Benny Binion, Budd Boettigher, Wilford Brimley, Jack Buschbom, Marilyn and Harry Carey, Jr., Lorie (Collins) Carnall, Stu Carnall, Lex Connelly, Deb Copenhaver, Alex Cord, David Corlew, Suzanne Creps, Lewis Cryer, Arlo Curtis, Charlie Daniels, Royal Dano, Doctor DeKock, Dawn Denzer, Beth (Tibbs) Donley, Pete and Olive Dunsmore, Manuel Enos, Pat Feeney, Bob Feist, Steve Ford, Ron Foreman, Clifford Fravel, Neal Gay, Renee (D'Balsac) Gonzalves, Alice Greenough, Margie Greenough, Turk Greenough, Jason Hagan, Bill Hancock, Sonny Hancock, Casey Hannum, Katie (Tibbs) Hannum, Lloyd Hannum, Ed Hayes, Jim Heard, Arnold Hill, Billy Hogue, Regina (Murphy Tibbs) Holloway, Billy Huckabee, Carl Huckfeldt, Betty Huff, Bob Hughs, Duncan Hunter, Stan Immenschuh, Buster and June Ivory,

Andy and Camile Jauregui, Andrina Jauregui, Maurine Jauregui, C.R. Jones, C.T. Jones, Ben and Carol Johnson, Burt Kennedy, Louis L'Amour, Carrie Lattimer, Rick Le Fevour, Anne Lockhart, Steve and Connie Long, Larry Mahan, John H. Manhold, Harley May, Doug McClure, Donnie McFadden, Larry McKinney, Bill Merkel, John Miller, Doug Moeller, Tony Moiso, Dolly (Tibbs) Muir, Pat and Grace Mulloy, Willie Nelson, Eddie Nordquist, Bob O'Donald, Chuck and Sheila Parkinson, George Peck, Joe Pepper, Homer Pettigrew, Jerry Potter, Gene Pruett, Glen and Lynn Randall, Dean Redfield, Ace Reed, Lloyd Ripkema, E.C. Roberts, Gerald Roberts, Jack Roddy, Cheryl Rogers-Barnett, Cotton Rosser, Rex Rossi, Fern Sawyer, Happy Shahan, Jim and Sharon Shoulders, Claire Anne (Douthit) Stewart, Adam Taylor, Buck Taylor, Harry Thompkins, Ancel Tibbs, Ardie Tibbs, Frank (Shortlog) Tibbs, Tommy Tibbs, Thad and Nyla Tibbs, Robert and Mikki Totten, Betty Ulmet, Billy Ward, Mike Warner, Harvey West, Bill White, Jo Jo Whitefeather, Dean Williams, Ruth Witeman.

With sincere thanks to the many talented photographers whose images of Casey Tibbs and others still continue to inspire us.

Ben Allen, George W. Baker, George and Lawrence Barrs, Ferrel Butler, James Cathey, Foxie, JJJ Photo, S. Haffey, J.B. Harris, Hasselbrock, O.J. Hebrank, DeVere Helfrich, L.E. Henderson, Irene's Studio, David Kovar, Miller Studio, Raymond L. Pound, Eddie Rocco, Ed Smyth, Stewart's Photography, Homer Ventners.

'

INTRODUCTION

The sun had not yet broken into the black of the sky. With cups of hot coffee warming our hands, my wife Amy and I sat and waited, filled with quiet excitement. The words of that old cowboy song rang through my mind: *I started up the trail October twenty-third...I started up the trail with the 2-U Herd, come a ti-yi-yippee....* As soon as it turned light on that chilly morning of October 23, 1983, we planned to go out to the old Tibbs home-place where Casey was born, where John Tibbs, Casey's father, had operated under the 2-U brand!

Amy and I had already driven fifty miles that morning from Fort Pierre where we'd slept under a handmade quilt made by Casey's mother, at the home of Casey Tibbs' sister, Katie Hannum and her husband Lloyd. Now we waited with Katie in the kitchen of Fio and Lory Tibbs, and when it finally grew light, we started out.

There was no road. As we drove over grassy hills and crossed through wire-gated fences, not a tire mark or a turned blade of grass signaled the homestead's location. At last we crested a small ridge, and there the house sat beneath us, nestled in a small drift of leafless trees.

The experience was unforgettable. The house and barn of hand-hewn logs still stood, though just barely. Part of the sod roof was missing, but where it remained I could see the stubble of dry grasses and the last remnants of wildflowers that still bloomed there each spring.

The corrals and sheds remained partially in place. Some were tumbled down, but I could see how it had all been. Katie Hannum pointed out another crumbling shack – Old Thad's shack. Ol' Thad had been John Tibbs' lifelong friend and business partner.

A wagon rested in the yard with the harness still in the seat where Casey's brother Shortlog had left it when he'd unhitched the team for the last time. Weathered over all those years of changing seasons, the leather looked so brittle that had I picked it up it would have fallen apart. On the walls of the barn rigid old bridles hung in a casual row, exactly where they'd once hung for daily use. Part of a hand-crank ice cream maker lay in the grass next to the house, and farther out sat the wheels and frame from Casey's baby buggy. The whole place made me feel as if I were peeking into the private lives of a wonderful, rugged, western family. The scene filled me with awe, and I felt moved by the experience.

I first met Casey Tibbs in the late fifties on a movie set, not long before he won his last World Champion Saddle Bronc Riding title in 1959. He'd always been a hero to me, like he'd been to so many other young men. In my teen years it would have been the thrill of a lifetime just to catch a glimpse of him through a knothole in the fence. My admiration bordered on worship, and I still marvel that, outside of my family, he became my closest friend.

As we drove back to California, Amy and I could think and talk of nothing but Casey Tibbs and that old home-place. What struck us was the reality that people of our generation – the generation of space travel, computers, high-rise buildings, automobiles, and supersonic jets – had actually lived so recently such a harsh, pioneering lifestyle. Casey had literally been raised in a log cabin, then later had dined with presidents and royalty. What a story!

"Casey Tibbs is such a great American character – a legend – I can't believe no one has written his biography," I commented to Amy.

"Yes," she agreed, and after a few moments of thought added, "And you're just the one to write it!"

Taken aback, I argued against the idea. I wasn't that kind of writer. Casey Tibbs' life story was too important to be fictionalized, or worse, not written at all, but I was not a biographer.

"This story has got to be written by a cowboy," Amy continued. "You've spent your life breaking and training horses, you've rodeoed enough to know the lifestyle, and you've worked in the picture business. You're acquainted with most of Casey's friends. You're so familiar with the main areas of Casey's life, I think you could do it."

Inspired by Amy's encouragement, I presented the idea to Casey. After some trepidation, he agreed. When I gave Casey a few completed chapters, I didn't hear from him for quite some time. But then I finally got an excited phone call.

"I like it! I like it!" he shouted over the phone. "My folks in South Dakota are gonna like it, too. Keep on goin'. Write me some more!"

I hope the reader agrees with Casey. I also hope the reader will see the man as I saw him – a giant among men who struggled to the top from humble beginnings to become a world champion with an unbeaten record, a man who amassed a fortune twice and lost it, an athlete who saw rodeo as a sport and not a spectacle, a man who loved to laugh and loved a good practical joke, a man who faced alcoholism and arose a champion again.

I give you my friend, Casey Tibbs.

Rusty Richards
November 2010

Casey Tibbs

Born to Ride

Rusty Richards

OUT OF THE ASHES

Around midnight, April 2, 1887, in Highmore, South Dakota, the wildfire hit, setting the sky and rolling prairie aglow as the billowing columns of smoke reached the perfect mixture of gas and air and ignited into huge balls of fire. The conflagration had traveled more than twenty miles when it struck Tom and Nettie Tibbs' place. The same wind that brought it blew it into a raging inferno.

Tom's first thought was for the safety of his family. It'd been only a little more than five years since Nettie and he had married on January 3, 1882, yet already their family had grown to include five children.

A wave of relief swept over Tom and Nettie when they finally reached the plowed ground where they knew their children would be safe. But their relief was to be short lived, for a tragedy of the highest magnitude was about to strike.

As Tom viewed the scene of raging destruction, his thoughts turned to his livestock. The animals would perish if he didn't take action to save them. Tom told Nettie that she and the children must stay in the safety of the plowed area while he ran back to release their trapped animals.

Nettie and the young children waited, huddling together, frightened and worried about Tom. Then the wind shifted, changing the course of the fire.

Nettie told the children to stay where they were while she ran to warn Tom of the change.

Afraid for his mother and dad, their eldest son, five-year-old Frank, also ran toward the barn to help. But Nettie and little Frank misjudged the behavior of the fire, and the flames surrounded them. When Tom discovered what had happened, he rushed into the fire to save his wife and child.

Tom suffered severe burns, but through his valiant actions he brought both of his loved ones out of the flames. However, eighteen hours later his little son died. Six hours after the loss of Frank, his beloved wife also passed away.

Tom endured unimaginable grief and pain. In an attempt to give him relief from the physical pain, members of his family rigged up a harness, and for two weeks lowered him into the cold water of the well.

Over time, Tom recovered his health and later remarried. His new wife, Kate, a gentle and good woman, was well liked and respected by those who knew her. For the next six years she did her best to replace the mother the children had so tragically lost. Even so, the day came when two of Tom's remaining sons, John (Casey's father), and Elza decided to run away.

The two lads took very little with them besides their horses. They decided to try their luck finding work in the area of Fort Pierre, South Dakota, but when they came to the Missouri River, they found it to be a formidable barrier. Their luck improved when they found a ferryboat captained by a kindly soul. He put them to work and fed them until they'd earned enough for the fare. When they landed on the other side of the river, the captain gave them a little money and wished them well.

John Tibbs later told his son, Ancel, that he and Elza immediately went to a bakeshop in Fort Pierre and bought rolls. Not long after their arrival, however, Tom caught up with them and returned them home to Highmore.

The two boys struck out on their own again a year or so later, taking only one horse this time, a somewhat cantankerous old mare who was hard to catch and would sneak off every chance she got. Some uncertainty remains about the exact age of the brothers at this time. A family member described them as having been "just little brats." This was true, but they were also capable, which is evidenced by a story they told in later years.

While still on the east side of the river, they spotted a rattlesnake. Not as common in that area as snakes are on the west side of the Missouri, the boys sure wanted to kill it. But they'd found themselves in a desolate place on a half-outlaw mare with nothing nearby they could use to kill the rattler. So, they eased down off the mare's back and John, knowing the horse's tendency to run off, locked his arms around her neck and hung on tight. Elza took her bridle off, killed the rattlesnake with it, re-bridled her, and the two remounted and went on their way.

Ahead lie the Missouri River again, only this time they saw no ferryboat, so their only option was to swim the horse across the river. With John on her back and Elza holding onto her tail, the old mare eased into the river, and they made the dangerous trip across to the other side without incident. This time their father decided that if the boys wanted their independence so badly, then that's the way it would be -- he did not go after them again.

Elza went to work for Scotty Phillips' Buffalo Ranch, and John soon found work as a wrangler for the Moore Brothers' Ranch. Dave Moore, a horse buyer, recognized John's natural talent with horses. That talent came into full bloom after Dave "took him under his wing." Folks who remember the boys say that both John and Elza were skillful with horses, and that John was an exceptionally pretty bronc rider.

Throughout John's teenage years he worked as a cowboy for David Moore, the Diamond A Ranch, Henry Angell, and the Turkey Track Ranch.

Henry Angell, an industrious man in Fort Pierre, had varied business interests. While working for him, John's life took a happy turn when he met the lovely Florence Leggett. Born in Mainsgrove, Iowa, on December 14, 1889, Florence had come to South Dakota with her parents, Ike and Nettie Leggett, and her brothers, Clarence and Wall.

Around the turn of the century, the Leggetts homesteaded at a place called Antelope Creek. As a teenager, Florence worked as a waitress in a restaurant in Fort Pierre owned by Henry Angell. This is where she and

John met. For their first date, John asked Florence to accompany him to a dance, and thus began a courtship that lasted several years.

John's chosen life as a cowboy made it difficult for him to call on Florence regularly, but mail service was available at the distant outposts where he worked, so the two stayed in touch.

John was offered more permanent positions wherever he went, yet he continued to move about. He wanted something more out of life than to be just a valued worker -- he wanted something to call his own.

He finally got a taste of true independence when he met Thad Benton, a storekeeper, moonshiner, trapper, and wild horse runner. Benton, or "Ol' Thad" as he became known, knew that part of the Dakotas as well as any man in his time. As a young man he'd come from Ohio with a surveying crew and had helped to draw many of the old maps. Thad had a "store" down on the Cheyenne River, at a place called Rousseau. Thad's store was the entire "town," for the log building contained the store, post office, and the whole population of Rousseau -- Thad Benton.

John and Ol' Thad really hit it off right from the start. They discovered they both liked the same kinds of things, especially the South Dakota horses, and they struck up a friendship that was to last a lifetime. During the winter they ran trap lines, selling the furs of animals they snared. These were happy times for both, and in later years John would often share stories from those days with his family. Casey, his eyes dancing with pleasure as he recalled his father telling of a particular incident, surely must have looked a lot like John looked when he told this story.

Casey recalled, "Dad loved to tell one story on Ol' Thad. They'd gone down at night to check some traps near their camp, and killed a big ol' bobcat down along a creek. Ol' Thad, he'd been alookin' at him and sayin', 'Damn! Boy, he's a big one!' Then they dragged him up out of there -- he was dead but still warm -- and Ol' Thad threw the big cat over his shoulder as they started back up the bank."

Casey chuckled, "Now Dad's walkin' along behind Thad in the dark, and Dad picks up a sharp stick and just reaches over and pokes the ol' cat hard, in against Thad. Ol' Thad lets out a holler and throws that bobcat out in the brush, jumps off the bank into the creek bed where he shadow-boxes him, yellin', 'Watch 'im, John! He's still alive! He damn near got me!' Dad was bent over laughin', tryin' to keep Thad from hearin' him. Damn, Dad used to love to tell that story!"

Both Thad and John were excellent horsemen, and they began to run horses on the open plains. Unmarked or un-branded horses were called slicks and became the property of anyone who could catch and brand them. John and Thad would break and train these horses, then sell them through auctions held in Fort Pierre, or private sales to families or ranches in the area.

During the time John worked for Henry Angell someone offered him a better job, but when he tried to quit the old man wouldn't let him go. Henry pleaded with John, saying, "Oh no! You can't quit me now, man. I need you!" So John stayed on another six months, but meanwhile he did everything he could to irritate the old man, trying to get Henry to fire him. John Tibbs had a keen sense of humor, and he drew pleasure from pulling pranks on his boss. It's also clear, however, that the two men actually cared a great deal about each other.

When Halloween came, John put Henry's surrey on top of Henry's barn. One neighbor, who'd ridden over just to see this sight and have a good laugh, asked the old man who'd done it. Henry looked up and squalled, "Gawd, oh Gawd! Tibbs -- Tibbs!"

The neighbor asked why he didn't fire John. "I have," he moaned. "But he won't quit!" Henry had become so exasperated with John's endless pranks that he'd finally fired him, but true to form, John had just kept on working, pretending he'd never heard.

On October 31, 1908, John Tibbs married Florence Leggett at the home of their friend, Henry Angell. Soon after their marriage, John spotted a section of ground on the south side of the Cheyenne River that seemed perfect for a homestead for him and his new bride. It consisted of a small, somewhat protected valley with a ridge that ran down into a steep walled canyon. The canyon had a sandy bottom, and the walls grew wider apart until they eventually spread out like two open arms onto the plains. The pattern made a perfect, natural trap for horses. John's plan was to build his big main corral right at the top of that finger, which extended down into the deep trap of the canyon.

It was an ambitious plan, as they had to build a house, all the corrals and chutes, barns, and outbuildings. Only when one considers that the wood for all this construction had to be located, felled, trimmed, dragged to the site by horses, fitted for placement, and finally put into place, can a person fully comprehend the enormity of this undertaking.

John's longtime friend, Thad, invited the newly married couple to stay with him at his store at Rousseau on the Cheyenne River. Three miles stretched from there to the new homestead, and the newlyweds spent their days hauling timber and building their new home.

Thad Benton became caught up in the spirit of the adventure; he pitched in and worked strenuously alongside his young friends. Occasionally, neighbors or more distant relatives would trek out to the site and lend a hand, but for the most part they labored alone, just the three of them.

They had no water source right at the home place, but a spring lie about a quarter mile away. They hitched a team to a stone-boat, which was nothing more than a heavy sled onto which they lashed barrels, dragged it to the spring, filled the barrels with water, then dragged it home again -- countless times.

Each day their livestock had to be trailed to the spring to water, morning and evening, then returned to the site. The horses had to be let out to graze and then caught again to work. These chores, repeated again and again, took a big chunk out of each working day.

Winter in South Dakota is sometimes severe, making it necessary to lay in copious amounts of firewood, food stores, and other supplies. As they faced their first winter alone in this desolate location without any modern conveniences -- no electricity, no running water, no phone, or any supermarkets -- it's difficult to imagine the amount of pressure this young couple must have felt. Still, it's not hard to see that it was also a time of joy and high adventure.

Florence became pregnant, but she worked on at the homestead until late in her pregnancy. When her time neared, she returned to her family home on Antelope Creek to be with her mother for the baby's delivery. John stayed on at their homestead near Mission Ridge and continued the work.

The love John felt for the family he'd left so long ago in Highmore, South Dakota, became apparent after his children were born. He named their first baby Tom after his grandfather; in later years they named another son Frank, after the brother John had lost in the horrific fire. Still later they named a daughter Katie, to honor the stepmother who had raised John after the tragic death of his mother.

Thad Benton eventually moved out to the Tibbs' place to live full time. They built a small dwelling behind the main house for him, and it became known as "Ol' Thad's shack."

The horse trap worked perfectly, and the operation succeeded in the way that John had envisioned it would at the outset. John and Florence Tibbs' family grew to include eight more children. They had ten children in all: Tommy, Velma (Dolly Muir), Ancel, Frank (Shortlog), Regina (Murphy Holloway), Katie (Hannum), Johnny, Ardie (Cook), Thad (Doc), and Casey. As each of them became old enough, they pitched in and helped with the chores.

The main corral proved to be the center of excitement for the whole family, and all the children, the boys especially, became expert horsemen. The last of the children, Casey, was destined to become famous the world over through the very skills that he would learn there. John Tibbs taught him, as did Casey's older brothers, his old friend Thad Benton, and a helpful and kindly neighbor, Albert Lopez, who was the head wrangler for the Diamond A Ranch. Of course, Casey also learned from the thousands of horses that passed through that trap and into the great corral. This background, coupled with a tremendous desire to excel, laid the groundwork for the youngster who set a goal for himself to become "the best damned bronc rider that ever lived."

John and Florence with Dolly and Tommy, ca. 1912

The Old Homestead, ca. 1934
Insert of John and Florence Tibbs

BORN TO RIDE

Florence Tibbs suffered great difficulties with Casey's delivery. A midwife came to stay with her, and Dolly, who was eighteen by then, also assisted. Florence's labor lasted for three days and was a time of tremendous anxiety for the entire family. Katie recalled hurrying home from school each day and running into the house asking, "Is the baby born yet?" only to be answered with a solemn, "No, not yet."

On the third day, March 5, 1929, Katie ran into the room, nearly out of breath, and once more asked, "Is the baby born yet?"

The midwife, Mrs. Duffy, turned around, still holding the infant in her hands. "Yes, and here he is!" Casey had just arrived, and with those words she placed the newborn gently in Katie's arms. Katie said it seemed to her as if she never put him down again, as it became her job to help with the care and raising of the new baby, a job she relished.

Katie glowed with affection whenever she remembered the endless hours of carrying Casey in her arms, saying that to her it was just as if he were her own baby. In later years when she married and had children of her own, she named one of them Casey.

As Casey grew, it must have seemed as if the whole world focused solely on him. His family loved him and played with him often. John loved to play with all the children, and his favorite game with Casey was to get down on all fours, wait until the boy was set with a firm double handhold on his big suspenders, and then "buck" as hard as he could.

Casey remembered with joy how this game grew in intensity, until John had to buck and whirl with all his power to throw him off, but buck him off he inevitably did. Casey said, "It's a wonder I never got any serious injuries, 'cause sometimes I would fly through the air until I'd hit the wall, sometimes clear up near the ceiling!"

Thad Benton was just like an uncle to the children, and they all love to tell stories involving him. He was really quite a character and remained so until he died. He always smoked, and he preferred roll-your-own cigarettes. He had the habit of sitting down cross-legged wherever he might be to roll one, even in town -- right in the middle of the sidewalk.

Katie said that one of the children's favorite games was to cook up mischief that would provoke Ol' Thad enough to get him to swear. "We loved to hear him cuss," she said, "because he did it so well.

"We really did love the old guy like an uncle," Katie continued, "but I used to get so mad at him! When Casey was about two, he'd go down to the corral when Thad was branding and castrating horses. Thad would feed him those oysters, black as coal, right out of the branding fire. Casey would stand there with that blood and black running out of his mouth, and I'd get so mad at that old guy!"

Laughing, Katie went on, "Then at night, when it was time for Casey to go to bed, Casey would follow me around and say, 'Seester, I wanna go to bed.' You know, he'd be tired, and Mother was too busy with cooking for so many and everything. But Ol' Thad would mock him, 'Seester!' he'd say, and I'd get so angry at him for picking on Casey.

"Mom and Dad went somewhere and I was supposed to be the boss. Casey got up in Dad's big chair -- he was no bigger than a minute -- and grabbed Dad's pipe, stuck it in his mouth, crossed his legs, and started giving orders." Katie laughed.

A strong bond of affection grew between Casey and Ol' Thad, but much to Casey's dismay, Thad took to calling him "Booger-face." Casey's skill with horses had developed at a very early age. His instincts for "thinkin' like a horse" were keen, and even though he didn't care much for his new name, it always made him feel a little proud when Thad would say, "I'll just take ol' Booger-face here, and we can gather the whole damn herd."

When Casey talked about Thad Benton, a certain respect crept into his voice for his old friend, the same respect that showed up whenever he spoke about his father. It tickled Casey that Thad had lost a spur, and as long as Casey could remember Thad only wore one. He'd tell Casey, "If I get one side goin', the other side will get goin' too!"

It wasn't only the girls who enjoyed provoking Thad into a good round of cussing; Casey took his turn at this game as well. One time, though, it didn't work. Thad had a big chunk of mirror that he'd prop up under a tree just outside his shack. One morning Ol' Thad was hunkered down in front of his mirror shaving when Casey spotted him. Casey circled quietly around behind the house and found a small rock. Peeking around the corner, he took careful aim and caught the mirror dead center, shattering it.

Pleased with his success, he waited eagerly for the creative outpouring he knew would follow, but Ol' Thad was a jump ahead of him. Without reacting in any way, he reached down, picked up a tiny piece of the broken mirror, put it into place, and continued shaving. Casey chuckled when he recalled the incident, and how easily Ol' Thad had gotten the best of him. Later, when Casey got within range, Thad, who had been biding his time, reached out and grabbed him, applying his favorite method of discipline -- a good hard pinch.

Although the Tibbs' homestead seems an odd place for one, Florence had a baby buggy for Casey. He rode in it during two periods in his life: first as an infant, then after he grew a little older and rediscovered it, he would drag it to the top of the hill above the house, climb in and coast down, crashing somewhere at the bottom. He continued until the buggy's wheels would no longer roll.

He dragged goats, calves, and even pigs up to the top of the hill, then rode them down. Little Casey became quite adept at staying aboard as the animals leaped and bounded down the hill. One old billygoat proved to be the most challenging. The whole process of getting him to the top of the hill and then riding him down became good entertainment for the whole family. An audience for Casey's antics made the bruises or black eyes worth it to him.

The Tibbs family thrived on humor, and Casey became a master of the practical joke at a tender age. His life included an endless chain of pranks, such as pouring out Ol' Thad's moonshine and replacing it with vinegar, or hiding behind the seat of Dugan Rheborg's car when Dugan drove Casey's sister, Ardie, up the hill so the couple could be alone.

"We heard him giggling," Ardie exclaimed, "and, oh! Dugan did get mad. He chased Casey clear down the side of the hill."

***

In the early thirties, times grew hard for John and Florence Tibbs and their family. They'd struggled through the Depression only to face the terrible drought that followed, which resulted in the loss of most of their livestock. They were finally forced to sell off half their land to raise enough money to pay the taxes in order to keep the remainder.

Pat Feeney, a long-time friend of the Tibbs, recalled, "A lot of people lost horses; most of the horses that made it through to wintertime were winter-killed 'cause there was nothing for them to eat. It was really rugged. Scores of people just packed up and left. You'd see them load up their old cars and head for California. The county wound up owning all the land in western South Dakota. I can't tally it accurately, but if I was to estimate, I think the county seized for back taxes at least 70 percent of all the land between here and the Wyoming line. This became an opportunity for me, and I bought all the land I could buy for fifty cents an acre, ten cents down and five years to pay for it. Folks have asked why I didn't buy a lot more…well, I didn't have the dime."

As a result of the drought, antelope and deer died off all over the area, as well as the horses and cattle. John lost a big percentage of his herd, as even those that had foraged on brush and whatever else they could find were unable to withstand the severe winter that followed.

Casey was only about five years old at the time and had been riding a little mare called Pee Wee. Deep into that terrible drought, Casey worried about his horse. But Pee Wee was one of those that made it through with an assist from Casey who fed her the corn silks that had been the stuffing in his own mattress.

"In the dirty thirties," Casey said, "Dad had to scatter his horses all over hell to try to find grazin' enough to keep 'em alive. He moved a herd of 500 head over near a place called Ottumwa, South Dakota. Red River was among 'em, and he was just a colt then. Of that huge herd only 23 survived the winter, but Red River was one of 'em!"

Through all of this, the Tibbs kept their spirits high. As Casey put it, "I didn't know we were poor until after I left home." Florence gave of herself tirelessly; she often stayed up all night making clothes on a treadle sewing machine. Whenever the girls had a special event of any kind coming up, she would be sure they had a new dress to wear for the occasion. John always arose early and fixed breakfast for the whole family so that Florence could get a little much-needed sleep.

Every one of the Tibbs family takes on an almost reverent tone whenever they speak of Florence, expressing gratitude for the many things she did for them and for others. Dolly recalled, "When I was young, my older brother Tommy and I would go to dances together on horseback. In the wintertime it would be bitter cold, but when we got home Mother would always have put heated bricks in our beds to warm them. It would feel so good when I'd crawl into that bed. She also sewed for all of us and did anything else she could for us. Oh, Mother was quite a woman. She was so good to us all."

One day while walking on the hillside above their home, Florence discovered water seeping from the ground. It was just a small wet patch, but the whole family turned-to and dug into the side of the hill. Before long the hole began to fill with water. They cemented the sides of the spring, covered it, then ran a pipe to the house. The spring provided just a trickle, but it kept the water barrel full. To Florence that trickle of water was pure heaven, and to Doc, who usually had the arduous chore of hauling water to the house, it was a godsend.

Excitement always brewed down at the corrals as John, Ol' Thad, and the boys worked endlessly at making "using horses" out of the wild-range broncs they gathered. It was not uncommon for the horses to "blow up and buck" in the early stages, but it was frowned upon if one of them did this after a certain point in their training.

One particular horse, Red River, had been given to Doc for his own use. Red River was inclined to blow up and buck whenever he took the notion, which was a habit Doc hated. One day Red River bucked so hard he threw Doc to the ground, breaking Doc's arm. The horse passed to five-year-old Casey.

Casey soon discovered he could ride the best that Red River had to offer, and instead of breaking the horse from bucking, Casey began to look for ways to get him to buck more. Keeping this from coming to the attention of his father, the horse served as a training aid that helped pave the way into Casey's future.

Of his father, Casey said, "Dad was a rugged individual who worked and played hard. It might be three months before he'd have a drink of whiskey or go into Ft. Pierre, but when he did he'd make up for it. When Dad got to wantin' to go to town, he'd always say, 'I gotta go after peanut butter.' I don't know if he even *ate* peanut butter, but I guess that was his way of lettin' Mom know he needed a break. But whenever there was work to be done, he'd save the toughest for himself; he was sort of the mainstay of the neighborhood. He had the only ice house, the best work teams and wagons, and the only saw-engine for sawing wood, which he shared with all the neighbors."

One of the Tibbs' few neighbors, Albert Lopez, spotted Casey's skill with horses and hired the ten-year-old boy to break colts for him. Casey's memories of Albert Lopez all seemed to be fond ones. Albert helped Casey acquire some equipment of his own, such as ropes and hobbles. Lopez wasn't a wealthy man in terms of dollars. He'd worked for the

Diamond A Cattle Company for many years and spent most of his life on the open range, coming to realize that the wealth he enjoyed came in many forms. Albert paid Casey five dollars per head for training his colts. He also paid him with equipment, advice, laughter, and most of all, friendship. He was a generous man, and he gave of himself and his time, especially to young people.

It's easy to see the great appeal Albert held for Casey when one sums up everything Albert had to offer. He offered not only friendship laced with a sense of humor equal to Casey's, but he also offered Casey a chance to earn money by riding a bunch of horses that could really buck. Moreover, Albert shared the same values that had already been instilled in Casey by his family, values such as self-sufficiency, love for the land and nature, respect for his fellow man, and most especially love of horses.

Albert Lopez's philosophy (practical experience along with book learning, learning about the weather, respecting a blizzard, saddling ponies, and learning the ways of the land) describes Casey's school years pretty well. Storms had to be taken seriously. Often the children were unable to return to their homes from school because of blizzards -- at times for a week or more.

Betty Ulmet, a fellow student, shared a few memories of those early days. "The weather was terrible! Only seven children attended the school at that time: my older sister Dorothy, a younger sister Ruth, plus four Tibbs children: Murphy, Ardie, Thad, and Casey. The school was located on the Tibbs' side of Bush Creek, built right down alongside it. We had to cross the creek to get to school. The banks were twelve to fifteen feet deep, straight up and down, so we had to ride our horses across a narrow foot bridge with a squat little rail on each side, about four feet high. Rainstorms often made the river rise six or eight feet. The water would rush down through there, and the horses would be really scared. We children had to whip our horses to get them to go across. It was very dangerous; I don't know how our parents let us do that. I guess they had no choice.

"In the wintertime, we took turns bringing beans to school, and we would hang them in a big pot down inside the wood stove and cook them for our lunch. The school had one room with a little entrance area attached, and rattlesnakes would get under the space beneath the floorboards. You could hear them rattling under there in warmer weather, and we would jump over the threshold because we didn't know if there was a rattlesnake under there.

"Casey was in the first grade when I was in the fifth. I remember him as being a very cute little boy with blond curls all over his head. He always wore a big smile, and he kind of swaggered when he walked, like he'd been riding a horse, you know?"

For Casey, breaking colts on the way to school became a major part of each school day. He often took a whole string of colts with him, checking his trap lines as he went. He recalled a time when all of his brothers were off doing things on their own. "Just Dad and I were home at that time, and I was helpin' him break these work broncs. We'd been arguing back and forth, jawin' at one another like father and son will. Dad was up on the seat of the wagon holdin' the lines, and we had one broke horse hitched up next to a green bronc. I'm settin' on Red River, holdin' what we called the 'g-string,' a line hooked to the green bronc I could easily dally off to my saddle horn and control the green bronc with. I could hold him back or let him out.

"Well, we cut them horses loose from the hitchin' post and I let them out -- dang near clear to the end of my line. Dad was just on this old flatbed wagon, and he could ride the hell out of it. So I let him go up over that first little ridge there, and then a plow and a road drag appeared and I let him hit it. The wagon bounced up over it and he was a hollerin', 'Eeee! Eeee! Eeee!' and just bitin' down on that ol' pipe. Well, he stayed on and when we got over the top, I let him out a little more, and he knocked over a gate post.

"There was a fill spot on the dirt road where we'd just dug a culvert, so I let him hit that, too. It was a hard enough jolt to knock a rim off a wheel, and then the spokes started goin', and we just barely managed to limp the wagon back in.

"He'd been too busy to hear me laughin', but I'd been havin' hell tryin' to keep from it. Dad never said a word. I knew he was mad, but he never said anything. I thought sure he was goin' to get out the razor strop, although he hadn't used it on me in a long time. We just unharnessed the horses and put them up, and it looked like that was to be the end of it....

"At the time, I was breakin' this squatty, three-year-old mare for Ol' Thad, and she was tougher than hell. I could just barely ride her in the corral. I'd ridden her inside the corral longer than I normally would have 'cause she was just so tough, and I was kinda hatin' to take her outside.

"I saddled the mare up and let her soak a little. Then Mother hollered us in for supper, so we went in to eat, and I filled up on bread and gravy. After supper, Dad saddled up a horse, figurin' he'd ride with me when I took that tough old mare outside for the first time.

"I come out and got on that son of a gun, and Dad and me went right down across the creek bed and up this little pinnacle. I couldn't figure out why he was headin' right for the top of it.

"Old Thad had this little dachshund he called Sittin' Bull that was always followin' us around. Well, as soon as we got up on top of that hill, Dad sicced ol' Sittin' Bull on me.

"Well, dang! That mare jumped and kicked and went to buckin', and that little dog just kept a yappin' at her. She bucked down off of there through a little lakebed and some weeds. I was just barely hangin' on, and then that dog would run up and grab her again. The mare *finally* bucked off into the fork of a creek and stopped. My tongue was hangin' out. Dad rode up and I yelled at him, 'Get that dog out of here!' He just said, 'I heard you hollerin', and I thought you were callin' him.' He'd found a way to get even with me."

Although some enjoyed it more than others, all of John Tibbs' sons inherited their father's ability to ride broncs. Tommy entered the bronc riding in only two rodeos in his lifetime, but he won them both. When asked why he didn't pursue it more, Tommy said, "Because Dad was so set against it."

John provided bucking horses for a number of rodeos, and although most of the men he dealt with were good men, he felt that all too often those who followed the rodeos were shiftless and simply dodging honest work. The fact that he had lost halters and even saddles in the course of having his stock used at rodeos, didn't help matters any. John felt that hard work was the way to improve oneself. Whether a man worked for himself or another man's outfit, he measured his own worth by an honest day's work. This was the standard John lived by, and he wanted his sons to follow in his way. All of them did, Casey included. For although his desire "to become the best damned bronc rider in the world" was not to be denied, no one who ever knew Casey would argue that he always gave 110 percent to whatever he had striven to accomplish.

***

Every year on the Fourth of July, Fort Pierre hosts a rodeo, and it's a big day of celebration there. The Tibbs family always made the fifty-mile trek to celebrate this holiday in grand style. John Tibbs often provided bucking horses for this rodeo, and it was here that the excitement generated by the roar of the crowd first trickled into Casey's veins. Surprisingly, it was not in the riding events that Casey first enjoyed attention from the grandstands.

The Fravels were probably the Tibbs' closest neighbors. According to Clifford Fravel, Casey first appeared in the Fort Pierre Rodeo at seven or eight years of age as a rope spinner and did that for a couple of years before he ever entered the riding events.

The Tibbs family enjoyed another form of entertainment: radio. They only turned it on briefly and for special programs, for the electricity to run it had to be stored in batteries charged by a wind generator.

John would make sure that the whole family gathered around before he turned the radio on. The prizefights were a particular favorite with Casey, and he daydreamed about one day becoming a fighter. He even sent away for a book entitled *How To Box*, by the great champion Joe Louis.

In those days many rodeos around the country broadcast the action over the radio. John loved to tune in to these broadcasts, as it gave him an opportunity to see how well his stock performed. Casey said he would never forget the night his father woke him up to listen to the radio broadcast of the rodeo from Sidney, Iowa. Casey was just about ten years old at the time. He later remarked, "Since Dad didn't want any of us boys to follow rodeo, he really made a mistake with me that night. When I heard the announcer saying things like, 'That was Wildfire, one of the great broncs from the string of John Tibbs of Fort Pierre,' I knew I had to be a part of it!"

Casey Tibbs, 1935. The future bronc-riding champion of the world!

Five-year old Casey on Red River ca.1934

BUSTIN' LOOSE

As Casey entered his teens, he never lost sight of his goal to become the best bronc rider in the world. Every year he attended the Fourth of July rodeo in Fort Pierre, and he'd seen what the older, seasoned hands had to offer. The more he watched, the more certain he became that he had to be a part of it.

John Tibbs remained unwavering in his negative opinion of rodeo; Casey, just as determinedly, had been honing his skills while dreaming of nothing else. Unfortunately, this conflict was not a passing thing, and it opened a painful chasm between father and son that was not to close for many years. When the family climbed into their Model A Ford for their annual Fourth of July trip into Fort Pierre, John noticed Casey's spurs lying on the floorboard. He must have known then that they'd reached their "moment of truth."

Casey recalled, "My dad didn't know I was going to ride until he saw my spurs, a pair of Baby Cross Ls with big old rowels. They might have been all right for bull ridin', but they were just about the worst thing you could use to ride saddle broncs. He asked me what I was gonna do with them, and I told him I thought I might do a little ridin'. That's all that was said about it. I was thirteen years old.

"When we got to the rodeo I entered the bareback ridin', the bronc ridin', cow ridin', and the kid's calf ridin' because I was under fourteen. Bulls were not used yet in rodeos in South Dakota.

"Dad might have been okay if I had just entered the calf ridin', but he got upset when I came out in the bronc ridin'. More than twenty bronc riders entered, and I rode a good horse that afternoon and made the six high. Some good bronc riders had entered too, such as Carl Huckfeldt and Les Stein. A lot of top hands rode at Fort Pierre.

"It was one of the better known Fourth of July rodeos in the area because the officials added the entry fees to the purse. They might only add a hundred dollars, or even just fifty, but those added entry fees meant a lot. In those days, that was the only difference between an amateur event and a professional rodeo. If the entry fees were not added to the purse, the event was considered an amateur rodeo.

"That night in the finals I drew a horse they called Black Bartles, a horse with a reputation in the area. I dang near had him rode, but he bucked down the track and crashed into the stands. I caught my spur in the woven wire they had along the front of the stands, so I lost my stirrup and bucked off him. He might have bucked me off anyway, I don't know, but I was lucky I didn't get hung up or crippled.

"Dad thought the experience would teach me a lesson, especially if he left me there broke to find my own way home. So he just left me there. There was no money in any of the other events which were just exhibition. I think I got a dollar mount money for my bareback horse. You could ride them any way you wanted to, with one hand or with two. They were just wild horses and you rode them with a loose rope."

Casey had made his decision and was now going to have to live with it. Luck was going to have to come his way, because other than for his skill, he didn't have much more than his spurs and the clothes he wore on his back. But he was definitely not of a mind to limp home in disgrace.

Billy Meyers, a friend of Casey's, lived down on the Missouri River. A couple years older than Casey, Billy had won the bronc riding at Fort

Pierre that year, putting on a frenzied ride that had caused some controversy between the contestants and the judges. The crowd had gone wild in response to Billy's giant effort to survive the ride. The judges, influenced by the crowd, gave him first place, but the other contestants correctly accused the judges of confusing wildness with bronc riding skills. The decision stood, however, and Billy won the event. Casey said, "They were just local judges -- one was the sheriff and the other the county commissioner."

White River is a town less than a hundred miles from Fort Pierre. The White River rodeo took place the following weekend, so Casey and Billy decided they would hitchhike together and enter the rodeo there. Casey was glad not to be going home to face his father.

Out on the highway, baking in the blistering July sun, the boys were not having any luck flagging down a ride. Finally, seeing a pickup coming, Casey talked Billy into lying down in the road as the truck drew near. The driver saw Billy stretched out along the road with Casey bent over him, fanning him with his hat.

"He's not feeling too good," Casey told the driver as the truck rolled to a stop. "But if we get him on into White River, I can get him some help."

"Put him in the back," the driver said, and Casey helped Billy into the bed of the pickup. When they came to White River, the first time the driver stopped at an intersection the two boys jumped out and ran for it.

At the rodeo grounds, Billy got entered okay, but when the officials looked at Casey they told him he couldn't enter because he was too young. "I cried and hollered and threw a little-kid fit, but they wouldn't let me enter. So I told them, 'Someday I'm gonna be a champion and the Crogmans are gonna want me to ride in their rodeo but I'm not gonna do it!'

"Later, when I became a champion, I got to be real good friends with the Crogmans, but when they offered me more money than they were payin' in prize money just to come there and ride, I refused to do it. Frank and Louie Crogman are my good friends, but I have never competed in their arena. I've ridden in it, but not as a contestant," Casey remarked.

Skill is the number one element in the making of a rodeo champion, but luck most likely determines success more in rodeo than in any other sport. The unpredictability of the animals is a major factor, and half the points in the final score are based solely on the animal's performance.

The same kind of good fortune that Casey's forebears, John and Elza, experienced when they found a ferryboat pilot willing to let them earn their way across the Missouri River, came Casey's way at White River. A rancher had brought into town a rank stallion to be tried out as a bucking horse. The animal was really on the fight and doing his best to make splinters out of the bucking chutes. The rodeo was over, but many ranchers and farmers stayed on to see how well the stallion could buck. Casey saw his chance and told them he could ride him. He remembers the horse as spectacular in the chute and hard to get down on, but he rode him well, whipping him with his hat and giving it all he had.

When the ride was over, the ranchers and farmers liked it so much they took up a collection for Casey that amounted to more than eighty dollars, more than was paid to the winner of the bronc riding! He would have had to ride sixteen of Albert Lopez's horses to have made the same amount of money. Most important, though, Casey had what he'd come for: public recognition of his skill. The youthful Casey celebrated his "win" by drinking all the grape-flavored soda he could hold -- enough to make himself sick on it.

From White River, Casey went on to Timberlake, South Dakota, and entered the rodeo there. The arena at Timberlake was nothing more than a bunch of parked cars with some snow fencing stretched around. He rode his bronc all right, but luck failed him here when his horse jumped the fence. Right out over the hood of a car they went, and then the bronc struck out for open country. After a bit, Casey decided to just bail off him, but when he did he broke his ankle.

Casey's sister Murphy and her rancher husband John Holloway happened to be at Timberlake when Casey got hurt. Casey stayed with Murphy and John while his ankle mended. He did go back home a few times, but his dad would not speak to him directly, and when he did communicate through Florence, he would not call him by name. Casey, remembering this difficult and painful time said, "If he wanted to give me an order or something, he'd say to Mother, 'See if you can get "Rodeo" to do so and so...' or something like that."

During one of these visits Casey asked his mother to write a letter of release, giving her permission for him to enter rodeos though he was under age. He gratefully recalled that his mother always "took up for him." She gave him the release and never told his father about it.

Getting around on his broken ankle proved difficult, as the bone was never set. Remembering the summer he spent with Murphy and John, Casey said, "I hobbled around all year with that broken ankle, but I could drive a team so I helped them put up hay. As soon as I could, I started ridin' again. I joined up with Bud Annis, a fellow who provided horses for many of the Indian rodeos. We trailed his stock from around the Eagle Butte area over to McLaughlin. I won my first day-money there on a horse called South Dakota, the horse that had bucked off a guy everyone was talking about -- Lee Garrett. Garrett, the wildest guy I'd ever seen with a loose rope on a bareback horse, lived up there on the Indian reservation. He'd broke ol' South Dakota, but he couldn't ride him.

"Anyway, on the way to McLaughlin my horse went lame. We'd had to cross these gravel roads and the pebbles caused him to pull up sore. We were about twenty miles out, so Bud caught up this horse, South Dakota, out of the herd for me to ride. I didn't know he was the same horse that had been bucking off Lee Garrett, the talk of the country. The only thing Bud said when he handed him to me was that he might try to buck.

"Well, that sucker tried -- all the way to McLaughlin! I had all my hitches taken up on my hackamore, which gave me a little control, and I'd get him pulled up after about three or four jumps. When we got to McLaughlin I drew him in the bronc ridin' and he bucked like hell. He was more of a showy horse, but they all thought it was a hell of a ride. He didn't have much power, but he'd turn back and buck like a wild horse, and I won the day-money: $87.50."

Casey continued, "I was holdin' that check for winter purposes, you know -- for security, but I got robbed in the Sam Houston Hotel when I stopped through Fort Pierre. I never did get to cash it.

"I especially remember McLaughlin. It was like the Waldorf of our Indian circuit because they had a nice sale barn that we could stay in, with fresh straw and everything, so we bunked there. McLaughlin was just a small town, but it filled with people during the rodeo.

"The Indians weren't allowed to buy alcohol back then, but I could. We got a couple of gallon jugs and I'd walk up about six blocks and get them filled with beer, making about three or four trips every night we were there. I looked too young to enter the rodeo, and yet I could buy beer, but the Indians couldn't.

"From McLaughlin we trailed on up to Williston, North Dakota," Casey concluded. "It was the first time I'd ever been out of South Dakota, and I rode out a-horseback."

Pat Feeney also recognized Casey's talent with horses. "Casey was not only a helluva good cowboy," Pat stated, "but he was also what I'd call an extraordinarily good stockman. One time I bought a string of twenty-five geldings from a fellow by the name of Everett Towne. The youngest one was six years old, and from there they went up to ten years old. They had some Morgan in 'em, and some thoroughbred. Anybody who knows much about horses knows that combination isn't easy to handle. So I hired Casey to come to the ranch and break those horses.

"Casey tied the first one up in the evening, and the next morning put a saddle on him for the first time. We were going to gather a pasture in rough country stocked all in cows and new calves. I wanted to gather 'em up and brand 'em before movin' 'em to their summer pasture.

"Casey got on this bronc and rode him in the corral, then I opened the gate for him and hazed him out. We rode down the road a mile or two before we hit the pasture. There we split up, and I didn't see Casey again until noon. When I did see him, he was packing a baby calf on that horse! I said, 'Casey, how in the world could you ever get that done?' He said, 'Well, I just kinda talked him into it.'" Pat shook his head, "I don't know very many cowboys who could do that."

Casey, around fourteen at the time, spent part of that winter with his sister Katie and her husband Lloyd Hannum on their place at Bad River. Casey was breaking horses for Pat Feeney while his brother, Johnny Tibbs, was living up on the Carr place along the Cheyenne River. Casey decided to trail his horses to Johnny's ranch so that Johnny could help him finish them out. Casey recalled, "I trailed them up there in the middle of winter, and they got through some gates. I spilled half of them and had to go back after them the next spring. Those were the Towne horses I was breakin' for Pat Feeney, big and rank, with a lot of age on them to be still un-broke.

"Johnny was a real good horse breaker, and we were breakin' this bunch together. While we were ridin' a couple of these broncs outside the corral, Johnny's horse jumped a fence, tumbled over, and broke Johnny's leg. I had to get Johnny into Fort Pierre to a doctor, and we were four miles from the gravel road. The only way I could get him to the road was with a team of horses and a wagon. I broke up some barrel staves and made splints, and I tore up some burlap to tie them on. I set his leg myself, loaded him into the wagon, and drove him over to the Cheyenne River Bridge.

"I stayed on alone at Johnny's place and finished breakin' that bunch for Pat. It was kind of spooky stayin' out there by myself. I was about half wild anyway, and it was a pretty remote place. I was always scared of the dark when I was a kid. Somebody at home could spook me, and I would run and hide under the bed.

"There at Johnny's, I never saw anyone, except once in awhile I'd see an Indian named Bullet Pearman who lived down by the river. Other than that I never saw anybody. This one night, I had got out Johnny's razor and decided it was time for my first shave. I propped up a mirror, got a pan of hot water, and had just sat down in front of it when Pat Feeney knocked on the door.

"I don't know why it spooked me so much -- maybe because I didn't think I was supposed to be shavin', but I let out a holler and knocked over the table. The pan of water went flyin', I was cussin' and jumpin' around, knockin' things over everywhere, and old Pat Feeney, he just took off and never came in.

"He'd merely come by to see how I was doin' with the horses I was breakin' for him, but I never heard him come up. He told everybody, 'Damn, somebody's got to go down there. That kid's gone plumb wild!'"

While still at the Carr place, Casey got a visit from Billy Maher who produced a number of rodeos around South Dakota. Casey remembered, "Billy had some little celebration rodeos around the state, and he was a real good guy. He always paid his people and everything. They'd heard about me ridin' a lot of broncs and how well I'd done at the different rodeos. Billy came up to see if they could get me to come to their rodeo in Redfield. He offered me a hundred dollars for one day. Well, a hundred dollars was more than I was gonna make in three months, so naturally I grabbed it. Billy came in person 'cause there was no phone out there. He paid my way up and back as well. At Redfield, I rode fourteen head of stock that day. It was all exhibition stuff, plus I worked the wild horse race and the wild cow milkin' and I got the hundred dollars."

The following year at Huron, South Dakota, Casey got his first introduction to Brahma bulls. Casey remembered, "You didn't see Brahmas much in that part of the country. I paid my entry fees and went over to the corrals to peek through the fence at these big-horned sons of bucks. I heard a bunch of cowboys talkin' about them sayin', 'When you get off or buck off, they won't bother you if you just lie still.' So, when I got off that's what I did. I just lay down like a jellybean, and boy! This son of a buck hooked me around and around! So now I had some broken ribs. I've got scars on my ribs yet where he hooked me."

At Huron Casey met up with Jack Buschbom. The two youngsters liked each other right off, and it was the beginning of a long friendship. Jack was also destined to become a great champion. He won the World Champion Bareback Rider title three times in his career. Many people from rodeo believe him to be the greatest bareback rider of all time. There's no doubt that he was one of the best ranking, right in there with Joe Alexander, Jim Shoulders, and several others.

Jack introduced Casey to Hugh Ridley, who was more or less a talent scout for producer Joe Greer's Wild West Show in Lancaster, Wisconsin. By this time, World War II was raging in full fury, making travel difficult, as gasoline was rationed and automobile tires were nearly impossible to get. When Hugh offered Casey fifty dollars a week plus transportation, he jumped at the chance. Jack had already worked for Joe Greer, so Casey knew this was a good opportunity and would fit into his plans to enter more rodeos. Casey remembered, "Hugh gave us a ride back there and the whole thing. Most of the time we slept in horse barns. Hugh got a hundred a week for us and paid us fifty. But I couldn't believe we were getting fifty a week!

"Joe Greer's Wild West Shows were approved shows, as were Colonel Eskew's. A few other good outfits came along, too, like the Miller outfit. The Cowboys Turtle Association had approved them. Many top cowboys emerged from these shows, like the McMackens, and Ken and Gerald Roberts. Unlike some other producers, Joe Greer always paid his people. He worked the hell out of us, and we did some pretty reckless things. We'd work the wild horse race, the bareback ridin' -- in fact, we worked every event.

"The chariot races were pretty intense. We'd take horses we'd been ridin' in the wild horse races and hook them up to the chariots. At night we set off rockets on the back of the chariots. As soon as we left the grandstands, it would be dark on the backside of the track, and damn! Those horses would be crashin' off the rails and fences -- it was a wild ride!

"Joe didn't want us partyin', and he also didn't want us datin' his daughter. We kind of stayed clear of his daughter, and we tried to keep him from knowin' we were drinkin' and partyin'. We all partied, though. One of our biggest thrills was to go raise hell with the carnival, 'cause Buschbom could start a fight in an empty closet and could fight pretty good. A carnival or a small circus always appeared in conjunction with the fair wherever Greer played, so in our spare time that's where we headed."

Besides exhibition riding for the Wild West Show, Casey and Jack also entered regular contest events. Greer would put up fifteen, ten, and five, and the cowboys would pay an entry fee of two, or sometimes five dollars, then compete for the purse. Whenever another regular contest rodeo came within striking distance they would enter it, so long as it didn't conflict with their performing in the Wild West Show. At times Joe would not have his show booked at all, and this worked out well for Casey and Jack. They could travel around entering rodeos, knowing they could go back and work for Greer when his next booking came up.

Casey continued, "There weren't as many rodeos then, so when there wasn't one to go to, Bush and I sort of made the Black Hills our headquarters. Deadwood had wide-open gambling then, and we hung out there a lot. We got to know the bus drivers, and sometimes they'd let us ride even when we were broke.

"One time a driver wasn't gonna pick us up, but in Deadwood he had to go up the cobblestone street, make a u-turn, and come right back through town. We'd scattered our stuff all across the street so he had to stop. 'Okay,' he said, 'but you're going to have to stand up all the way.' We were just going to Newcastle, which wasn't too far, but after that uncomfortable experience I designed a dog-harness that I wore underneath my clothes. I threaded it under my arms, and it had a strap with a snap on it that I could hook into the luggage rack. I'd just snap myself on, and sleep standing up.

"Once, in Rapid City, we got kicked out of the Harney Hotel for sleeping on the couches in the lobby. We didn't have any money for a room, so I went over to the coat rack, snapped my harness onto it, and slept with my legs and feet stretched out on the floor. I'd love to have some pictures of some of the stuff we went through. We never worried about being busted or being poor -- we always managed.

"When we'd go to a rodeo, I always liked to get into town ahead of time. Almost always there'd be a few old farmers and ranchers who'd bring some horses to try out. They'd pay you a few dollars to get on them, and 90 percent of the time one of them would take up a collection, 'cause as many as they had, I'd get on. I became the local hero before the rodeo would even start! Sometimes they'd collect as much as seventy-five to a hundred dollars, and give it to me. It seemed like a lot of money."

Somehow, throughout all this, Casey managed to save enough money to buy a 1934 Chevrolet. But because of the war it was hard to buy gas and tires for it, so he kept it stashed out at Pat Feeney's place. Instead of taking money for trying out broncs, sometimes he would trade for rationing stamps, which were called T stamps. Soon he had built up quite a supply.

Whenever the subject of this old car came up, Casey laughed or else talked in amused tones as if still amazed that the car rolled at all. "But I had a car and some gas stamps, so Les Stein, Jack Smith, and I headed for Cheyenne," Casey continued. "In that three-hundred-mile trip we put eighteen tires on that old car. One would blow out and we'd get to a gas station where they'd sell us another old retread, but pretty soon that one would blow out, too. It seemed like it took us forever to get there, but there just weren't any good tires to be had.

"We finally got to Cheyenne and looked for the cheapest place we could find to stay. We found a place by the railroad tracks that looked more like an old boardin' house than a hotel. The room cost us a total of three dollars per day.

"After we got moved in, the guys sent me out to the drugstore with a few dollars to buy some shavin' stuff they needed. I didn't even shave yet, but I was the youngest, so they sent me. Cheyenne was the biggest town I'd ever been in. I left at ten o'clock in the mornin', and I found the drug store all right, but when I started back, every place looked the same. Ours was an upstairs room, so I walked up steps, and I walked down steps.

"Finally, I walked all the way down to the rodeo grounds, about three miles from downtown Cheyenne, and I barely got there in time for the bronc ridin'. I couldn't believe I'd gotten lost on my first day in town. But I found the guys, got my equipment, saddled my horse, and I won the day-money."

Actor Ben Johnson, who won an Academy Award for his performance in the film entitled *The Last Picture Show*, was one of the best-liked men in the motion picture industry. Ben had always loved to rope, and throughout his movie career he continued to enter rodeos. In 1953 he decided to give rodeo his full attention, and by the end of that year he'd won the title of World Champion Team Roper. He was a close friend of Casey's, and in recalling the first time he saw him, Ben said, "He was tryin' to enter the buckin' horse ridin' at Cheyenne, but he was just a young, skinny kid, and they weren't goin' to let him enter. I was in the office when he came in, and when they told him no, he pulled out a letter from his mother. Well, he got in it and won it!"

Casey entered the amateur bronc riding at Cheyenne. The amateur events were open to anyone. As Casey said, "They were often full of wolves."

Casey, reflecting on his first trip to Cheyenne, said, "I wasn't quite ready for all the top hands that showed up there. Guys would go there that had competed in the pro events all year. When they got there, if they thought the professional division looked too tough, they just entered the amateur. Old Vern Elliott would always put some of the toughest horses into the amateur riding 'cause he liked to buck guys off, and he knew he had a good chance there. Vern liked to see those fallin' bodies.

"Everybody thinks I won the Cheyenne bronc ridin', but I didn't. Jack Smith won it. I won more money than he did, but he won the average." One of the horses that Casey won on was a tough bronc called Wildfire. Ironically, Wildfire was one of the horses that had come from his father's herd.

On this trip to Cheyenne, Casey met Ken Roberts who was later to become one of his best friends. During a bronc ride, Casey landed hard with most of his weight on his hands. The jolt popped a wrist bone, so that it stuck out like a big knot from his wrist. Ken was already a world champion all-around cowboy, and Casey, showing him his wrist asked, "Mr. Roberts, does my wrist look like it's broken?" Ken replied, "Do I look like a doctor to you?"

Casey laughed, recalling, "That's all the help them old-timers would give you. You just didn't go up and ask one of those guys where to take your rein on a horse or to help you saddle or anything. Now, you know, a lot of these old-timers are makin' a livin' off these kids by puttin' on clinics for them. In those days you had to prove yourself before they would accept you. Rodeo was a little clannish then. You just didn't mix with everybody."

Casey first joined the Rodeo Cowboys Association at Cheyenne. Ken Roberts' brother, Gerald Roberts, an RCA officer, approached Casey about becoming a member. Casey remarked, "In those days cowboys tried to avoid joining, but when Gerald came up to me and asked, I just gave him the ten dollars and got my card."

One of Greer's big rodeos took place in Minneapolis, and it was there that Casey had a run of bad luck. Knocked unconscious in one event, he didn't know where he was for two days after he came to, although the head injury did him no lasting damage. Then, while bull riding, his bull came down on top of him and broke his leg.

Casey found his way back to South Dakota, but he couldn't go home. He didn't want his father to see him with his leg broken, and he'd also heard a rumor that if he returned he might be put into some sort of reform school.

Casey's sister Dolly and her husband Lyle Muir had a place out in Washington State. Casey's sister Ardie had stayed there while her husband, Dugan Rheborg, was away at war. When Dugan was discharged the young couple flew to South Dakota to be with their folks at Christmas. When the holiday ended and it was time to return to Washington, Casey went with them.

He was sixteen years old, and things had been bad for him at home. His problems with his dad were just as painful as ever, so he thought he'd try his luck in Washington. They decided to drive Casey's old Chevy, carefully planning out the long trip. Ardie remembered telling Casey that there were ever so many little towns along the highway. She laughed at the needling she took from him during the whole trip. As they drove across the vast expanse of empty, open country, Casey frequently repeated her words, mimicking her. "Oh, you'll just be amazed at all the little towns there are out here!"

The trip went smoothly and they laughed most of the way. "The steering wasn't good on the old Chevrolet," Ardie recalled, "but we made it back home with no problem. But the next day when we went to take it to the market for groceries, the whole engine fell out -- right in the driveway!"

While living in Washington with Dolly and Lyle, Casey got a job at a dairy. He did all the chores that come with life on a dairy farm -- feeding cows, shoveling manure, milking -- all of it. He worked hard, but he didn't like it.

Looking back on his job at the dairy, Casey said, "I wouldn't recommend that life to anyone. I didn't even like doing those chores at home. I guess that's why whenever it was my turn to milk, somehow the calves always got in with the cows and sucked them dry."

A youthful 14-year old Casey Tibbs bridling a horse in his father's corral, ca. 1948.

DANCES WITH CHAMPIONS

A phone call from Jack Buschbom rescued Casey from the drudgery of dairy work. Jack told Casey that he'd met a rich woman in Rapid City who wanted a bunch of horses broke and was willing to pay thirty-five dollars per head plus provide all the feed to boot. To this day Jack swears such a woman existed, saying she weighed as much as he and Casey put together. Casey said, "Jack was just wantin' company, 'cause when I got back to Rapid City there was no rich widow, no horses to break, nothin'. I didn't know anybody in Rapid City other than a few barmaids, so I called the Diamond A lookin' for work. In those days a big outfit like that wouldn't take on a guy that rodeoed, but due to the war they hadn't had any horses broken for over three years, so they were short on broke horses.

"Albert Lopez was the horse boss and he, of course, liked me. Ivan Fluharde was the foreman. My brothers had all worked there and had good reputations, so they hired us. We went up there and started breakin' horses. We each got a hundred dollars a month plus ten dollars for each horse we broke and turned over to a line camp. That was the most money ever paid by the Diamond A for a couple of cowboys breakin' horses.

"We started that winter and with the spring thaw comin' and the war over, things were lookin' pretty good. On Saturday nights we'd trail our horses over twenty miles one way to go to an Indian dance. It got a little wild once when we cut through some Russian farmers' corn fields and they took after us with shotguns."

Casey and Jack found that the Saturday night Indian dances were a great place to let off steam. They not only danced but they could drink, fight, and sometimes get lucky with the girls.

Buschbom said, "It was never me that started those fights! They were the result of Casey's warped sense of humor. I don't want to dispute anything Casey has said about this except that I know damn well whatever he said is a lie. He's the one who could start a fight in an empty closet, and then sit back safe somewhere and watch me and laugh.

"He always did that when we worked for the Diamond A. Every Saturday night we'd saddle up a couple of horses and push some others ahead of us and head for his sister's place. We'd leave the horses at Murphy and John Holloway's and then hitch a ride the rest of the way to the dance. And every Saturday night, just like clockwork, we'd get into a fight, and he tries to say that I started them? Shoot! That's a good one!

"Murphy always knew, just by lookin' at us, what had happened. She would fix us a big breakfast every time, and she would invariably have a chocolate cake waiting for us. When we got ready to leave, Murphy's husband John would say, 'Wait a minute, boys. My neighbors down the road brought a horse or two for you to ride. They're good horses, but they just want you to take the edge off 'em. If you'll just ride 'em around the corral a couple of times, that's all they'll need...'

"Well, I mean we rode some of the rankest horses. You can't believe how some of them would buck. As word spread it got to be a regular thing. Every Sunday there would be anywhere from four to a dozen tied up out there, and all the neighbors would come, just like a Sunday picnic, to watch poor me 'n ol' Casey, and both of us hung-over so bad.

"We'd have to get on them horses though, 'cause we couldn't disappoint all those people. Ol' John Holloway, that booger, he knew what he was doing. He'd set us up like that every week."

Jack said of the horses he and Casey broke for the Diamond A, that all were at least eight years old, averaged in weight around twelve hundred pounds, and had never been touched. Jack elaborated, "We got us a hold of some bad boogers! It was a hundred square miles of ranch with five camps, two men to a camp, five horses to each man, and we had every camp outfitted when we left. When I say outfitted, I mean that Mr. Lopez had approved all the horses we'd broke. He rode every horse before turning them over to a camp.

"Casey and I already knew what tough horses were, though. The first time Casey went back with me to work for Joe Greer, Mr. Greer asked me how I'd been doing. 'Fine, Mr. Greer,' I said, 'I've been doing real good. I haven't bucked off a horse all year.' Well, I'll tell you, he bucked me off seven in a row and I'd look up at him, and that grin of his would just get wider and wider. But there was no malice in the man's heart. Casey bucked off his second horse at Minneapolis so hard that he was unconscious for two days. I didn't think we'd live through those times -- we were just kids."

When the spring thaw came, their "good deal" with the Diamond A began to crumble; their horse breaking got interrupted more and more by other work, such as pulling cattle out of bog holes. But one incident that took place during an evening meal really caused a dramatic change.

One night the camp cook, a moonshiner with a short fuse, caught the fencing crew foreman pilfering biscuits before supper. He pulled out a gun and shot the foreman in the belly. It was eighty-five miles to the nearest hospital. After the foreman had been shipped off on the long trip, Albert Lopez turned to the gathered hands and said, "Don't worry about the dead, boys, just worry about the living."

The fence crew was mostly young men from the East, and Albert's remark didn't settle them down. In fact, the whole bunch quit the next day. Ivan Fluharde, the ranch foreman, needed a crew in a hurry, so he put Jack and Casey to work on fencing. It'd been bad enough pulling cattle out of bog holes, but working on fences was worse. Jack wasn't keen on any kind of work that didn't pertain to breaking horses.

"Every night he'd want to quit," Casey recalled. "And every morning I'd talk him into workin' one more day. Finally, we trailed our horses over to Eagle Butte to have it out with Fluharde."

"We were hired to break horses," Jack told him.

"That's worth ten dollars a head," Fluharde responded. "What the hell do you think the hundred dollars a month is for?" The meeting ended with Ivan paying them off. Their days with the Diamond A fence crew were over at last.

When the two youngsters left the Diamond A that day in Eagle Butte, it's unlikely that Fluharde could have imagined what lie in store for them. Many years later, after Casey had achieved the World Champion Saddle Bronc Rider title, Casey found himself having a drink with a group of his old South Dakota friends in a tavern in Fort Pierre.

Fluharde, who by then no longer worked for the Diamond A Ranch, was there as well, evidently feeling in a boastful mood. He walked over to Casey, put his arm on Casey's shoulder, and said, "I made a world champion out of this boy!"

Which prompted Casey to respond, "You sure as hell did. If you hadn't put me on that fence crew, I would have still been workin' for that chicken-shit outfit."

***

South Dakota has turned out its share of top hands over the years: Carl Huckfeldt, Les Stein, the McMacken brothers, and Bill French, to name just a few of the big guns during Casey's early years in rodeo. Huckfeldt was one of the first to recognize Casey's talents and helped him with occasional advice.

Casey remarked, "Carl Huckfeldt wasn't a flashy bronc rider, but he sure was a good one. He could ride a really tough horse, and he rarely ever missed one out of the gate. He drilled that into me, 'Be sure and spur them out,' he'd say, and then he'd make me rough-lock them out for a jump or two. That advice helped me a whole lot.

"Huckfeldt was a hero around South Dakota. He was from Fort Pierre, and he'd ridden at Madison Square Garden and many other big rodeos. He liked me right off. Eventually, Carl, Billy, and I ran around together."

Carl remembered when they were sharing a room in an old hotel. "I was shaving at the sink with my shirt off when Casey came out of the shower naked and threw ice water on my back. I jumped across the room, grabbed Casey, and shoved him out into the hall. Then I locked the door on him. He went to hollering and banging on the door, trying to get back in, but I wouldn't let him in.

"Finally, the hotel manager came so I let Casey in, but while Casey was in the other room getting his clothes I told the manager, 'I'm very sorry about this, but he just can't help himself. He's a real talented bronc rider, but he's so proud of his body that he wants to run around naked all the time. I keep him locked up in his room until time for the rodeo, but he slipped out on me.' The manager left, shaking his head."

Through Carl Huckfeldt Casey got to know the Roberts family better. World champion Ken Roberts, the same tough hand who'd told Casey in Cheyenne that he "wasn't a doctor," was teaming up with his father to form a rodeo stock contracting company. Ken and E.C. Roberts needed a good string of broncs, and Ken had asked Carl for some help getting horses from the Diamond A, the Sioux Indians, and other ranches in the area.

"Ken wanted bucking horses, so I bought a bunch for him from Albert Lopez," Carl recollected. "Ken wanted me to go into producing rodeos with him, but I didn't want to. I did sell him one of my horses that I called Dutchman. I never even saw those horses of Lopez's but I'd heard about them, so I gave Lopez some money down on them.

"Later, when Ken came up for the horses, Lopez said, 'I can't get those horses in, so I'll have to give you your money back.' Ken was about to blow his stack, as he really needed those horses. I said, 'Ken, I know who can get them damn horses! Casey Tibbs knows that reservation like the back of his hand.'"

Ken and E.C. Roberts hired Casey to help them buy broncs from the Indian country around South Dakota. Casey said about it: "Old E.C. handed over his signed checkbook and told me I could break the bank if I wanted to, but to just get him those horses! E.C. trusted me," Casey said.

"I never paid over a hundred dollars for any horse, and I bought some of the best buckin' horses. I trailed that bunch for a hundred and five miles, by myself; some of them I trailed even farther.

"It was in the middle of winter and I had horses from probably thirty different bunches. How I ever got them all the way in, I don't know. I'd stop at an Indian camp, buy a few, throw them in with the rest of the herd, and keep going to the next place.

"Ken had loaned me an old association saddle to use to try out some of the broncs. It had to be the worst saddle in the world for ridin' across country, but I thought it was okay, and I rode it the whole way. Some of those horses I tried out right there in the open -- with no corral, no nothin'."

Any cowboy or stockman, no matter how skilled or seasoned, will agree that this project would be difficult for several good hands, but for one lone teenaged boy, it was an amazing feat. His justifiable pride showing a little, Casey continued, "A snowstorm hit me about thirty miles out of Fort Pierre, just before I got to Jim Everett's place. Jim was a rancher who'd been blinded during the war. He was just weanin' his calves and they were already in his corrals. He had hay out for 'em and everything, 'cause he had just cut them off the cows.

"He couldn't see, but he could hear me comin' with those broncs. One bunch would break this way, and I'd ride and whip and holler and turn 'em, then another bunch would break, and I'd have to turn them back. It was all I could do to hold 'em.

"Jim finally hollered, 'I ain't got no fences that'll hold them sons of bitches!' And he opened his corral gate and kicked his calves back outside. He kept those horses in his corrals for a couple of days until the storm cleared; he was quite a guy. Not too many people would have put their calves back out with their mothers after they'd just gotten 'em separated, let alone put up a bunch of wild broncs.

"When the storm broke, I trailed them the remainin' thirty miles on into Fort Pierre. There I shipped 'em on the railroad to Ken and E.C. in Strong City, Kansas. I went back to Strong City on the train with 'em, to try 'em out, and let E.C. and Ken see what I'd bought. I was pretty proud of that bunch of horses. I shipped them eighty-seven head.

"As it turned out, I stayed on there with the Roberts, and they were sure a great family. They combined their rodeo business with ranchin' and farmin'. We'd buck hay in the fields all day, then come in and try out buckin' horses in the evenin', and I really got in good shape from both the work and the ridin'.

"We'd go out and enter all rodeos within reach, and Ken and Gerald helped me quite a bit. Ken was probably as good a bull rider as ever lived, and it used to make him mad whenever I'd draw a good bull and beat him in the bull ridin'."

Luck was again running with Casey, and yet it certainly was more than just luck that brought him to live with the great Roberts family. He was a mere teenaged boy, yet by himself he'd located, tried out, purchased, gathered, ridden, trailed over a hundred miles, shipped by rail, and then re-tried out a herd of eighty-seven broncs. The herd contained some of the toughest bucking horses in the world, including School Boy Rowe and Spanish American. And he was hired to do it by a family that had already produced two world champions. No, it wasn't luck alone; Casey had definitely earned their respect. He was living among champions who respected his skill and treated him just like a brother.

While Casey lived with the Roberts family, his rodeo career really began to blossom, and his gratitude and affection for them grew steadily over the years. Due to the differences between Casey and his father, Casey couldn't go home. The Roberts family must have filled this void considerably. Mrs. Roberts loved Casey like one of her own sons; she no doubt felt compassion for Florence Tibbs, who missed Casey a great deal. Mrs. Roberts knew what it felt like to have a son riding broncs and bulls -- she was the mother of two world champions.

Although Casey couldn't return home, he lived in a home environment, thanks to the Roberts family. They also allowed him to ride just about all the tough bucking horses he cared to mount, and he got their good advice and friendship at the same time.

Casey was quick to give credit to those who assisted his career and helped him learn his trade, but it was Casey himself, and the broncs that he rode that were his primary teachers. He remembered his father's corral could be as hard as cement at times. In that corral Casey devised a way to tie the feet of a bronc with a certain knot. He could pull the knot loose himself to release the bronc's feet while he was still aboard the horse and set to ride. His favorite horses to practice on were the biggest work broncs that he could find, and the harder they bucked, the tougher he got.

Most of Casey's recollections of the days he spent with the Roberts were punctuated with laughter, warmth, and affection for his old friends. Casey said, "Back in the mid-forties while staying with the Roberts we had a lot of good times, but I pulled so many tricks, I'd get blamed for everything that happened.

"E.C. was a good hand and a good pickup man, but he had this whip, and he was always snappin' it too much. I'd holler, 'Throw that damn whip away!' We'd be at all these rodeos, like Abilene and different places, and the committeemen thought I was the boss 'cause I was always yellin' at him. They'd ask, 'Does that kid own this outfit?'

"When nylon first came out, E.C. had a brand new nylon rope he was so proud of that he took it with him everywhere. He'd even pack it into the restaurants with him. One day we were out in the bull pens, and while he was busy talkin' to this committeeman, I said, 'Let me see that rope.' So he just absentmindedly handed it to me. That rope was so nice and clean, I just thought I'd break it in a little. I put it down in this nice big pile of fresh bull manure. I was mashing it in real good when E.C. looked around and -- oh, man! He took that whip to me, and did he ever cut some Ws on my back! But it was real funny -- up to then," Casey finished off in laughter.

"There were two other brothers who didn't rodeo much -- Clifford and Howard Roberts. They mostly ranched and farmed. One time I was settin' up on top of this load of hay that was stacked way up high on a flatbed trailer. The trailer was hooked behind a truck that Clifford was drivin'. We had to go up a hill, around a turn, and then over an auto gate.

"As Clifford drove up the hill, the damn pin dropped out and the flatbed trailer cut loose with me up on top of it. It happened that E.C. was followin' us up in another truck, so all of a sudden here I come down that hill, sittin' on top of that flatbed, and it's windin' down the road. It was a pretty good ride, too. E.C. could have gotten out of the way, but he didn't. He just froze and hit the brakes and the whole thing crashed right into him. I was gettin' up a pretty good momentum, so it's a wonder that it didn't hurt him and demolish his truck. But he was okay.

"He blamed me for it, though, so I got to puttin' people up to askin' him what happened to his truck. He'd have to answer 'em about ten times a day, and he still thought I jimmied it, or had a wire and pulled the pin out. I'd say, 'Hey! You think I'm crazy? I've got some pride for my life. I'm not gonna do a suicide attack for nothin'.'"

Casey gave Gerald a good deal of credit for helping him during his early years. Gerald passed on essentials such as where to take the rein, and whether the horse is apt to turn to the left or to the right. Casey recalled, "Gerald was good at knowin' where to set a saddle. I usually set my own saddle, but Gerald could set a saddle for me just the way I wanted it, and sometimes we'd set each other's saddles. He helped me a lot, especially in bull ridin'. One year at Colorado Springs the other bull riders entered me in the bull ridin' 'cause they didn't have enough guys entered to cover all the performances. Lee Roberts reminded me of it. He said he told them, 'Don't put him in -- he'll beat you!' Sure enough, I drew a bull they called Jasbo that hardly ever got rode, and I won the bull ridin'.

"I wasn't ridin' bulls much in those days -- my mother didn't really want me to -- but Gerald was a real good instructor. He helped me a lot and eventually I rode lots of good bulls. I rode Gentleman Jim and won the biggest day-money ever paid to that date. I got Blue Bell rode also.

"I hung up quite a few times though, too. Once in Birmingham, Alabama, I think I set a record for the longest time anyone was ever hung up on a bull. I'd bucked down over my hand and I couldn't get loose. The ride went on and on, and finally they cleared the arena. Everyone thought I was dead. Cy Taillon, the announcer, was goin' on and on about this being one of those terrible things that happen. No one knew it yet, but I wasn't even hurt.

"Well, I had so much rosin on my glove that you could hear it squeakin', and it sounded like that bull was takin' my arm off. But it was the cowboys who were hurtin' me worse than the bull was. They were throwin' boots and riggin' bags and everything they could get a hold of at the bull to distract him, but they were hittin' me. I knew I couldn't get loose, so I just hooked my arm around the bull's neck and hung on.

"That ol' bull finally played out and dropped to his knees with his tongue stickin' out, and I just feebly reached up and untied my hand. I was a little short of air, but I wasn't hurt, so when I got loose I kinda showed off and shadow boxed him a little, but he just laid there.

"One thing that hurt my bull ridin' was listenin' for the whistle. I rode many rank bulls right to the whistle. I'd open my hand and let 'em fling me out. Sometimes I'd land on my feet but I would never get hurt. Still I would have been a much better bull rider if I'd never listened for the whistle."

Charlie Beals, who was an RCA cowboy and one of the top contenders of Casey's day, said that Casey Tibbs won more money on fewer bulls than anyone he knew. He said that Casey would just enter where the biggest purses were, and win them time after time.

***

Casey's love of fun and his elaborate sense of humor kept him busy thinking up new pranks and jokes to pull on both friends and strangers. When recalling events that happened, in some cases well over forty years ago, Casey laughed as if they were something that just happened the day before.

During the 1985 National Finals, E.C. Roberts reminisced about those early days in Strong City, Kansas, when Casey lived with the Roberts family. E.C.'s eyes danced with pleasure as the 93-year old let his mind journey back some forty years. His voice rang with joy, as if he were trying to hold back a great flood of laughter.

48

He chuckled as he recalled, "We had quite a time with Casey when he first came. He'd got a lot of buckin' horses for us up around the Fort Pierre area.

"Casey took me to a dance out on the Indian reservation. I was just beginnin' to get acquainted with him. Well, there was a young Indian girl that had gotten married to some feller, and he was jealous of Casey. Boy, he was gonna shoot us! Shoot Casey, anyway, but I was with Casey. So we lit out of there real quick and took off down a grader ditch with that guy a-shootin' at us!" E.C.'s eyes glistened from laughing. "I never went to any more dances with Casey.

"If you had a bronc you wanted tried out, why Casey'd do that for you, all right. That first year he was with us, he was just like one of my own boys, but he was always pullin' some damn joke. He got more kick out of that than anybody I ever saw.

"He was with us pert' near two years, and he was with us after that some, but he got along so good and he come on so fast in the bronc ridin', I think it kinda went to his head.

"He'd won some money, so he bought himself a new bronc saddle. Them new saddles are hard to ride at first -- they don't fit your form. He was tellin' Ken, and Ken said, 'Well, soak it overnight and then get on it the next mornin' and set your stirrups about where you want 'em, and it'll dry out that way and fit your shape. Casey had a room down at the old hotel with only one restroom, you know. So one night Casey had gone down about ten o'clock and put that saddle in the bathtub and filled it with water and left the saddle there to soak. He'd crawled out over the transom leavin' the door locked. Folks was tryin' to get into the bathroom all night."

Finally, some woman pulled a chair up and looked over the transom. Looking down into the darkened bathroom she saw the red dye in the tub and thought it was blood, and what could be seen of the saddle looked like a dead body! She screamed, the manager came, they called the police, and newspaper reporters quickly arrived.

When they broke in and found the saddle, they collared Casey since he was the only cowboy staying there at the time. The police said he was to remove the saddle and scrub that bathtub till it shined.

Casey grumbled that he had a heck of a time getting that tub clean, but worse yet, the reporters thought it such a good story they waited till he was scrubbing the tub, then took pictures of him doing it.

Casey got up early the next morning and made a run on the front lawns of the honest people of Strong City in an effort to get all the papers before the cowboys saw them. This huge effort failed, and for some time thereafter he "Booger-face," they hung a new one on him: "Bathtub Tibbs."

E.C. remembered, "We were goin' to a rodeo with a load of doggin' steers, and we had a pickup horse up in the front end. We had trucks that were pretty good sized, 'cause we cut ensilage into 'em and then drove to the silo to dump 'em. Well, we were drivin' through Harrington, Kansas, and right in the center of the town Casey pulled the dump lever.

"This man runs out in front of us wavin' and a hollerin', 'Your truck's a dumpin'!' Well, Ken looks over and gives Casey a cussin', and Casey says, 'I thought this was just as good a place to put on a rodeo as to go a hundred miles farther to put one on.' Those cattle had slid clear to the back, but he didn't dump any of them out, and we got the bed back down. Then when we got on up there to Abilene, the old truck's battery was kinda down, so Ken says, 'I hope we can get these doggin' steers and horse unloaded before we kill this truck, 'cause I don't think we can get it started again without jumper cables.'

"Why, that damn Casey just reached down and pulled the choke out and killed it right there! He'd do things like that all the time. Everybody liked him, but he was ornery.

"He went farther in rodeo, faster than anybody I was ever around, or anyone else I know of. I had a couple of boys who were world champions, but Casey went to the top faster than either of 'em."

E.C. hesitated here for a few seconds, as if debating with himself, then went on to say, "There's one deal yet, and I don't know whether you oughta tell it here, or not...it was so ornery. But Casey and Ken ate at the hotel there in Strong City quite a bit, 'n there was this girl around town who went with everybody, and one thing and another. I don't know too much about her. But anyway, Ken and his wife were in the hotel eatin' breakfast this one mornin' when Casey gives this girl's kid brother a dollar. He pays the kid to go up to their table and say to Ken, 'I want you to stop takin' my sister out at night.' Well, my gawd! Ken hadn't been takin' her out, but his wife heard that. By gawd, she was mad! She was redheaded, anyway, and boy, I tell you that was awful. Ken never convinced her otherwise. I don't think to her dyin' day she ever believed him. Casey gave that kid a dollar to get Ken into trouble, and Ken was one of his best friends!"

This photo shows both Casey Tibbs and Nugget in perfect form. It doesn't get any better than this! LA Livestock Show and Rodeo.
(Photo by Raymond L. Pound. Used by the kind permission of his son, Leland Pound)

Coliseum, L.A. '55   Photo by R. L. Pound

Casey won the first money ever paid on Andy Jauregui's Gentleman Jim. He received the most money ever won for a single ride to that date. *(Photo by Raymond L. Pound. Used by permission of his son, Leland Pound)*

1953 World Champions: Todd Whatley, Eddy Akridge, Ben Johnson
Ross Dollarhide, Casey Tibbs, and Bill Linderman.
(Photo Courtesy of The Donald C. and Elizabeth M. Dickinson Research
Center Archives of the National Cowboy & Western Heritage Museum.
Photo by DeVere)

FROM LOGS TO CONCRETE CANYONS

It's interesting for several reasons why Casey became an expert in his chosen field. Consider the tremendous amount of rank bucking stock he climbed aboard, then measure that against the various ways he found to make it pay. One year Albert Lopez paid him for breaking sixty head of horses, and as Casey said, "That was a lot of horse breaking for one year." Looking for more stock to ride was the name of the game, and Casey not only got on each horse, he took them as they came and rode them honestly.

It's possible that he set a record for the sheer number of broncs ridden because of his eagerness to try out horses for extra money. Once, in trying out horses for Ken and E.C. Roberts, he rode an incredible thirty-three head of bucking horses in one day.

It's almost unimaginable how many broncs Casey rode. That he did so without much injury gives silent testimony to his great skill.

In Gordon, Nebraska, he rode twelve head of big work broncs in one day. They were all powerful, and all of them bucked. The collection taken up for him came to eighty-five dollars, and he remarked, "I done had the day-money won."

Earl Sellers, an RCA member from Marion Junction, Alabama, a bucking horse man who scouted broncs around South Dakota and Montana, often hired Casey to try them out. These were all good horses, and Casey frequently rode as many as fifteen or twenty in a day.

Another time in Elk Creek, Earl had a bunch of tough horses that he'd gotten from another contractor, Harley Roth. Among them was the great horse Empty Saddles. Earl'd hired Carl Sattafield, an RCA member from Cheyenne to try them out. Casey remembered Carl as a pretty good bronc rider who also fought bulls. After his first bronc, Carl took off his boot and said he thought his foot was broken. Casey said of the incident, "His little toe was hurtin', but he had a point. He had some contracts for fightin' bulls, and he didn't want to get hurt and lose the work."

Casey rode all those rank broncs that day, but when he got to Empty Saddles, that mighty horse bucked him off seven seconds into the ride and then took after him. Broncs that will attack a rider are rare, but Empty Saddles was certainly one example. This vicious horse tried his best to trample Casey, but Casey was able to duck away under the fence.

Casey and his brother Shortlog had fun recalling an incident that involved another horse. Casey began, "The only horse I ever really stole broke me of horse stealin'. This guy had a big old stockin'-legged horse, a chestnut with a bald face. He was really outstandin' lookin' and sure stuck out in a loose bunch of horses. The guy wanted me to catch him and break him.

"Shortlog was livin' down on Agency Creek, about seven or eight miles from the home range. So he and I went down together and gathered these horses and put 'em in his corral. Of course I had to ride that chestnut first thing, so we fore-footed him, threw him down, and just rolled him into the saddle right on the ground. I cinched him up and stuck a foot in the stirrup and let him come up under me. That sucker never did make a jump. He had a natural runnin' walk and he lit out around that corral, and liked to never stopped.

"He just kept on a-goin' round and round. First he was a-runnin', and when he got wore down from that, he went to single-footin', but he never got over close enough to the fence for me to jump off. He was a big ol' horse, and I think Shortlog just wanted to see me get bucked off." Casey laughed as he went on, "We called him Go Devil, 'cause he'd just go and go, and he had a pace, a trot, and a single foot, all at the same time.

"Now, Shortlog's gettin' tired of waitin', and he can't get me off him. Hell! It went on for hours. Shortlog finally said to hell with it, and he went

56

to supper. So he left me on that sucker while he went and ate. When he came back it was already startin' to get dark, and I'm still ridin' him. It's too late to head for home now, so Shortlog said, 'Find a way to get off him. You'd better stay overnight and try it tomorrow.'"

Laughing heartily at the memory, Casey continued, "I finally bailed off him, and the next day I cut out a big gray horse about four or five years old without a mark on him. For that part of the country, he was pretty good lookin'. I needed this other horse to help me take the chestnut home, 'cause it's easier with two when they're not halter broke. It would have been a long way to drag the chestnut home by himself, so I head and tailed the two of them together and took off. Shortlog helped me for a ways, but it was a wreck for awhile -- one of them jumped a creek and the other one got down in the creek -- it was a mess.

"Anyway, I got 'em home and then I got to thinkin', 'Damn! I don't want to get caught with this gray horse.' But the country was full of horses, so I just took my pocketknife and split his ear. That way I'd know him myself, and anybody else would know he'd been had. Then I just turned him out.

"That fall when puttin' together all those horses for Ken and E.C. Roberts, I threw that split-eared gray in with the herd that I trailed into Fort Pierre and shipped to Strong City. He was one of the few horses that ever took to me. I don't remember tryin' him out in Strong City, but he ended up in the draw at Olathe.

"The arena at Olathe was woven wire with thick posts, and he tried to jump the fence. Every time he hit it he broke my leg someplace else. E.C. Roberts was the pickup man, but he couldn't get me off him, 'cause when the bronc first hit the fence it crushed the stirrup in against my foot. I finally got my foot loose and bailed off him, and that sucker took to me. Here I am with a broken leg, and he's really after me. E.C. was tryin' to get him off me when I rolled away from him under the fence. They took me in and put some plaster on my leg and I came back to the rodeo. I tried to get on my bull, but they wouldn't let me.

"I'd just thrown that gray in with the bunch. I think E.C. gave me about a hundred dollars for him, but there I was crippled, so I said right then, 'I'll never attempt to steal another horse.'" Casey went on, "I'm not even sure I got paid for him, but what about the hospital bill? We didn't have insurance then, and I was unemployed for quite awhile."

***

In 1946 many good things happened for Casey. That year, not only was he entering lots of rodeos under the eyes of two world champions, but he was starting to travel a great deal and win enough so that he could plan and save in order to participate in events that'd been on his mind for some time -- New York's Madison Square Garden, and Boston Gardens, to name two.

In the meantime, the Fourth of July weekend was coming, and it offered Casey a number of rodeos to enter. He decided to try his luck in his home state of South Dakota because he could ride at Mobridge and then make it to Mandan, North Dakota, and ride there, as well.

Casey recalled, "Mobridge was close to home, but I decided to take a chance on it. I left Strong City and headed for Mobridge, and when I got there my gamble paid off, 'cause there was my dad. He was still against my rodeoin' but he could see I was doin' okay, and I knew he was thawin' out a little. I did pretty good at Mobridge, too. I don't remember exactly what I won, but I got some of the bronc ridin' and some of the bareback."

Casey was relieved to be able to come to some understanding with his dad, and he was grateful for his father's guidance. He recalled, "Dad and I talked awhile and he offered me some helpful advice. One of the things he said was, 'If you're goin' to rodeo, you better go with the best.'

"Bill McMacken from Trail City, South Dakota, was a big name in that state, as well as a leading contender throughout the country. He usually came in second or third in the world standings for bronc ridin', steer wrestlin', and all-around," Casey continued. "Carl Huckfeldt had talked to Bill about me, so McMacken asked me if I'd like to ride up to Mandan with him.

"Bill came from a family of good cowboys. His brother, Fritz McMacken, lived in the same building in Spearfish where my sister Murphy lived. They say their brother Joe was a better cowboy than all of them, but I never knew Joe. He was killed at a rodeo while bulldoggin' a steer," Casey reminisced.

"Ken Roberts told me before I left Strong City to be sure to look up Shirley Hussey when I got to Mandan and to ask his advice on my stock. Hussey was probably the very best at knowin' where to take the rein on a horse, and the best judge of buckin' horses that anybody ever knew.

"Ken had called ahead and talked to Hussey, so Hussey knew I was gonna be lookin' him up. Ken had said to me, 'You may not like Shirley 'cause he's a little rough, but he's a good guy and he'll treat you right. Tell him I said to ask him about the horses you draw, and he'll tell you where to take the rein on 'em. But whatever you do, don't let Cremer know he told you.'

"Leo Cremer was the stock contractor for Mandan and many other rodeos. His featured horse was called Golden Fan, and he kept him in a separate pen. That horse could not only buck, but he was a beautiful sorrel with a flaxen mane and tail. Cremer almost had a heart attack when I rode Golden Fan." Casey continued, "I also rode Madam Queen, another of his top horses. Only the week before they'd thrown off both Bill and Bud Linderman.

"Cremer got all over Cy Taillon, the rodeo announcer, because Cy'd been announcing my age. 'You'll never announce another one of my rodeos!' he told him. 'No sixteen-year-old kid is gonna ride my good horses!'

"I should have won Mandan, but McMacken had gone to Heavy Henson who was judgin', and told him, 'This kid is going to be a hell of a bronc rider, so make him spur them out.'

"Heavy goose-egged me on one of my rides, and I sure hadn't missed that horse out. McMacken didn't mean anything against me when he said that to Heavy. In fact, he was upset when it happened. 'You never missed him,' he later told me. 'But in the long run, that'll pay off for you.'"

It was in Mandan that gambler Buddy Malone approached Casey. Malone worked for Benny Binion, who owned the Golden Horseshoe in Las Vegas and was a supporter of rodeo. Binion's stagecoach, with its beautiful matched blacks in silver harness, had been seen at many of the major rodeos throughout the United States. Malone had flown into Mandan in a luxury airplane, bringing several top cowboys with him. He told Casey that he would pay all his expenses and entry fees, and Casey could keep everything he won if he wanted to go with them. He meant at all rodeos, not just at Calgary, which is where they were headed next. Casey stated, "It was a cinch deal. I stayed with Buddy that night, and I watched him count out thirty-five thousand dollars in cash. It was just a little too spooky for me, sleepin' on top of all that money. I got thinkin' about Dad's advice -- he never approved of gamblin', but he did say, 'If you're goin' to rodeo, you better go with the best.'"

When the rodeo at Mandan ended, Casey headed for Wolf Point, Montana, with Bill McMacken. "Wolf Point was the wildest rodeo I'd ever been to," Casey chuckled. "They had Indian races around the arena, but no race track. They just cut a swath out with a road grader that left a ridge about a foot and a half high, so that six or eight jumps out of the chute a horse would have to go up and over it. The buckin' stock were all wild, and they used shotgun chutes. Those chutes were really something. You'd get down on your horse, get all set, and three men on each side would pull the chute apart. The chutes all came out from under the grandstands but in different areas. There would be a pen full of horses over here, another pen back there, another one way over on this side, and you'd have to walk all around that enormous arena tryin' to find your horses that they'd painted big old numbers on.

"If you got a re-ride, and you usually did, you'd have to run maybe plumb across the arena to another chute to get on your horse. Oh, it was the damndest thing you've ever seen! Instead of a couple of pickup men, they just offered a dollar per head to anyone who wanted to pick you up. There would be twenty pickup men in the arena and it was a really huge arena."

Casey laughed as he went on, "On his ride, McMacken had about three guys fightin' for him. They each wanted that dollar, so one of them had his rein, and two of 'em were tryin' to pull him off the other side. He had a hold of the rein, too, and was whippin' the guys over their heads with it, tryin' to get loose from them. It was those kinds of rodeos that got me in the habit of steppin' off my horse and hopin' I wouldn't get run over."

Casey remembered, "McMacken won the bronc ridin' at Wolf Point, and I got second and won the bareback ridin'. We kept goin' and made a bunch of rodeos together. I always wanted to travel in the daytime so I could see the country, but McMacken wanted to travel at night. We'd pull into town and he'd call some gal up and take off. I wouldn't know if we were goin' to spend the night or not, but if I wasn't in the car when he came back, he'd just drive off without me.

"I used to ask him about different cowboys, but he'd just drive down the road and wouldn't talk. He'd pull into a town, and if there was a poker game goin' on he wouldn't check into the hotel for two days -- he'd just sit there and play poker while I just stood around waitin' and wishin'," Casey complained.

"One time we pulled into Ogden, Utah, and he went to playin' poker with Buckshot Sorrels and a bunch of other guys. I was ridin' fairly good then, but I saw these big old broncs back there that old hard-hearted Shirley Hussey had brought in, and he asked me if I wanted to try 'em out. I told him hell, yes! 'Cause Hussey could just look at a horse and tell you where to take the rein on him. These were big ol' rank sons of bucks and I rode thirteen head of them. I'd just ride 'em out about as far as I wanted, and then just step off 'em, and I got five dollars a head for it," Casey recalled.

"McMacken was in the shed row playing poker when someone told him I was out there tryin' out these buckin' horses. And oh, boy, did he raise hell with me! He came out there and shouted, 'Damn it! If you're goin' down the road with me, you ain't gonna be gettin' on these sons of bitches!'

"I didn't pay any attention to him 'cause I was gettin' some good practice and makin' some money on top of it. Bill went back to his poker game and went bust, and that was the first time I kind of popped off to him. As we were drivin' back into town, I got to countin' my money, all five dollar bills, that I got for gettin' on those horses, and there he was -- broke! We weren't splittin' or anything. We each paid our own way and then shared the cost of the gas, rooms, and whatever. We'd borrow money back and forth, but that was all. Later on we did split 10 or 25 percent once in awhile." Casey added soberly, "McMacken was killed in a light airplane crash while on a fishing trip in Lewiston, Idaho, but he was a good bronc rider right up to the last."

At Newton, Kansas, Casey won his first trophy saddle. To qualify for it he won the all-around for that rodeo by winning the bronc riding and bull riding and placing second in the bareback riding.

Casey'd been saving his money carefully. He knew it was going to take a lot of cash to enter New York and Boston, as well as pay his expenses while he was there. "I'd saved all summer to go to New York, because I thought that goin' to the Garden was out of this world," Casey acknowledged.

Ken and E.C. were producing a rodeo at Saint Joseph, Missouri, and Casey went there on his way to New York. Then, with his suitcase, riggin' bag, and bronc saddle, Casey headed for New York City. To a young kid raised in a log cabin in the middle of nowhere, the Madison Square Garden Rodeo was the thrill of his life and a dream come true.

Madison Square Garden ran for thirty-three days with over a hundred thousand dollars in added money, and an even greater amount added to that by the cowboys themselves in entry fees. Every top hand in the rodeo world had converged on New York, so the competition was especially tough.

After the first go-round and they'd all gotten a look at him, several of the biggest names in rodeo approached Casey, asking him if he'd like to split winnings with them. Splitting was a form of cowboy insurance. It made sure that when the pie was cut you'd at least pick up a piece of it.

Casey accepted and split with several of them, but it was a costly move. When it was over he'd won so much more than the others, but then had to split. Even though he didn't win first in any event at New York in 1946, he won over two thousand dollars in day-monies and was able to enter Boston Gardens with money to spare.

The Boston Garden Rodeo went much the same as New York, except he did win the wild horse race but didn't win any other event. Still, he won so many day-monies the rodeo was profitable for him.

When 1946 ended, Casey'd won over forty-five hundred dollars. That's nothing by today's standards, but in those days it was a goodly amount. Considering that he would've had to ride for his friend Albert Lopez nine hundred broncs every day for a year, or one bronc every day for nine hundred years, this was an astronomical amount of money.

Throughout 1947, Casey Tibbs' star continued to rise. He created an absolute sensation, not only with the professionals within the sport, but with rodeo fans as well. Florence loved hearing from Casey, and she loved to keep track of his progress. He wrote her often and sent her clippings from the various magazines and newspapers throughout the country that contained articles and pictures pertaining to his skyrocketing career. He continued doing so throughout the years, much to his mother's delight, and eventually to John's great pride as well.

Florence carefully saved every letter, postcard, and clipping. She stored them at Casey's sister Katie Hannum's home.

Movies and stories sometimes perpetuate the absurd idea rodeo cowboys drink to bolster their courage in the arena. It would be no more ludicrous to believe a great prize fighter would get drunk before entering the ring than to think that a bronc rider would prepare himself in this way before riding a bronc.

Sometimes, however, alcohol does play a role in the lives of rodeo cowboys. For instance, fans, friends, rodeo committees, and various other supporters of rodeo will host parties, wanting to make the incoming cowboys feel welcome. Rodeo Week is one of the major events of the year in most towns, but the cowboys are just coming from Rodeo Week in some other town and are going to another one as soon as the present one ends. Unfortunately, this scenario ascribes to the true role that alcohol plays in the life of many a rodeo cowboy.

Casey, a young rising star, was being asked to attend more and more social functions. The need to perform in and out of the arena began to put considerable pressure on him. He became aware that he was gaining a reputation that needed to be defended. He was being heralded as a sensation, and he knew that each time he rode he was being watched -- not just by the judges and fans, but by all the cowboys, their wives and girlfriends, the stock contractors, and increasingly, the press.

The ropers and their wives generally left the arena to head for dinner or a party just as soon as their event ended. But these folks began to find themselves staying to watch the bronc riding if they knew Casey was up. The roping end of the arena would virtually fill with spectators whenever he rode.

He felt so complimented by this, that at times he would forget all about the judges. He'd spur wild and high on the side of the horse positioned toward the ropers, even when the judges couldn't see that side of the horse.

Reflecting on some of these events, Casey said, "If I'd only had the sense to just slow myself down a little, I probably could've won the bronc ridin' easily in '47. I rode as good then as I ever have in my life, but I was tryin' to ride better than I was capable, or anyone else was capable. I was also partyin' and travelin', goin' on sheer energy, tryin' to keep up with the big boys."

Since half the points for any bronc ride are based solely on the performance of the animal, Casey devised ways to take what he'd labeled a mediocre horse and make him look better. For instance, while maintaining his "feel of the head," he would give extra slack in the rein to allow the horse's head complete freedom. Since this meant he couldn't pull on the buck rein, he had to ride almost on pure balance and agility while leaving his rein hand extended to throw slack in the rein.

Casey also left his cinch loose on this type of animal to give the horse the impression the horse was winning. The spurring lick he used was fabulous. Stacks of bronc riding pictures reveal an amazing similarity. Photo after photo show Casey's spurs in the neck, just under the mane at the beginning of the stroke, and remaining in contact with the horse all the way back until both spurs hit the cantle board of the saddle.

All this combined gave Casey a reputation for what became known as "floating" his horses. Many people in the rodeo business today give Casey credit for being the first to full stroke a saddle bronc. Once he was asked if this was true.

"No," he answered. "There were other bronc riders who used the full stroke. Actually, they didn't get all that much credit for it, I don't think. I might have improved on the technique a little, but you see, the good solid bronc riders had a stroke from over the point of the shoulder on the right-hand side, and back to about the cinch or maybe six inches behind the cinch.

"Most of those guys used a left rein, and on that side they full stroked 'em. They were hard to beat 'cause they seldom bucked off. It was pretty much a standard thing that they would mark two or three points higher on the left side, though they probably should have marked six points or ten points higher.

"I could see right away that a guy could just as well spur 'em with both feet, so I tried to ride every horse the same on both sides. There were guys like Burel Mulkey who spurred with both feet, and Jerry Ambler was pretty good, too," Casey commented. "Ambler was one of the better bronc riders I knew at that time, anyway. He could fake it, dependin' on how hard he had to ride. He could miss 'em but still make it look like he was double strokin' 'em and gettin' his spur into 'em when he wasn't. But he was still a hell of a bronc rider.

"Then there was Bill McMacken who rode about every horse and spurred 'em with both feet. Billy Ward was pretty good at it, too. But some guys would spur back then wouldn't spur ahead, yet still get credit for it," Casey mused. "Not all of them, though. Mulkey, Ward, and McMacken would all get up in the neck, but sometimes they wouldn't spur all the way back. I tried to ruffle the hair all the way back, and I tried to improve my stroke on every one of 'em," Casey asserted. "The worst problem I had was tryin' to over-ride horses instead of just ridin' 'em good.

"On some of those big ol' rank horses of Cremer's, I'd get my foot plumb up in the saddle like this," Casey laughed, pulling his foot up. "My knees aren't in that good of shape. I can hardly get my foot up onto this bench now," he remarked, "but I'd sit on my damn foot! My spur would come right up into the saddle with me and I'd sit there and jump and try to get that sucker down.

"Golden Pheasant was one of the worst ones for that. I could just ride him so good. He was a big honker, yet you could reach way up in the mane. He had such perfect timing, and he was stout as well. I'd get into the habit where my legs would come right up over the swells almost, so I could spur him a little higher in the neck, and I'd just feel them spurs come all the way back, then I'd know I gotta slow down or I'm gonna get up in the saddle again. But damn! Every once in awhile he'd do it to me again," Casey whooped.

"I wanted to ride him so bad in Chicago once 'cause I was havin' a runnin' feud with old Cremer, but I was lookin' off and I was feelin' so good, and then -- damn, I sat on my foot.

"Gawd, it was great in those days, though." Casey explained, "You didn't worry about good draws -- you just worried about keepin' your pack on a lot of them suckers, 'cause there were so many good buckin' horses.

"You could draw a horse in those days that maybe wasn't the best, and still take up the slack and win, 'cause a lot of others were so rough that they were just barely gettin' ridden.

"What hurts today, I think, is the fact that all your good buckin' horses are rideable, just about all, and they're rideable in a good fashion. Today guys will turn out what's a mediocre horse in the class 'cause they know all the others are gonna be rode. You never figured on all of 'em gettin' rode then.

"I think there was more honor in it, too -- guys just figuring they had a responsibility to get on the stock just 'cause they entered, whether it was good, bad, or indifferent. Course, they were a little more lenient with the re-rides then, too. You could get just about as many re-rides as you wanted.

"I've seen Hawkeye drive halfway across the country to get on a horse he knew they'd given a re-ride on the day before. He just figured, 'I'm in the standings and they expect me to be there.' That's the difference between some guys and others.

"Brad Gjermundson's a good guy, and I don't think he'd turn anything out if he had a chance to get on it. He's quiet and he rides broncs, and nothing bothers him much. He just wants more stock."

When asked if he was worried Brad might break his record of six world titles in saddle bronc riding, Casey said, "Hell, no, I hope he does. Records are made to be broken, and Brad's a heck of a nice kid with a good attitude. He gives his best on everything he gets on, which is good for him, and good for the sport. If he does break my record, it'll create some excitement, which'll be good for rodeo and it'll make more people aware of what I've accomplished in the past. It can't hurt my name any."

THE BEST DAMN BRONC RIDER
IN THE WORLD!

1947 found Casey's name in the standings for the first time. At that time the standings consisted of only the top five ranking men in the world for each event -- today it's the top fifteen. His bank roll had grown into a considerable pile of money, and he always carried every bit of it on him.

Casey began having his shirts tailor made, as well as his boots. No doubt the time he'd spent with Bill McMacken was at least partially responsible for the taste he'd developed for tailored clothes. People had always noticed Bill wherever he went, especially women, a fact that had not escaped Casey. Now Casey not only rode like a star, he was beginning to dress like one as well.

Again, he did well at New York in 1947, winning day-money after day-money. The last horse he drew was a tough bronc called Hell Diver. When the chute gate opened, the horse whirled out with his rear end toward the judge. Casey said, "By all means, I should have won the bronc ridin', but didn't. I had that horse necked out perfect but the judge couldn't see it, so he goose-egged me. There were about a half dozen guys sittin' across from me who could see that I'd marked him out. There were other times though, when I should have been egged and wasn't, so it all evens out.

"I actually won more money in the bronc ridin' than the guy who won it. I was ridin' as good then as I ever rode in my life, so when I went to Boston, I was feelin' pretty cocky. One night a bunch of us were playin' poker when Bill Eiler jumped me out. He said, 'You're so damn smart, I'll just bet you two hundred dollars that you don't win the bronc ridin' here.'

"This happened just at the startin' of the second go-round. We got twelve horses there that year, and it was pretty bad odds, but I was a little ahead in the poker game so I just called him and won the bronc ridin', even though I drew a horse called Howdy Doody who'd bucked everybody off, most of them right out of the gate. I also won the bareback ridin' and the wild horse race."

Besides the money Casey was paid in cash, he won three beautiful hand-tooled trophy saddles. He also went straight to a new car dealership and bought a brand new Studebaker. "I'll take it," he told the astonished salesman as he counted out the money, paying for it in cash. "I drove the Studebaker straight to the ranch," he went on. "I didn't even stop at Fort Pierre. I went directly to the old homestead. It was about four o'clock in the mornin' when I pulled up to the house. Dad got up and put his suspenders up over his shoulders, and we sat down at the kitchen table.

"I pulled out the cash I had left and laid it out on the kitchen table and started countin' it. Mother got up about then, and when she saw all that money she let out a scream. She thought I might've robbed a bank or somethin'. Just over seven thousand dollars in cash lay on the table, and the new car was full of saddles and trophies. Dad and I had a long talk, and he thought rodeo was all right after that.

"I went into Fort Pierre and bought a house for my folks, and that spring we moved them into it. It had six lots that went with it, so there was plenty of room for a garden. There was a little barn in the back, and Dad kept a cow back there.

"He'd never believed in gamblin' -- always hated it, but he got to goin' down to the pool hall and bettin' that I'd win, wherever I went. He just had to bet on me to win. I kidded him about it. I told him, 'Dad, you're spottin' 'em too much.' But he knew I could ride a tough horse before I ever left home. I used to love to sneak around when I was just a kid and listen to him tell how tough a horse I could ride.

"After that Dad went to a few rodeos and watched me ride. He went to Deadwood and he went to Denver, but he wasn't doin' well. He'd had a couple of strokes -- he'd even had several he'd never told anybody about before he left the old home-place.

"They'd found him once up by the spring where he'd had a stroke, but he just thought he was feelin' bad and havin' a 'bum spell,' as he called them. I was at a rodeo at Huron when they called and told me he'd gotten worse. So I left and came home, and I was there when he died. Dad didn't get to enjoy the new place very long, but he did enjoy it while he was there."

John Tibbs died July 7, 1948, and his death was a great loss to the Tibbs family and friends. Casey bore not only the sadness and grief, but also disappointment that his father would not be there to share the excitement he knew the future held for him in the world of rodeo. It was truly fortunate, however, that before John died he and Casey had resolved their conflicts. As Casey put it, "At least we got to be friends again, and he'd begun to think rodeo was okay."

March of 1948 found Casey and Gerald Roberts in Phoenix, Arizona, looking at an old converted army airplane, a twin-engine Cessna dubbed the *Bamboo Bomber*. The plane belonged to Luther Finley, one of three brothers who'd all made names for themselves in rodeo. Larry Finley was a world champion bareback rider, and his brother Frank was a tough contender for the title. Luther Finley won two world championships in wild horse racing.

Luther was known by the cowboys as Chipmunk. They'd given him the nickname because of the way his head bobbed around in the chute as he was getting ready to ride. He'd check his horse, then the judges, pickup men, gate men, etc., and the cowboys said he looked just like a chipmunk. He was an aeronautical engineer with a doctorate in mechanical engineering, as well.

During the war in the Pacific, Luther was wounded and shipped home. Five days after his release from the military hospital he bulldogged a steer in Chicago in 5.1 seconds, setting a record for that time. He hadn't had time to go home for his clothes and was still wearing his Marine Corps uniform. On his release from the Marine Corps, he'd taken up flying and had bought the twin-engine Cessna.

Gerald owned a Packard convertible with about twenty thousand miles on it, and he was considering a trade for the plane. Of the swap, Gerald said, "Luther talked me into trading with him, and I never should have done it 'cause I sure could have made a better deal. Casey helped me with all the expenses, and if anything went wrong with the plane, he helped pay for it."

Whenever Casey talked about this airplane his expressions changed rapidly: looks of amusement, disbelief, glee, and thankfulness for just being alive crossed his face. He said, "You could stick your thumb right through its skin. It was one of those fiberglass planes. They called them bamboo bombers in the war. Neither of us knew how to fly, so we went lookin' for a pilot. We made a deal with a cowboy named Lee Harris. Lee rode bulls mainly and broncs a little. He'd been in the Air Force, and we used that to help us get other cowboys to go with us to help pay for the gas. We talked to Bud Linderman, Harry Tompkins, Jim Shoulders, and different guys, and the first thing they would ask about was the pilot. I'd tell them, 'Hell! We got us a good pilot. He was a captain in the Air Force.' It even sounded good to me, but I didn't find out till later that he'd been on the ground crew the whole time -- he'd never even been *in* an airplane!

"We painted the old airplane red, white, and blue, and we did a good job on it. It was a fancy lookin' sucker on the outside, but nothin' worked on the inside. The compass didn't work, and whatever other equipment the old plane had didn't work, either. It would only go a hundred and sixty, and Lee would bring it in at about a hundred and forty, bouncing all over the runways and out into the corn fields. At first he'd only land in some little crop-duster fields because he didn't have a license. Later, after he'd practiced on us awhile, he took to landing in the bigger airports.

"He landed at Casper, Wyoming, on a clear, quiet evening and used up the whole runway. Everything was fallin' on us, and saddles were hittin' us in the head. So I told him, 'Lee, I'm tired of you makin' these crash landings on a two-mile runway!' But we always did overload it and usually had one too many guys in it as well.

"I'd see the old plane go over in the early mornings and I'd think, 'Damn! He's sure burnin' up a lot of fuel. But he's a good pilot, I guess, 'cause at least he's out there checkin' it out.'

"What I didn't know was that he was loggin' his hours so he could get his logbook filled so he could get his license. He dang near killed us in the process, but he eventually did get it -- at our expense. He couldn't read an air map at all, and he was lucky if he could read a road map. We were lost all the time.

"We were entered at the rodeo at Cheyenne, but we heard they had a midnight rodeo in Kansas City, of all things, so we had to make that. There wasn't much prize money, but it was there, so we went. We were the first of the flyin' cowboys. For some reason we thought the *Bamboo Bomber* was the answer because it'd carry the weight. It had two engines, but it was a gas-eatin' son of a gun! We had to win first and second most everywhere we went just to keep it in the air. Gerald was wantin' to win the all-around that year and he did, but sometimes I was sure I could have driven faster than we were flyin'."

After Casey and the guys rode their first stock at Cheyenne, they decided to fly over to Kansas City and ride in the midnight rodeo there, then fly back to Cheyenne in time for their next go-round. The trip was harrowing to say the least. They made it to Kansas City in pretty good shape, then rode in the midnight rodeo held on the outskirts of town. But a storm front moved in after the rodeo, and the main airport shut down. Lee Harris (still unlicensed at the time) had his aversion to major airports, so he'd used a small outlying field. The remainder of the important Cheyenne Frontier Days Rodeo was still beckoning and couldn't be kept waiting because of a few raindrops, so the *Bamboo Bomber*, loaded to the roof, took off. On board were Lee Harris the pilot, Gerald, and Casey, accompanied by Larry Finley, Bill McMacken, and Billy Weeks, a bareback bronc rider.

Casey exclaimed, "We took off and Lee flew right into a squall line, and suddenly that old puddle jumper started goin' three hundred feet up in the air then droppin' another three hundred feet, and now the old plane started comin' apart. You could hear a piece of that old fiberglass flappin', goin' rat-a-tat-tat-tat-tat. The plane was makin' screamin' noises. I mean just screamin'!

"I kept myself from bein' scared by jokin'. I was sayin' things like, 'Damn! I wish I would have cashed these checks. I've got about twelve hundred on me, and now I'll never get a chance to spend it.' I was tryin' to cool everybody down, 'cause there was panic settin' in. Finley, who was damn tough -- he loved to fight and brawl -- was really scared. He actually had sweat runnin' out of the palms of his hands."

Casey's jokes didn't seem to be going over well, but he tried another one. "One thing about it," he told them, "these things are supposed to burn up in twelve seconds, so we won't have to worry about anything for long." But that bit of humor didn't go over too well, either. "I wasn't scared," he continued, "until I looked up and saw Gerald's eyes. He doesn't scare too easy. He'd been on every rank bull in the world, but his eyes looked like two saucers lookin' back at me from the copilot seat. I knew then that we were gonna burn, and I remember thinkin', 'This ain't nothin' to joke about.'

"Little ol' Billy Weeks, though, he stood tough through the whole thing. He was plenty scared like the rest of us, but he just drew a breath and said, 'The undertaker has done wiped our ass!'" Casey laughed as he continued, "He said it straight and he meant it. But we came out of that storm and ended up in St. Joseph, Missouri, and we were tryin' to get to Cheyenne. We didn't know where we were, 'cause none of the instruments worked. We were just barely skimmin' the tops of the trees when we landed.

"We waited for the weather to clear, and when it didn't, we took off again anyway. We headed straight for Cheyenne again, but when we got there, we were in Topeka, Kansas, instead. We made two more crash landings before we ever got to Cheyenne. We were always runnin' out of gas 'cause we were travelin' three times farther than we should have.

"So we were runnin' out of gas again and had to stop in Scottsbluff, Nebraska. It's only about a hundred miles from there to Cheyenne, but by now that old plane had taken so much abuse any of the electrical components that had been workin' before weren't workin' now, and we couldn't get the landin' wheels down. We got a crank out and started crankin' 'em down by hand. Larry Finley cranked for awhile till he got sick and gave out. We were in serious trouble, too, because we were also runnin' out of fuel. It was hotter than hell in the plane, and everybody had been sick and throwin' up all over it.

"It was hard goin' and we were almost out of gas, with no wheels, and now it was gettin' on towards rodeo time, so Billy Weeks said, 'Let me have that damn crank!' I had to laugh at him, 'cause he was so damned tough. He had a crooked arm that had been broken several times, and I'll never forget how he looked crankin', sweatin', and throwin' up all at the same time."

This whole frightening, miserable situation, struck Casey as so funny that he could hardly tell the story without laughing uncontrollably. He said, "We finally landed, got gassed up, and made it on into Cheyenne, but when we got there they'd already turned out Gerald's bull." Casey said with a thoughtful look, "It was a bad deal, as there were still two or three bulls left in the chutes. Normally, they'd have held his bull back. If they had, Gerald might have won the world bull riding championship as well as the all-around that year."

Casey had already drawn and ridden some outstanding horses at Cheyenne, but he needed a good one for his last horse. He drew a horse called the Old Gray Mare. No one knew much about her, but since she was gray and no one knew her name, she was referred to simply as the Old Gray Mare.

When Casey approached the chute with his saddle and bronc halter, she went crazy. She was determined not to let him put the halter on, and whenever he tried, she reared up so hard that a number of cowboys quickly jumped in to lend him a hand.

No matter what they did, as soon as they started to halter her, she thrashed and kicked and tried to tear the chutes apart. Some of the time she would drop her head to the ground where she couldn't be reached for haltering.

To those unfamiliar with rodeo, this might seem like just the kind of horse a rider would want for a good draw in the bronc riding, but usually just the opposite is true. That's because usually when a horse fights the chutes it takes something out of him, and then the animal doesn't perform as well in the arena.

Casey was feeling sick and weak from the unbelievable round trip to Kansas City in the *Bamboo Bomber*. He had disembarked from the plane only minutes before, and he hadn't slept since the night before when he'd ridden his last horse right there in Cheyenne.

"I went through one full section of broncs just tryin' to halter her," Casey remembered, "and I had some help, at that. They were goin' to turn her out, but I finally got my pack on her."

Chute fighter or not, when the gate opened, the Old Gray Mare decided it was time for her star to shine. She came unwound and helped to write a new page in the annals of rodeo history, for when it was over, Casey Tibbs became the youngest contestant ever to win the professional bronc riding at the great Cheyenne Frontier Days Rodeo.

"I never saw a horse buck so hard after fightin' the chutes so long," Casey exclaimed. "There was some money won on her after that, but she never became one of the great ones like you might've expected. She could buck, though she was probably as rank a mare as I ever rode in my life. I was pretty seasoned by that time, but they still weren't lettin' kids win like the older pros. I drew all good horses there that year: T Joe, Jersey Joe, and then the Old Grey Mare in the last go-round. Sick as I was, I guess I got a second strength when it came time to ride her."

The ride was certainly one of those spectacular matches, so much so that those who saw it will never forget it. One of the judges, Tom Knight, told Casey after the ride, "Every time I think about it, I've got to put you farther ahead."

Casey finished 1948 in third place in the saddle bronc riding. Gene Pruett took first place, while Carl Olson placed second, with Casey trailing him by only 82 points.

***

Casey's youthful appearance often fooled people. It was impossible to believe that this curly-haired boy was actually an athlete with tremendous ability. Gene Rambo once overheard a security guard speaking to Casey behind the chutes at the Salinas, California, rodeo. What he heard so tickled the great champion, he often repeated the following story. At that time, Casey had already won his first world title, and he was busy behind the chutes getting ready to mount up. A security guard walking by noticed him. "What are you doing back there, sonny?" the guard asked him.

Rambo perked up his ears, grinning, then nearly fell off the chute laughing when he heard the frustrated Casey reply, "I'm fixin' to kick the shit out of this bronc as soon as you get out of my way."

Although Casey knew his young age to be a disadvantage when he'd first started in rodeo, very early on he figured out how his appearance could be turned into an asset. Casey said he learned to "drink with the big boys," yet swallow very little, then become boastful and brag that he could ride the toughest horse in the string. Older hands, not knowing who he was, would think this baby-faced brat needed a lesson. Often they would cover his bet and his phenomenal skill won him considerable money. "I actually won more money on side bets than I did in regular competition," he said.

Once, while driving past a sprawling ranch, he saw a bunch of cowboys gathering a large herd of horses. Dressed in slacks and a polo shirt, Casey pulled up in his rather gaudy looking purple car and began to pop off. "You call these horses?" he taunted them. "There isn't a one in the bunch that can buck!" Knowing he was about to be sent packing, he pulled out a roll of bills. "You haven't got one here that I can't ride!"

On seeing the money, the boss turned to a younger cowboy and told him to go get Old Rattler. Turning back to Casey he said, "You're on, kid." After the horse was led up, Casey opened the trunk of his car and lifted out his saddle and equipment, pulled on his boots and spurs, then started saddling the bronc. The sight of his well-worn gear and the skill he showed as he handled the bronc while saddling him, made the foreman start to get nervous. With the horse blindfolded, Casey eased up in the saddle and began to take his rein. The foreman, sensing that his money was in jeopardy, tried to change the rules a bit. "You've got to take the blindfold off him yourself," he told Casey.

"Okay," Casey answered, "but that's gonna cost you an extra hundred."

"You're on, you little punk!" the foreman shot back.

Casey just reached up and jerked the blindfold off. What happened next can best be described by lyrics from the Western song, *Zebra Dun*: "He thumped him in the shoulder and he spurred him when he whirled/ And he showed us flunky punchers he was the wolf of this ol' world!/ And when he had dismounted once again upon the ground/ We knew he was a thoroughbred and not a gent from town."

When 1949 came to a close, Casey Tibbs was not only a thoroughbred, he was the world champion saddle bronc rider.

Young he was, and though he looked even younger, Casey was, nonetheless, a nonstop, goal-seeking mechanism of tremendous will and energy. Casey was on his way to being recognized as "the best damned bronc rider who ever lived!"

Casey Tibbs, Gerald Roberts, and the *Bamboo Bomber*. 1948.
*(Photo Courtesy of The Donald C. and Elizabeth M. Dickinson Research
Center Archives of the National Cowboy and Western Heritage Museum.
Photo by DeVere)*

Casey in perfect control on Payday.
(*Photo Courtesy of The Donald C. & Elizabeth M. Dickinson Research Center Archives of the National Cowboy & Western Heritage Museum. Photo by DeVere)*

Casey Tibbs on the Old Gray Mare, Cheyenne, Wyoming, 1948.
A spectacular, unforgettable match. *(Photo Courtesy of The Donald C. and Elizabeth M. Dickinson Research Center Archives of the National Cowboy and Western Heritage Museum. Photo by DeVere)*

HIGH ROLLIN'

Casey was off and running with his great looks and talent and a world champion buckle on his belt. His biggest regret was that his dad couldn't share his success with him. His mother was quoted in a Huron, South Dakota, newspaper as saying, "I worry about him, of course, but since that's what he wants to do, I wouldn't spoil it by nagging him. He is always good about writing and phoning home, and I'm very proud of him."

Casey kept his close family ties intact with frequent visits, calls, and letters. He invested in a tavern in Fort Pierre, along with Dolly's husband, Giles Rheborg, who managed the business. Casey was too young to buy a drink legally, yet he owned his own tavern.

Besides the tavern, Casey undertook other investments. Some were as small as staking a competitor down on his luck for entry fees, while others were of a larger nature. He was also generous with his money and quick to lend a hand if someone needed help.

Regarding Casey's handling of money, Harry Tompkins had this to say: "He was the only man I know who could go into Fort Knox with a wheelbarrow and a scoop shovel and come out with his wallet missing."

Where his father disapproved of gambling, Casey loved it to the point of obsession. Throughout his rodeo career he nearly always carried a pair of dice in his pocket and was quick to pull them out whenever he thought he might get a little action. Casey said, "While my father was alive, I fought off the urge to gamble because he was so dead set against it, but in rodeo your life really is more or less a gamble. Every time you put your entry fees down, you're bettin' you can beat any other guy ridin'. If you don't, you don't eat." Speaking of gambling during those early years, Casey said, "Like any other kid who tried to gamble, I got screwed pretty bad around the old pros of rodeo. They used to start a game and just sit back and wait for me, like a bunch of vultures. I was their number one sucker."

***

Rodeo is a sport for cowboys, and nobody knew this better than Casey. But he also knew it was the people who filled the bleachers that made it possible for rodeo to exist as a sport. Casey always gave the best he had, with whatever stock was drawn for him, and he always dressed to please the crowd. He wore flashy purple and lavender shirts and scarves for the fans, but if his attire happened to rankle a few of the cowboys, that tickled him all the more. Purple hues eventually developed into his trademark.

He made trip after trip to the pay window, yet the cash flowed through his hands like water through a sieve. He bought tailored clothes for himself, always with a flash of lavender or purple. He wore suits and tuxedos as easily as the finest models, and he did so with the best of taste.

His automobiles included Cadillacs and Lincolns, which were often painted purple. He had a regular police siren installed in his car to clear his way through traffic or the crowds at the various fairgrounds. He used the siren as he raced from rodeo to rodeo, sometimes barely arriving in time to get on his stock.

He admits that he got an incredible amount of tickets for speeding, and although his siren saved a lot of rodeos for him, it generated even more traffic tickets than his speeding had.

"Harry Thompkins always drove a Cadillac, too, but whether it was his car or mine, it burned me up, because whenever he came to a stop sign he was always revving up the engine and hot roddin' it as he pulled away," Casey said.

"This once he came up to a stop sign, and luckily he went too far into the intersection 'cause then he had to put it into reverse to back it up a little bit. He slipped it back over into drive, but when he looked up into the rear-view mirror, I just reached over and dropped it back into reverse again, and Harry never noticed. Some guys in a pickup had pulled up behind us just as Harry gunned her. Whambo! And boy, he just whacked their heads into the windshield." Casey laughed as he finished the story.

Once during Rodeo Week in El Paso, Texas, Casey took a little trip across the Rio Grande into Juarez, Mexico. He found a Mexican barbershop that not only cut his hair, but also put hot towels on his face and massaged his scalp and shoulders while he steamed under them. Sometime during this luxurious treatment, Casey's prankster mind began to plot a most devilish joke to play on his buddies.

"It's the greatest thing you've ever experienced," he told them. "I don't know what it is about it, but after they've given you a shave and a haircut, they put these hot towels on you, and then reach under and massage your face. It hurts when they're doin' it, but if you just tough it out it's just like magic. You feel years younger when they're finished."

Later, as he browsed along the little tourist-trap stores, he finally saw Harry Tompkins enter the barbershop. He kept out of sight until Harry had his shave and haircut. After the barber tipped the chair back and the hot towels had been applied, Casey hurried over to the barbershop. He signaled the barber with the hush sign of his finger to his lips, then tiptoed up to the chair. He gently pushed the barber to one side and began massaging Harry's unsuspecting face. Reaching under the towel, he began to pinch harder till Harry's knuckles on the arms of the barber chair began to turn white. Casey laughed so hard at the memory of this incident that he could hardly tell it. "Harry really went for it," he chuckled. "I'm puttin' blood blisters on this poor guy's face and he's just lovin'it. I put it on him so hard that his feet started risin' up off the stool, but he just hung on. Now, I'm thinkin', 'My gawd, how much more of this can he take?' My arms were givin' out. I mean, I was really gettin' tired. I laughed so hard, and the next day was even worse, 'cause here comes poor Harry and he's got these cherries on his cheeks!

"Billy Weeks had been shoppin' around down there, and he'd bought a pair of cheap Mexican boots. They were kind of yellow and had black stitchin' on 'em. A lot of guys used to buy 'em in Juarez. He had 'em on and had showed 'em to me, and later on I walked by the barbershop, and there he was lyin' in the chair. You couldn't miss him with those new yellow boots on, so I tiptoed up to the chair and took over again.

"I started in on his face, but he didn't seem to take it as good as Harry had, and he started really squirming around. I knew I had to work fast, so I reached up and grabbed his nose. I really gave it a twist. I mean, I tried to take it off.

"He jumped up out of that chair and, gawd! What a shock! I'm lookin' into the enraged eyes of some guy I'd never seen before in my life. I started backin' for the door. 'I'm sorry,' I said. 'I thought you were a friend of mine.' And as I took off down the street I heard him scream, 'That's a hell of a way to treat a friend!'"

While Casey was lucky to have gotten away with a prank that had obviously gone awry, the following hair-raising account further shows how incredibly lucky he was to have survived some of them. Casey's friend, world champion Gerald Roberts, shared this story: "It always made Casey kind of embarrassed whenever I told this story. We were at the rodeo up in Eureka, California, and we rented a boat and went deep-sea fishing. There was Dave Campbell, Carl Mendes, Casey, myself, and three or four other guys, plus the captain of the boat. We had a bar on board and everything, so we had a few drinks.

"We were catching sharks about three or four feet long, just as fast as we could throw our lines in. Casey got bored with the fishin', so he just went to drinkin' and playin' around. The water was just as smooth as glass, and it was a warm day, so Casey said, 'I'm just gonna dive in.' And old Dave Campbell said, 'Why don't you?' Well, of course, Casey couldn't swim a stroke, but he went ahead and jumped. The water was smooth but the current was goin' in, and I mean it had him past the boat in just nothin' flat. I tried to throw my line out to him, but he went right on by me. I nearly jumped in after him, but it was a good thing I didn't because we would have both drowned.

"The captain of the boat jumped off after him, but then there was nobody left to run the boat. Like I said, the tide was goin' in, and they were a hundred yards from the boat in just no time at all. The captain got out to Casey and got him out of his boots, then got his own shoes off and held Casey up. Me and Carl Mendes pulled up the anchor and got the boat started. Neither one of us knew how to run it, but we managed to get it goin' and got it around to the other side of them. Heck, they never would have made it back to the boat. Casey never liked me tellin' that story, 'cause the incident ruined our fishin' trip.

"The captain had quite a bit of money in his pocket, and he lost it all when he took off his clothes to save Casey. Well, Casey had to pay him back all that money. I think it was about five hundred dollars."

Jack Buschbom remembered one of Casey's little scams that backfired on him. In those days a hundred dollar bill went a lot farther than it does today, and they were a lot harder to cash.

Jack said, "Bill Linderman, J.D. McKenna, Casey, and I were traveling together, working the rodeos at Omaha, Chicago, and New York. We were on the run, and wherever we stopped to eat and went to pay the tab, Casey would pull out a hundred dollar bill. Now, he didn't do this on the spur of the moment. He had it all set up. We were in a hurry, and he'd do it whenever he knew darn well they couldn't cash it, so that Bill or I or J.D. would have to pay. This went on for a whole week, until we got to New York.

"We finally had an evening where we weren't in such a rush 'cause we were going to stay there awhile. We sat back and had us a good meal and a few drinks. The tab came to thirty or forty dollars for the four of us, and Casey said, 'I'll get this!' and he pulled out that hundred dollar bill and handed it to the waitress. 'Oh, I can't break that tonight,' she said. Right then, Bill Linderman grabbed it and stuffed it in her pocket and said, 'Just keep the damned change!'"

GROWING POPULARITY

Casey won a total of nine world championships in the RCA. He was six times world champion saddle bronc rider. He won his first championship in saddle bronc in 1949, and he placed in the all-around standings, too. In 1950 he was in the standings for all-around, saddle bronc, and bareback bronc. In 1951 he won the all-around championship, the saddle bronc championship, and the bareback bronc riding championship. In 1952, he again won the saddle bronc championship and was in the all-around standings as well. He again won saddle bronc championships in both 1953 and 1954, and was in the all-around standings both years. In 1955, he won the all-around title, placing second in saddle bronc. His last title was for saddle bronc in 1959.

His six saddle bronc titles gave him the record for the most titles ever won in that event, and his record still holds today, although it was tied by Dan Mortensen in 2003 -- forty years after Casey set the record.

Casey's star as a saddle bronc rider shines so bright that his achievements as a great bareback bronc rider could be overlooked. He finished in fifth place in the bareback bronc riding in 1950 against many tough competitors. 1951 was another prime year for the great bareback riders of rodeo history. Top competitors that year were Jim Shoulders, Jack Buschbom, Sonny Tureman, and Del Haverty, to name just a few. Other wolves were knocking at the door in the bareback riding that year, making life tough on all of them. Harry Tompkins, Wallace Brooks, and

Buck Rutherford were doing their best to win, not to mention the ever-present threat from the Linderman brothers, Bill and Bud. Casey won the 1951 bareback bronc title 2,779 points ahead of the second place, Jim Shoulders.

The October 22, 1951, issue of *LIFE* magazine ran a full-page profile photo of Casey on its cover. With his hat tipped back on his head, arms akimbo, and straddling a bucking chute, he looked more like a model than the man who was winning the titles: world champion saddle bronc rider, world champion bareback rider, and all-around champion of the world.

The lengthy article described his great skills as well as his flamboyant lifestyle. The twenty-two photographs ran the gamut of his activities: riding broncs, steaming sore muscles, shooting craps behind the chutes, talking a cop out of a speeding ticket, sitting on a horse on Broadway in New York (with a skyscraper for a backdrop) visiting an injured Gerald Roberts in the hospital, and charming pretty girls, including a New York model at the Copacabana. They'd even included a shot of a brief reunion with his mother and family taken in a tourist court near Ellensburg, Washington.

Although Casey's first world championship came in 1949, he'd made the standings for two years before that. Of course back then, to be listed in the standings, a cowboy had to place in the top five. It's the top fifteen now, so obviously there were far fewer who made the list.

He placed fifth in 1947 when a Canadian, Carl Olson, won the title; then third in 1948, the year Gene Pruett became champion. Casey finished only $82 behind second place Carl Olson that year. Then in 1951, Deb Copenhaver, a tough competitor of Casey's, burst on the scene. It was Deb's first time in the standings, and he finished second in the saddle bronc riding ahead of greats like Gene Pruett, Bill Linderman, and Buster Ivory.

1951 proved to be Casey's biggest year. He won three world champion titles: saddle bronc riding, bareback riding, and the all-around cowboy -- the biggest sweep of his whole career. It must have been a rugged year, as whenever asked about it, Casey always referred to having been jinxed by the *LIFE* magazine thing.

Growing Popularity

Also in 1951, movie director Budd Boetticher convinced Casey to go to Hollywood and work in the picture business. This decision perhaps caused Casey to lose some of his focus on the big prizes in rodeo. Casey met Budd Boetticher at the rodeo at Cheyenne, and Budd had just agreed to direct a film with John Lund and Scott Brady called *The Bronco Busters.*

"Rodeo was not my cup of tea," Boetticher admitted, "so I took the picture on the condition that I be allowed to go to Cheyenne to live and learn among the top cowboys then bring them back with me to make the picture," Budd explained. "I'd gone to many rodeos, but I'm convinced that people making films should be very careful to know their subject. Neither John Lund nor Scott Brady could ride, and when you have actors who are playing great boxers or bullfighters or rodeo performers but can't really do these things, you surround them with the best who can -- it helps make them believable. It's a great trick. I did that in *The Bullfighter And The Lady* while filming in Mexico. During the filming, I surrounded Robert Stack and Gilbert Roland with the best bullfighters in the world.

"I had just finished shooting *The Bullfighter And The Lady,* and I was riding high in Hollywood, so I got my way and went to Cheyenne. While I was there I met Casey, Dan Poore, Pete Crump, and the Linderman boys. Casey was very thin and curly haired and good looking, but he looked like the son of a Hollywood producer instead of the best rodeo performer in the whole world.

"I really liked Casey, so I asked him to come to Hollywood with me. I told him about my trick of surrounding actors with the best, etc. He said, 'I don't want to go to Hollywood. They're a bunch of sissies out there.' But I told him, 'No, there are some pretty tough boys out there, and you'll love it.' Anyway, I talked him into it, but I had to promise him I'd never do anything to embarrass him.

"One of the funniest things that happened while filming a picture with Casey occurred when we were shooting a street scene with Robert Ryan and Rock Hudson. The street was asphalt underneath, but we'd covered it with about six inches of dirt in order to date it back to about the 1880s or '90s. Casey was supposed to come barreling down the street shooting and get shot off his horse.

"We were setting up the scene, and Casey was way down in the background with his leg hooked over the horn of the saddle, talking to some very pretty girls. He wasn't paying much attention to what we were doing. The cameraman, Charlie Boyle, came over to me and said, 'Budd, we didn't notice it, but the sun is setting so fast that I'm afraid when Casey rides by here we're going to see our cameras reflected in the window of the store across the street. We better have him ride through so we can check it.' So, I hollered down to Casey, 'Casey! Ride on through!' The camera wasn't even set up. I was just looking through the finder. Well, here comes Casey just flyin', and he bailed off that horse and plowed through that ground, and he looked like the waves of a battleship till he came to a dead stop.

"I walked right up to him and bent over, looking at him through the finder and said, 'Cut! Print!'" Budd roared with laughter at the memory of it.

"After that we worked together a lot, and he always stayed with me when he was in town. If he'd have listened to me, he would have been another Randolph Scott or Gary Cooper, but it's very difficult to take an athlete like that and put him into a new branch of the service, because to him making pictures wasn't as much fun as rodeoing. But Casey had the talent.

"I remember one night in New York. We were just leaving the Capitol Bar, which is across the street from Madison Square Garden, when a young cowboy with his number still on his back walked up and said, 'Mr. Tibbs, I'm so and so.' I couldn't catch the name, but I heard him say, 'They told me if I asked you, you might help me out. My wife, Sally, is going to have a baby in a couple of days and I don't have a penny.'

"Casey peeled off I don't know how many hundred dollar bills and gave them to the kid, and the kid walked off backwards thanking him. We took a couple of steps and Casey said, 'Budd, did you get that kid's name?' I said, 'No, what do you mean? Don't you know him?' He said, 'Never saw him before, but it doesn't make any difference.'

"Every time I'd get something together for Casey that I thought was really going to turn into something good for him, he'd take off for Denver or Houston or Fort Pierre to fill a rodeo commitment. But I made him work because he was so damn good and nobody could ride like him. Casey could have been a big star, but his first loyalty was always to rodeo, and I've got to admire him for that," Budd concluded.

It appears that the picture business sidetracked Casey. He obviously enjoyed it, but he would pass up great opportunities there to make a rodeo. It's difficult to guess how much Casey's continuing to rodeo while working in films cost him in lost breaks in the motion picture business. At the same time, it's impossible to determine what else he might have won in rodeo had he not taken the time away from the sport to work in films. In any event, he did remarkably well in both businesses.

***

Audie Murphy is America's most highly decorated hero. For service in World War II, he was awarded a total of thirty-seven medals. Eleven of these were for valor, including The Distinguished Service Cross, The Silver Star, and the Congressional Medal of Honor. Audie's shy and vulnerable good looks did not go unnoticed by Hollywood scouts, and after the war he became a successful actor.

Casey remembered Audie as a complex, often moody individual, whom few people really got to know. In recalling how their friendship began, Casey said, "I met Audie in 1951 at Universal Studios. I was working on a picture that Budd Boetticher was directing called *The Bronco Buster*.

"We became friends over one little thing I said. An incident happened shortly after I first met him -- I mean, I hardly knew him. We went into the steam room and I saw that one cheek of his butt was gone from a wound he'd received in the war. So I said, 'Mr. Murphy, if you're so damn brave, how come half of your ass is missin'?' Well, he laughed, I mean, he thought that was the funniest damn thing! He told it to everybody. One friend remarked, 'Who the hell could have gotten away with that but Casey?'

"We started runnin' around together. We bought some race horses to-gether, and we dated the same women. He'd tell the ladies he was Casey Tibbs, and I'd tell them I was Audie Murphy. One airline stewardess never did know who she was goin' out with. Audie and I spent a lot of time together.

"Little things would bother Audie, though, like the time he backed out of his driveway and ran over a kitten. That just tore him up. He got about half hot at me once because I was invited to the Governor's One Shot Antelope Hunt, and I wanted him to go with me. But he refused, answering, 'I don't want to kill any animals.'

"I never worked with Audie much in pictures. Universal was always going to do something, like have us play brothers or something 'cause we were similar types, but it never happened.

"Audie often seemed preoccupied, and yet he'd let go at times and laugh and cut up and really enjoy himself. He had his problems, I'm sure, because of what all he'd gone through in the war, but I really liked him a lot," Casey concluded.

Murphy died in a light airplane crash on May 28, 1971. He left a wife, Pamela, and their two sons, Terry and James, many loyal friends, and a multitude of fans who miss him very much.

THE DEVIL MADE HIM DO IT!

As the youthful sensation in bronc riding, Casey was asked to come to Hollywood to make an appearance on the television program, *You Asked for It*. Art Baker interviewed him, and film clips of several of Casey's bronc rides were shown, demonstrating what has been called "the greatest spurring lick in all of rodeo."

Casey, dressed in loafers, slacks, a polo shirt, and wearing makeup, stopped for a drink at the Cinegrill in the Hollywood Roosevelt Hotel where he was staying. He thought the lounge would be a good place to have a cool one. Instead, he nearly had to fight his way out of there.

Gene Autry had a sound stage not too far away, and the Cinegrill was full of cowboy extras who'd been working on one of the Westerns. When they saw Casey they started to question him. "What are you working on?" one of them asked.

Casey replied, "I'm out here doin' Art Baker's show, *You Asked For It*.

"Sure, kid, what's your name?" demanded one.

"Casey Tibbs," he told them.

"Yeah, I'm Joe DiMaggio!" one of them shot back.

"I thought I was gonna have to fight them," Casey said. "I guess people thought I should be a two-hundred pounder and stand six foot six. I think the reason I was impersonated so often is probably because a lot of people really didn't know what I looked like. I guess they visualized me as somebody with one ear missin', or whatever. One guy up in Nevada was part Indian and looked nothin' like me whatsoever, but he was able to buy a Cadillac in my name, and he married a woman in my name.

"He wrote a check for the down payment on the car up in Hollister, but he made the mistake of driving it to Salinas where I was fairly well known. He checked into the Town and Country Hotel and started signing my name to his bar tabs. The bartender called the front desk and told them, 'This guy that's registered here isn't Casey Tibbs.' It was just lucky the bartender knew me.

"They called the cops, but the guy found out that they were comin'. The cops arrived just as he and his wife were startin' out the front door, so they turned and ran out the back across a beet field and escaped.

"They got back to Nevada somehow and stopped in Winnemucca. It was early mornin' when they arrived, and there was an all-points bulletin out on 'em. As it happened, an old sheriff was on duty who'd punched cows with my brother Shortlog when he'd gone out to Nevada back in the thirties. The sheriff's department was checkin' out any couples that fit the description, so they asked him his name and he told 'em it was Casey Tibbs. That old sheriff had never seen me, but he knew the guy didn't look anything like my brother, so they hauled him in.

"There was another guy who knew more about my life history than I did, just about. He was writin' his life story about me. I even read some of it and it wasn't worth a damn, but he was goin' around tryin' to sell it, callin' it *Casey Tibbs Autobiography*.

"He was about twenty years older than me, but he would call me from different places all over the country, at all hours of the day and night." Casey chuckled, "I couldn't ever get my hands on him. One guy up in Colorado even bet a hundred dollars that it was me.

"Another couple, a man and wife who called themselves Casey and Jerry Tibbs, made a hell of a run on me, but they never wrote any big checks, just twenties and thirties. A lot of those checks actually went through my bank. They wrote checks on me all up and down Route 66."

In addition to impersonators, other criminal types sometimes targeted Casey. Once, in New York, he came close to being seriously harmed, if not killed, for the roll of money he invariably carried.

The Devil Made Him Do It!

Casey loved the rodeos at New York and at Boston for the thrill of winning and the money it brought him. But he also relished them for the excitement, the crowds, the many friends gathered together and, of course, the showgirls and models who were equally interested in him.

Casey recalled, "I dang near got hit in the head there once, and it was not in the arena. Ham Fisher, who did the *Joe Palooka* comic strip, was a good friend of the cowboys. He liked to hang around with us and would always throw a big party during the New York rodeo.

"I carried a lot of money on me in those days, and I ended up with two party gals in a cab going through the Lincoln Tunnel. I'd been drinkin' quite a bit, but I know that the cab driver was in on it, 'cause I was hollerin' at him, but he wouldn't stop or turn around.

"We ended up in a scroungey end of town, over in New Jersey. They took me to this joint -- it was a bar with rooms upstairs. We'd spent quite a bit of time in the cab, so I just went to actin' like I was drinkin', and actin' a lot drunker than I really was -- although I was drunk enough.

"There were people runnin' upstairs and down, and by now I was certain the bartender was in on it with them. Finally, I sensed I was in deep trouble, so I took off and broke out of there. I ran down the street thinkin' I'd get picked up by the cops -- hopin' I would. I tipped over trashcans and ran down the middle of the street stoppin' cars. It was about three or four o'clock in the mornin', but there wasn't a cop to be seen anywhere. I ran down alleys, and I finally got a taxi to stop, and I got the heck out of there."

In every city there are always those people who think that cowboys should be fair game for their rudeness. "What do you say, Tex?" or "Hey Tex! Where'd you leave your horse?" are just a couple of the jeers.

In New York one year, as Casey and some other cowboys were arriving at their hotel, the doorman became so obnoxious and abusive that Casey cold-cocked him with a single punch. He picked him up, still unconscious, and placed him in the back seat of a waiting taxi. Peeling off several bills, Casey handed them to the driver saying, "Take him over to the other side of town and drop him off." Then the cowboys cheerfully continued checking into the hotel, as if nothing had happened.

Casey said, "A lot of famous people and a lot of socialites liked the cowboys. Ham Fisher and Barbara Walters' father, Louis "Lou" Walters, who owned the Latin Quarter, both liked the cowboys a lot. Barbara was about my age, and I socialized with her a little, but her dad put a stop to that pretty fast."

Casey's addiction for pranks and practical jokes have made him possibly the most memorable cowboy ever to come along. He carried some of his gags to the extreme; some of them did not come off according to plan, and some of them caused Casey to reflect, "There are a few things I've done that I'm not too proud of." In later years, after Casey had joined A.A., he often remarked, "That was definitely alcohol related!"

Casey said, "Rex Allen was makin' his first big appearance in rodeo, and he was really wantin' to make a good impression with the cowboys because entertainers were sort of frowned on by them back then. The cowboys just weren't all that friendly toward them. But Rex was billed as the Arizona Cowboy and all, so he was really hopin' that the cowboys would accept him.

"Rex was just gettin' ready to go on at San Antonio and was signing autographs when I spotted him. Well, I'd gotten this disappearing ink, and there Rex was in that white costume with red roses embroidered all over it and covered with rhinestones. A whole bunch of kids had gathered around him, so I just walked up to him and said, 'Mister Allen, I really would like to have your autograph.' He was kind of thrilled because I'd just won my first world title.

"'Yeah! Sure!' he said, and I pulled the top off the pen and just laced that ink across his rhinestones. It looked awful, but after a few minutes that disappearing ink didn't even leave a water stain.

"Well, that went over so good I went down where all the trick riders were with their new white hats and white costumes, and I said to them, 'Hey! Let me give you my autograph!' And I pulled the cap off the pen and laced them good.

"Norma Shoulders jumped down off her horse and threw a real good Stetson on the ground and stomped it she was so mad. She just ruined it; she stomped a perfectly good Stetson into the tanbark. I mean, she was ready to kill.

"One of the cowboys and a good buddy of mine, Dan Poore, was standing there watchin' this and laughin'. When he saw what the ink was, he came over to me and said, 'Hey! Let me borrow that a minute so I can get Gordon Davis and those guys.' So I told him, 'Yeah, but I'm almost out of ink. Wait here a minute and I'll go fill it.'

"I went up to Fred Alvard's office and filled the pen with regular old desk ink and then took it back and gave it to Dan. Well, he just ran amuck with it. Lex Connelly had on one of those candy-striped jackets, and Gordon Davis had on a gabardine suit. Dan just let 'em both have it. They thought their old friend had gone crazy.

"Now, Dan turned and walked down by the doggin' chutes, and there sits all these people in the front seats who have put on a lot of muck to go to the rodeo. In San Antonio they wear mink stoles and everything else, and he's just lettin' 'em have it with that pen. 'Let me give you my autograph,' he's tellin' 'em.

"Well, when I saw that, the cold chills just started goin' up my neck. I wasn't up for a couple of days, so I just went and got in my car and drove to the Gunter Hotel and stayed in my room. All these people were comin' into the rodeo office and just raisin' hell. They called in Colborn, the rodeo producer, and everything, 'cause there was no way of cleanin' anythin', with that old ink.

"When Dan Poore saw me two days later, he headed toward me with his hands out like this...." Casey held his hands out, indicating a strangling position. The whole time he was shaking with laughter.

Casey lit up again, his eyes dancing with mischief as he recalled one trip he took with Benny Reynolds. Benny was the lanky, likeable cowboy that appeared on the once popular television program *Name That Tune*. His shy, smiling, good-natured manner had a Gary Cooper-like quality, and his "yep" and "nope" way of answering the questions literally charmed all those who saw the show.

Casey chuckled as he said, "I always stopped at the trick stores in every town to see if anything new came out 'cause they would have stuff there that you could use to pull tricks on almost everybody.

"We were goin' back to Minneapolis to a rodeo -- Benny Reynolds, Jim Shoulders, and myself. Jim was in a hurry to get to Minneapolis 'cause he hadn't been married too long and his wife was goin' to meet him there. He fell over in the back seat and said, 'You guys take over, 'cause I'm gonna sleep a bit.'

"We'd all been rodeoin' and travelin' like hell, and there was an old bar there, so Benny and I just left the car set right there. Well, at three o'clock in the mornin' Jim wakes up still sittin' in the same place.

"Benny and I are still drinkin' and playin' the slot machines, and we got a bunch of the town gals there and everything. It was Jim's car, but he was so mad at us he wouldn't ride with us anymore. I forget where he flew out of, but he got a plane and went on ahead and left us there.

"We just had enough time to get to the rodeo, and we had to ride as soon as we got there. Benny's knee was already hurt a little bit, and he hurt it again in the first go. We'd wasted about six hours in that old bar and now Benny's got water on his knee after the first go-round. And damn, it was hurtin' him, so he got his stock held back.

"We were roomin' together, so when he left the room I got out this itching powder and put it in his bed. Well, this poor booger is crippled and he can't get no sleep anyway, and now he's got this itching powder all over him. I'd put the itching powder in the bed, then made it up real nice, but finally he got wise to it. I came in and here he is hoppin' around on one leg." Casey laughed so hard here that he could hardly tell the rest of the story. "He's got the beds tore apart and is tryin' to put his mattress over on my bed. He was changin' the sheets and the mattress covers and everything. That was Benny, and his brother John and I had a lot of good times together, too."

The ProRodeo Historical Society has sponsored several reunions for retired rodeo people and their families. They call these gatherings "Wild Bunch Reunions," and they provide a great opportunity to laugh and reminisce. Naturally, Casey Tibbs stories abound. During the meeting of the Wild Bunch at Fort Worth, Texas, in January of 1986, Charlie Beals, an RCA cowboy from Tulsa, Oklahoma, and a friend and competitor of Casey's, recalled one of the pranks that kept Casey "on the lam" for a couple of days in Fort Smith, Arkansas.

Charlie told about Casey and another cowboy going for lunch together, and when they went to pay their bill, Casey noticed a big, cut-glass bowl on the counter that was level full of toothpicks. At the same time, he felt a big firecracker he'd been saving in his jacket pocket. The temptation was just too great. Casey "set the charge" while his friend was busy paying the bill, and Casey cut out the door.

Charley said, "Well, that firecracker went off with a big boom. I mean, it filled that room with toothpicks! The woman behind the counter came a runnin' out the door after Casey who'd run down the alley and had got up on top of the buildings. She called the cops."

According to Charlie, Casey spent his time on the rooftop of the hotel and moved about the city by jumping from roof to roof, knowing the police were after him. Finally, some very congenial inhabitants of a house of ill repute befriended him.

"The cops hunted Casey all day and half the night, and he didn't surface for a day or two 'cause he knew the law was a-huntin' him," Charley remarked. "They never did catch him, but it was a mess!"

Harry Tompkins remembered several good stories about his days traveling with Casey. Harry's eyes lit up with delight as his memory wandered through the interesting subject matter. "We had some airplane experiences that were really something. How we're still all here today, I don't know."

Harry continued, "This was back when they had those air sick cups on the airplanes that looked like coffee containers, you know, with the cardboard caps on them. Planes back then, they flew right into the storms at times. They didn't go around 'em. Sometimes when it got bumpy and rough -- hell! It was like a buckin' horse almost. I mean, especially at night, when they didn't know a storm was there until they were in it.

"Anyway, we were on this airplane and Casey was sittin' across from this old gal, and he saw her ask for the sick cup. So he called the stewardess and had her bring him a cup, too. Well, this gal is just actin' like she might be gettin' sick, but she never had gotten sick yet. So Casey gets his cup out, and he acts like he's really bein' sick. You know, he's makin' all the noises, pretending he was throwin' up and then settin' there, holding his cup up in front of him. Well, pretty soon Casey caught her lookin' at him, and he just tips up the cup and acts like he's drinkin' it! Well, this old gal never even hit her cup, she just threw up right on past it.

She threw up all over the long hair of the lady sitting in front of her. That damned Casey, I mean, he'd sure plan 'em!"

Buster Ivory and Harry Tompkins once told about a rodeo announcer at Calgary named Sparrow. They both laughed heartily at how mad Sparrow used to get at Casey. Sparrow used a megaphone to announce the rodeo, so he was continuously picking it up and putting it down. Buster and Harry said that Sparrow had a little mustache. Well, Casey spotted some old black grease oozing from a hinge on the bucking chutes, so when Sparrow wasn't lookin', Casey smeared it around the mouthpiece of the megaphone. Of course, the first time Sparrow used the microphone, it left a black ring around his mouth.

"After about the third day or so, Sparrow was really mad," Harry added. "Then he got so that he wouldn't put the megaphone down on the ground at all. He carried it up under his arm at all times. He had this little ol' board and pad where he'd jot down things. But Casey would grease that too, while it was still under his arm. Sparrow would get so mad he'd just scream at him."

One time Casey had to appear before a judge in Tucson, Arizona, on a speeding violation. This was back in the days when Casey carried all the money he owned in his pockets. "That'll be fifty dollars," the judge pronounced, as he started to tap his gavel.

"That's easy," Casey retorted, "I've got that right here in my pocket." And he pulled out a big roll of bills.

"And ten days in jail," the judge added, raising his voice. "Have you got that in your pocket, too?"

Billy Hogue told another good one on Casey. "A long time ago, when Casey had his office upstairs in one of those brick buildings on Sunset Boulevard in Hollywood, he was supposed to meet his bookkeeper at the office. They each had a key to the place and they were both busier than hell, so they were gonna meet there about eight o'clock at night.

"Casey knew the guy was real skittery, so he got there about twenty minutes early and let himself in but left all the lights off. The building looked like one of them old court houses, and Casey went upstairs and hid behind the banister at the top of the stairs on his floor. It was real dark in there, and he waited and waited. Finally, he heard the guy unlock the door and let himself in and start climbing the stairs.

"When the bookkeeper got right in front of him and came around the end of the banister, old Casey squalled and jumped up and grabbed him by the ass! But it was the maid! It wasn't the bookkeeper!" Billy's voice rose here, and he became animated, waving his arms about as he said, "She screamed and threw that bucket of soapy water in the air, and her brushes and the mop went flyin' too. Stuff was scattered all over. Casey had gotten wet, of course, and he apologized. When his bookkeeper got there, he found Casey on his hands and knees cleaning up all that ol' soapy water. Now, Casey told me that story on himself," Billy remarked.

Rodeo cowboy and later motion picture stuntman Arnold Hill related the following story: "This happened after the rodeo at Carlsbad, New Mexico. Casey, Bill Linderman, and I were waiting to get paid so that we could leave for Deadwood when Bill got into it with a guy.

"Bill used to get into scraps pretty often. Well, before we left Carlsbad, this guy beat the hell out of ol' Bill, and when it was over we all got into the car and headed for Deadwood. Casey was drivin' and ol' Bill, he's just a settin' there, but when we'd got about twenty-five miles down the road, ol' Bill reaches over and hits ol' Casey and says, 'Turn around! I think I can handle that guy. I'm gonna go back and whip his ass!'

"So Casey turns the car around and drives back to Carlsbad. Well, ol' Bill goes out and finds this guy, and the ol' boy beats the hell out of Bill again! So now Bill is completely flattened 'cause he's had the crap beat out of him twice by the same guy. We all get back into the car and drive about twenty-five miles out of town and ol' Casey just turns a brodie and spins the car around and starts headin' back to Carlsbad. Ol' Bill Linderman says, 'What the hell's the matter with you, you bronc ridin' little bastard?' And Casey says, 'We've gone far enough. I think you can handle him now. I'm takin' you back.' And Bill says, 'No! No! Turn this car back around -- I've had enough!'"

***

Throughout Casey's career, traveling by car was a usual mode of transportation, and Casey drove his cars at top speed, sometimes up to a hundred and thirty miles per hour. On one trip he drove from Houston, Texas, to Palm Springs, California, in nineteen hours and five minutes, a total distance of fifteen hundred and sixty-three miles. "We were going so fast that the cops couldn't catch us," he said.

Once, when Casey and Eddy Akridge were traveling together, they stayed over in Las Vegas after the Helldorado Days Rodeo. Their plan was to leave the next day for Killeen, Texas. Casey had gotten up early and had gone down to the casino to gamble.

"I got cleaned up and went down to the coffee shop to have breakfast with a guy that I'd arranged to meet with," Eddy said. "I was just finishing a cup of tea when Casey walked up and asked me if I had any money. I'd won the bull riding the night before, so I told him I had a check for nine hundred and eighty dollars. So I endorsed it and gave it to him. Well, when I finally finished that tea and walked into the casino, Casey had about eighty dollars left of that nine eighty.

"So I stood there and started watching him, and he won back about eight hundred of it and I went over and I said, 'Give me back about five hundred of that,' and I took five hundred of it and went over and cashed the chips in.

"By the time I went back over there, Casey had another eight hundred. So I told him to give me another five hundred. And I did that five times in a row and picked up twenty-five hundred dollars. When I went back over again he had another eight hundred, but I thought, 'I won't bother him anymore.' He lost that eight hundred and came to me to get some more money, but I told him, 'No, we've got to get started to Killeen.' And oh, he was mad at me for not giving him any more money.

"So we went out and got in his car and took off for Killeen. I didn't give him any money till we got to Kingman, Arizona. I took my nine hundred and eighty out and gave him the rest of it, and he snapped, 'Thanks!'" Eddy laughed as he continued, "And that was all that was ever said."

Besides sticking him with some of their tickets, the other cowboys took their turn at evening the score with their prankster friend whenever they

102

could. Once in Las Vegas, at the old Cashman Arena, Casey received an ovation from the crowd that he would rather have done without. Animated and laughing, he related the incident.

Casey said, "That was a big arena. Looking up at the crowds from the chutes, it looked like a solid wall of people. There was an infield right behind the chutes where some outhouses were lined up.

"It was right before the bronc ridin' when my stomach hit me, and I had to go. There was a clown act goin' on or somethin', so I told this security guard to cover for me 'cause I had to run to the outhouse.

"Just as I closed the door I heard the crowd holler. I thought they were watchin' the clowns, but they hollered 'cause they saw about six cowboys run toward the outhouse. It was not too clean in there, so I was settin' up on the top of the seat like I was out on the range. I had just got my pants down when those damn guys hit that thing and rolled it over!"

By then the crowd had forgotten what was goin' on in the arena and were focused on me. I heard everybody roar when the latrine tipped over, so I thought I'd better stay in there a little bit and maybe they wouldn't see me when I came out. I waited, but it started to get bad in there so I rolled out. I was tryin' to pull my pants up when I got a standin' ovation. If they'd have set that outhouse over on the door, I'd still be in there."

Casey was an unforgettable sight in his purple car. Once, when leaving Kansas City he lost his way, so he pulled off the interstate to ask for directions. Two old men were sitting in rocking chairs in front of a little country store, and they looked somewhat amazed as the purple-shirted Casey in his purple car asked them for help. They put down their flyswatters long enough to point out the way Casey should go.

Exactly one year later after the Kansas City Rodeo, Casey found himself confused by the same road, and before he realized it, he'd pulled up in front of the same store. There sat the same two old men, staring at him with their mouths hanging open as the purple-shirted Casey climbed out of the purple car to ask them the same question he'd asked them a year before. Before he could speak, one of the old guys knitted his brows and barked, "My gawd, man! Are you still lost?"

FATHER OF THE NATIONAL
FINALS RODEO

That Casey won the saddle bronc title in 1952 was nothing short of an incredible achievement because in July of that year he was severely injured at the Snake River Stampede in Nampa, Idaho. He'd drawn a bronc called No Doz, and although the horse didn't turn in his usual pattern of spinning, he bucked hard and Casey spurred him in spectacular style.

After the whistle blew, the two pickup men moved in from both sides, but at the exact moment Casey stretched to reach behind the pickup man to dismount, No Doz and the pickup horse veered apart. Casey fell head first between them and was knocked unconscious. As he lay there, face down and out cold, No Doz and both pickup horses trampled him.

In the hospital in Nampa, Casey didn't regain consciousness until the next morning, and when he did, he was shaken to discover that he was paralyzed from the waist down. He had a badly torn shoulder ligament and a blood clot on his spine which caused the paralysis.

The future looked black for Casey. Doctors told him he would probably never walk again. While lying there in his hospital bed, he became determined that this would not be the case. He worked with heroic resolve at getting his legs to move, and before the week was out he could wiggle his toes, then move his legs a little. Just nine days after the accident, he picked up the phone and called Frank Finley, who lived there in Nampa, and asked him if he would come and pick him up and drive him to Cheyenne, Wyoming.

Lee Riders Jeans had been using Casey's photos in their advertising. His image appeared in magazines and on billboards all over the country looking lean, fit, and handsome. He'd promised the Lee Riders advertising folks that he'd be at the Cheyenne Frontier Days Rodeo to sign autographs for them, and Casey meant to keep his word.

Casey dressed and was trying to leave the hospital past a wall of doctors and nurses by the time Finley arrived. The hospital staff finally let him go, but only after he signed a release that absolved them from all responsibility for what might happen.

Just the day before, Casey had gotten up on a pair of crutches for the first time, and he now used these crutches to maneuver himself down to Frank's car. When he got to the car, he opened the door, then smashed the crutches one at a time over the top of the door. After pulling himself inside, he looked up just as Frank motored away from the curb. Concerned faces of the doctors, nurses, and staff filled the hospital windows. Casey took off his hat and waved them a cheerful goodbye with it.

In less than a month he'd tied down his torn shoulder and won the bronc riding at Rapid City, South Dakota. The bronc he rode was a previously unridden buckskin called Boomerang.

Casey placed first in saddle bronc in 1952. Not only did he win the title, he also amassed the second highest number of points ever earned in that event. The highest number had also belonged to him for the previous year. Deb Copenhaver placed third again, ahead of Buster Ivory and Gene Pruett, but behind Bill Linderman.

Then, in 1953 and 1954, Casey again placed first and Deb second. In 1955 Copenhaver finally edged Casey out of first by a slim margin of just $174 for the saddle bronc riding title. Still, by finishing second in the saddle bronc riding and third in the bareback bronc riding, Casey emerged again as the all-around champion in 1955, even though he'd begun the year with a serious injury in January at the Denver Rodeo: he'd been trampled after hanging up on his bronc.

When asked by a friend if there was ever a time in his career where he'd come from behind and beaten all the odds for an important title,

Casey's first response had been one of irritation. "Rodeo's not like that," he'd snapped. But later, upon reflection, he said, "It was the all-around title in 1955. I was trailing for the all-around, and then in New York I drew bad in both the saddle bronc and bareback. They ran out of broncs in the bareback, so they put some horses from the wild horse race into the draw. I'd drawn a wild son of a buck, plus I'd drawn Chief Tyhee in the saddle bronc. Chief Tyhee was a bronc that had never been qualified out of the chute. He'd just rear over on you out of the gate, so I didn't figure I had any shot at the all-around championship.

"Well, I got lucky, 'cause my wild horse did buck. I made just enough points on him to win third in the world bareback by the skin of my teeth. But when I was gettin' ready to come out on Chief Tyhee, I could never even get down on his back 'cause I knew what he'd do. So I just stood on the chute over him. I had them hand me my stirrups, and I put them barely on my toes.

"I asked for the gate just as I dropped down onto his back, and I qualified him out, and the ride went perfect. I won the all-around title, and believe me, I didn't stand a chance, but the name of the game is try."

Although Casey seldom worked the bull riding event, he entered several times in 1954. He did well, winning in Reno. Then at the Los Angeles Coliseum he drew Andy Jauregui's bull, Gentleman Jim. This famous bull had remained unridden for six or seven years. Gentleman Jim came by his name because he was by nature a rather tame animal that could, in fact, buck. They say that cowboys sometimes took their families out to Andy's ranch in Newhall, California, for picnics. While Gentleman Jim grazed in the fields, they would take their children out and let them pet him. Sometimes they would set their children on his back to see how many he could hold. They swear that bull would just peacefully continue to graze, to all appearances oblivious to his riders.

Gentleman Jim was a Charlaise-type bull, having the light color peculiar to that breed. He was a good traveler and would seem at times almost to be dozing in the chutes, waiting for the bull riding to begin. When the cowboy who'd drawn him began to set his rope and get ready to ride, Jim seemed to settle deep into the chute. When the gate was opened, he'd look back at the cowboy, almost as if to say, "Are you ready?" If there ever was a bull that loved to buck, then Gentleman Jim surely was one of those. On that day in 1954, Jim, who was used to winning these kinds of battles, "turned the crank" as the saying goes, yet he had one major problem. For on his back was the great Casey Tibbs, and when the dust cleared, Casey was still there, and he picked up a check for $1,500, the most money ever paid for a single ride up to that time.

***

The fierce, competitive rivalry that took place between Casey and Deb Copenhaver was serious business but laced with humorous incidents. The two often traveled together and even helped each other at the bucking chutes, trading information on horses or helping with equipment, but the banter between them was often one of challenge as to who was the better bronc rider.

"Nobody knows what Casey was like in those days better than I do," Deb began. "I spent a lot of time with him, and we went to an awful lot of rodeos together, sometimes in an airplane, sometimes in a car. And it was one continual trick of his after another.

"Once, we left Denver, goin' to Fort Worth. It'd been a rather long night, and I was glad it was over. Casey was feelin' pretty sick and had laid down in the back seat and covered himself up with a blanket and gone to sleep.

"We were travelin' through the country when I came to this little town," Deb recalled. "There was an old guy in a pickup in front of us, and he was goin' only about five miles an hour on an overpass.

"A sign was posted saying not to pass, but the old guy was practically stopped, so I thought, 'Heck, it'll be all right,' and I pulled on around him. Just as I did, a cop caught me doin' it, and he pulled me over.

"I was really pleadin' with him. I told him, 'Shucks, with that old pickup goin' so slow, it was a hazard in its own right, so I just got out of there.'

"I'd come within an inch of talkin' that cop out of that ticket when Casey reared up out of the back seat and said, 'Officer, I've listened to this old malarkey all I'm goin' to. I've come all the way from Denver with him, and he's broken every law in the book. Somebody's got to stop him or he's goin' to kill himself, and kill me, too. Something has to be done about him.' Well, the cop wrote me a ticket and it cost me thirty dollars. Casey really enjoyed it -- he thought that was the funniest thing he'd ever done in his life.

"Even though we were competitors and constantly jawed at each other, I truly loved him like a brother. I can truthfully say, and I thank God for it, we never did actually fight. You'd have thought we were going to the very next minute, but we never did ever go to battle.

"Lookin' back now, I'm so grateful because it would have hurt something between us that I really treasured. I just thank God that even though we were at each other constantly and carryin' on, we still always seemed to be good friends when the mornin' came."

Casey pulled enough pranks on Deb to really try Deb's patience. Once, in a club in Kansas City, Deb sat down at the piano and began to play. He became absorbed in the piece he was playing and was really turning in a masterful performance. While he was busy, Casey began moving from table to table with his fingers to his lips giving the hush sign. Table by table he ushered folks out the door. Other people began catching on and soon, grinning silently, they'd all slipped out of the club. He placed a large bill on the bar as a tip, and motioned for the two bartenders to duck down under the bar, then Casey left the club, leaving the place empty. When Deb reached the grand finale and turned around for approval, he found himself completely alone.

***

Matched bronc riding contests between Casey and Bill Linderman were staged several times in different towns. Whoever promoted them would put up a thousand dollars, and they would each ride six broncs. The one with the highest score on all six horses got the thousand.

In 1954, *LIFE* magazine covered one of these matches in the little town of Bridger, Montana. Bridger is right close to Red Lodge, Montana, where Bill Linderman was born and raised. The population of Bridger is only eight hundred and fifty, but seven thousand people from all over the state flocked there to see the match.

LIFE titled their article "The Big Buck at Bridger," and they ran six photos of the event. One photo featured Casey and Bill standing together watching the preliminary events; three pictures were action shots of Casey on three different broncs; another was of a shaken Linderman being helped from the arena after being thrown from a bronc. The last photo pictured a smiling Casey receiving his check while Bill, also smiling, looked on.

It was by no means a runaway for Casey when these events took place. These were hard-fought competitions all the way, and both he and Bill had been victorious on different occasions.

At that matched bronc riding at Bridger in 1954, Casey and Deb very nearly tangled. Deb had been traveling with Casey, and Deb recalled the skirmish happened like this: "Me and J.D. McKenna just went along for the show. Shirley Hussy was the bucking horse man for Leo Cremer, and he brought the horses for the matched bronc riding. He'd gotten them from a man called Lawyer Rankin. Rankin had one claim to fame: he owned more land in Montana at one time than anybody else.

"Well, when Rankin bought out some of those ranches, he bought the brand and everything else. This one ranch had a bunch of palomino horses that were six to eight years old. They were wild and had never even had a halter on them, and that's what Hussey brought for the matched bronc ridin'." Deb laughed before he continued, "If anyone ever played a dirty trick on somebody, that was it. They were big, tall horses, and so wild you couldn't even get a halter on them.

"Casey and Bill rode six head apiece that day, and it was a rough day for them. The horses had no pattern and they were just wild. They'd climb up out of the chutes and there was no way of knowin' what they'd do next. They'd fall down and fight the chute -- it was just a horrible day.

"Mike Quinn was the guy who put the thing on, and he owned the bar there at Bridger. He had asked me and J.D. if we'd like to make a hundred dollars apiece. He had a couple of tryout horses, and he said he'd pay us to ride them.

"I told him shucks, I'd break 'em for that, and J.D. said the same thing. Well, they turned out to be the best little class kind of 'nice draw' horses you could ask for. Mine was a little gray horse, and he just stood in the chute there and he let me halter him and saddle him, and he just popped his lip and never even moved once. He let me get on him, and man he jumped out there, and you could have won day-money on him anywhere in the world.

"He was just that kind of a horse, and J.D.'s was the same way, and boy, those rides brought the house down. So that night down at the bar, I was kiddin' Casey and said, 'Shucks, you can't ride nothing. I brought the house down!'"

Casey laughed as he remembered the incident. "Deb was a good guy and my friend and a top bronc rider, but he had some little old chicken-shit ways! He was leadin' the bronc ridin' for that year, and he was maybe a hundred-and-twenty-some points ahead of me for the year. But it was only the month of May, so that meant nothin'. He was havin' them announce that he was the leadin' champion and all that.

"Anyway, that night at the bar he was gettin' on me, and I started pushin' it until we darn near got into a fight over it. So Deb finally said, 'I'll just bet you a hundred that I beat you for the year.' We had a big audience and I had just won the thousand in the match, so I said, 'Hell! If we're goin' to bet somethin', let's bet a thousand.'

"I knew Deb probably wasn't packing a thousand on him, but about that time Mike Quinn stepped in and said, 'Why don't you both write a check and I'll hold them here on the back bar. I'll send them to whoever wins.'

"I milked it up a little more," Casey went on. "I said, 'I'll take his check if he can get someone to cosign with him.' We finally agreed and Deb made his check out to 'Casey Tibbs, if he wins', or something like that, and Mike put them in the safe.

"They'd been usin' my picture on the championship buckles, but when Deb started to lead that year, he got with Buster Ivory who was the secretary-treasurer that year, and talked him into changing to a picture of him on a horse called Miss Klamath. He did get out in front for awhile, so he told them, 'Look, if I'm goin' to win the buckle, why can't I have my picture put on it?'

"Well, at the end of the year, I'd won by a pretty good margin, and by that time they'd started to have a nice little presentation out in the arena at Denver. They had a showcase with the trophies in it showing who had won, and so forth.

"Well, when I walked in and Deb saw me, he didn't say, 'How are you, Casey? How was your Christmas? How was your New Years?' Nothing! He just hollered, 'Hey! Casey Tibbs, look here! Do you know whose picture that is on that buckle?' And I said, 'No, Deb, but I know whose buckle that is.' And he never spoke to me again for the rest of that rodeo. A lot of guys heard it, and they just bellied-up laughing.

"Deb knew I packed credit cards, and he never would buy a tank of gas. He'd always say, 'Just put it on your credit card.' I was gettin' kinda tired of it, and he was always hookin' a ride. I really got him this one time. I knew he was goin' to come and ask me for a ride, and I was ready for him.

"Deb came up and asked if he could have a ride to Strong City. So I said I'd been thinkin' a lot about goin' to California to that rodeo in Long Beach instead. Well, he started in on me sayin' it wasn't that far out of my way -- only about three hundred miles more to go by Strong City. So I just said, 'Hell, that's great. I'll just put you on a bus and you can sleep. You oughta try it. It'll make you ride better.'

"Anyway, I pushed him a little farther and finally I said, 'Well, okay, if you buy all the groceries, all the grub, hotels, and everything, I'll drive and we'll swing by there.' Well, he thought that was a pretty good deal, but right away he wanted to play that old-time Texas music. I just reached over and turned the radio off and said, 'Put a quarter into the slot if you want to play music. Just drop it into the ashtray.' I just nickeled and dimed him to death, till I took all his change away from him.

"It wasn't all that far to go, but every time we got near a cafe or truckstop, I'd say, 'I'm hungry!' and we'd go in and I'd order a big old T-bone steak. He'd pay the bill, and by the next truckstop I'd be hungry again.

"When we got to Emporia, Kansas, I stopped at the hotel and ordered a suite of rooms. It wasn't much of a hotel, but I insisted on a suite. It was just getting daybreak, and Deb didn't want to get a room at all sayin' it was darn near rodeo time.

"But I said, 'No, we've got to have rooms,' so we checked in for just two or three hours. I finally took him on in to Strong City, which was only about twenty miles from our hotel. We pulled in at the rodeo grounds and picked up a program, and I already had the best two horses drawn, School

Boy Rowe, and another real good horse. I'd been entered there the whole time, see, and Deb didn't know it."

Casey was still so pleased with the memory that he shook with laughter all the way through the telling of it. "Oh, Deb got mad! He slammed the door in my face and yelled, 'You're as dumb as Gene Pruett!'" Casey roared with laughter at that conclusion.

By the end of 1954, the year of the bet, Casey had won by a margin of 2,666 points. He'd amassed the greatest number of points ever earned in any event to that date.

Both in written articles and in personal conversations, the question as to who was the better bronc rider, Casey Tibbs or Pete Knight, has been discussed by some of the old-timers. Casey said whatever the answer to that might be, he'd always been proud to be mentioned along with Pete Knight. "I never knew Pete Knight and I never knew Fritz Truan, but I always admired them," he said. "I liked Lewis Brook's style of bronc ridin', and when I first started, I got to watch him ride.

"One time up in Lewiston, Idaho, an old boy almost challenged me. He said, 'You're a good bronc rider, but you ain't what they say you are. You can't start to ride broncs like your dad could. They couldn't knock him out of a saddle with a stick.' I was always kinda proud of that.

"Another thing people would ask me was, with all this sponsorship money, wouldn't I rather be ridin' now, with all that money to ride for? And I'd just tell 'em, 'Hell no! I liked to killed myself with two or three hundred thousand [in prizes money], what would I have done for a million?

"In many ways, it was a lot tougher in those days, and not just in the arena. We had no insurance. If a guy got busted up, it was his buddies that would be at the hospital with him. You couldn't even get [admitted] into some hospitals without insurance.

"You know, a lot of people didn't know Bud Linderman like I knew him, but many a time some kid we didn't even know would get hurt and we'd swing by the hospital and leave a few dollars."

Casey's expanding goals began to include serving on the board of the RCA, helping the cowboys in any way possible, and furthering his goal to push rodeo into the position of an acknowledged sport. It was his idea to rename their paper, *Rodeo News*, to *Rodeo Sports News*. After they changed their association name to Professional Rodeo Cowboys' Association they amended it: *The ProRodeo Sports News.*

From April 25, 1954, through October 4, 1956, Casey served as second, first vice-president of the RCA under president Bill Linderman and vice-president Lex Connelly, then soon after, Harley May. Casey continued to serve in that position until Bill Linderman's tragic death, which brought Harley May to the presidency, making Casey the first vice-president through 1957.

The vice-presidency of the RCA was most certainly not an empty title. Casey took very seriously his participation in promoting and furthering the sport he loved. While serving on the board, Casey originated the idea of the National Finals. The idea, however, wasn't an easy sell.

"I hounded on it and wouldn't let up, and I was cussed and cussed over it. I was even run out of meeting rooms, mainly by Bill Linderman who threatened to kill me over it. Gene Pruett, who was my good friend, also battled me tooth and nail, but I fought it on into reality. Yet, I must say, when the National Finals became a fact, Gene was one of the top supporters of it.

"I would probably have never gotten it off the ground by myself, not bein' a businessman, had it not been for John Van Cronkhite. I'd heard what he'd done with Steiners and that he was a livewire promoter. I bumped into him while I was checking into the Gunter Hotel in San Antonio, Texas. I told him I had a hell of an idea, and I gave him my room number and asked him to call me 'cause I wanted to talk to him about it.

"When he called, I hadn't told him but three lines of what it was about till he hung up and came right over to my room. I explained that rodeo was never, ever going to get any recognition as a sport if they kept quietly crowning the champions six weeks after they'd already won. Until recent years, the champions had simply been handed their buckle in some scroungey old motel room when they came to Denver. If rodeo was ever going to be recognized as a sport, we were going to have to bring it more public attention, and the National Finals was the way to do it.

"Well, John really took to the idea. I mean, I bounced the ball, but he picked it up and made the basket. The first thing he asked me was, 'How much of this do you want?' I told him with my being on the board of directors, I couldn't take a dime of it. I told him I'd maybe have to pick fights with him in the meetings once in awhile just to help the cause.

"I don't want to take any bows, but it does kinda gripe me when guys who fought against the National Finals take credit for it now. After it was a reality, Bill Linderman, of course, did support it, but I admire Pruett because, although he was really against it in the beginning and he'd just get livid when I'd talk about it, he backed it when it first started to gel.

"Harley May was on my side, and also Lex Connelly, but on the cowboy end of it those two were just about it. Of the stock contractors, only Lynn Beutler and Harry Knight supported it.

"The Bucking Horse of the Year award came about when I pointed out that there were good buckin' horses around, just as there were in the days of Midnight and Tipperary. The difference was, they were just not gettin' the credit they should. But I didn't get any opposition on that idea. I got good support. Lex Connelly was real good. Lex had an energetic mind.

"People sometimes give me the credit for the Rookie of the Year idea, but I tell them hell no, that was Lex Connelly. But I was a one-man band in starting The National Finals."

Casey deserves serious recognition for elevating ProRodeo to sport status and for the development of this highly successful and prestigious climax to each year of rodeo. Casey Tibbs most certainly was the "Father of the National Finals Rodeo."

Casey Tibbs on Bull #212, Cheyenne, Wyoming, July 30, 1955.
(Photo Courtesy of The Donald C. and Elizabeth M. Dickinson Research Center Archives of the National Cowboy and Western Heritage Museum. Photo by DeVere)

WORLD'S FAIR

Even though a bronc ride only lasts for ten seconds, rodeo life can be hectic and time consuming, especially for the top contenders. They are often called on for personal appearances and publicity and photo sessions to help promote the sport. Called on repeatedly for promotional appearances as he traveled from town to town, Casey gave of himself generously.

The hours spent traveling were long and rugged. Planning his strategy as to which rodeos would yield the most points, and mapping out the distances between them, took time and thought. Calling rodeo secretaries and paying his entry fees before the cutoff dates also took time and organization. This process was crucial to his career, because most rodeos did not allow post entries. If you didn't get your entries paid in time, you didn't get to compete. Hanging on the phone line was part of the life.

By 1956 Casey had become a great draw at rodeos and was advertised heavily while making personal appearances with his trained horse, Midnight. By this time he'd become quite famous, and the public loved the fact that they could come to a rodeo and meet the star. They could not only see Casey perform with Midnight, but they could see him ride the rankest broncs as well.

He outdrew some of the biggest names to ever appear at rodeos; however, he felt out of place in his "Hollywood Cowboy" costume. The other cowboys didn't make things easier for him with their constant razzing and catcalls. It was their chance to even the score with him for his past pranks at their expense, and they were making the most of it. During one performance in Lubbock, Texas, Jim Shoulders compounded Casey's embarrassment by running out in the middle of his act and handing him a guitar. The cowboys got to calling him Captain Midnight after the kids' television show character of the same name, and this really bothered Casey.

Pranks and devilment of one kind or another have always been commonplace among cowboys, and when one dishes it out as both Jim and Casey often did, it is almost guaranteed that one's bound to get it back. Casey frequently sounded embarrassed when he recalled these times.

"I was making appearances at all the parades and hospitals, wearing my costume with the purple gun holsters, and naturally all the cowboys were laughin' at me and makin' fun of me. I would come in at night from makin' a show, or visitin' a hospital or whatever, and I'd fire a bunch of blanks by the door where the guys were stayin'.

"We were stayin' in a Travel Lodge in Pomona, California, during the rodeo there, and one mornin' just before we were to go out to the rodeo grounds I came back from makin' an appearance somewhere. I had my guns on and the whole bit.

"Well, there were three or four guys sharin' a room: Billy Hand, who's gone now; Harry Tompkins, who still remembers it; and Shoulders. Shoulders had gone out to the pay phone in the parkin' lot to make a phone call. The guys saw me comin', and they stuck their thumbs in their ears. Full-load blanks in a room do sound just a little loud. And they were sayin', 'Oh, damn! Don't fire in here! Go get Ol' Jim. He's down there makin' a phone call.'

"So I ran down there and slipped up behind the phone booth and cranked off a couple of blanks. It scared hell out of Jim, and he got instantly mad. He came out of there with his knife in his hand. Well, I treaded backwards about ten paces or so, and I'm tellin' him, 'Don't stick me with that thing!' But he had just cut me right across there!" Casey indicated his abdomen with his hand.

"I didn't even know I was cut. It didn't hurt, at first. But I went to my room and saw that I was bleedin', so I unbuttoned my pants and realized I was really cut.

"Well, it was just gettin' time to go out to the arena, and the other guys were leavin', and I waved and hollered from the door of my room, but they didn't know I was hurt, and they just took off.

"Shoulders hadn't left yet. He was still there, sittin' in his car by himself. So I run over and stuck my head in through the window and I said, 'You've got to take me to the hospital. I've got to get sewed up!'"

Casey got in the car with Shoulders, who by now was upset that he'd cut his friend. He drove until he found Pomona Cottage Hospital.

On May 28, 1956, the Pomona Progress Bulletin reported: "Champion cowboy Casey Tibbs underwent major surgery at the Cottage Hospital for a knife wound in the lower left abdomen. Dr. William G. Stahl, who performed the surgery, said the wound was three quarters of an inch long and two inches deep, scarring, but not penetrating, the intestines. Dr. Stahl called the police at three twenty P.M. just as Tibbs was coming out of the anesthetic. They were unable to question him until five forty P.M."

When Tibbs was finally questioned, he told the police he'd had an opened knife in his hand and was running and fell on it in the motel parking lot. When the police asked him where the knife was, he told them, "By this time some kid has probably picked it up."

"I had it coming, though. My morbid sense of humor had finally caught up with me. I also received a letter from Jim Shoulder's wife, Sharon, saying how sorry she was." Casey and Jim remained on friendly terms for the rest of their lives. It was an unfortunate incident, and one that both wish had never happened.

***

"I look back on when I was workin' in pictures and makin' those personal appearances, and I wish I'd just forgotten about the black horse [Midnight] that I had Glenn Randall train for me. He was really a good horse, and Glenn was such a great trainer, but I was sorta embarrassed by it. I felt kinda like the guy in the movie *The Electric Horseman,*" Casey reflected.

"I felt a knot in my belly every time I had to show that son of a buck. A lot of it was just the idea of bein' stuck out there with him and everything. I'd have probably been better off if I'd have just gotten about a half dozen head of tough buckin' horses, and just hauled two of 'em to the rodeos. I could have made a bronc ridin' appearance at each rodeo, 'cause that's what they knew me for anyway.

"I had some good buckin' horses about then, too. Joe Schomer and I were raisin' them up in South Dakota. We had horses like Johnny Cake, OK Red, Nutra Bio, and Whizz Bang. Oh, and World's Fair was another good one. You could buck him out at every performance -- he'd fire every time. He went to the National Finals four times. He was that saddle horse I took to Europe and everywhere.

"World's Fair, though. That sucker, I'll tell you, was one of the toughest horses I ever knew," Casey reflected. "I knew there was something wrong with him, but he was such a good lookin' horse. I knew he'd bucked ol' Pettigrew off, but Homer told me, 'You gotta get that horse. He'd be an outstandin' horse for you to ride in pictures and whenever you do personals.' I had quite a few jobs then.

"I got a costarring part with Maureen O'Sullivan and Will Rogers, Jr. in a picture called *Wild Heritage*. Rod McKuen, Judi Meredith, and a bunch of young actors were also in it. When I got the part, I asked the studio if I could use my own horse.

"By then I'd bought this horse, World's Fair, from Buck Abbott up in Victorville, California. I wanted to use him in the picture, although I'd really had problems with him.

"So I told the picture people that the wranglers could have the money for him, or whatever, I just wanted to ride my own horse because he was just a good cowboy lookin' horse. He was a buckskin with dapples and a black mane and tail with just a little bit of white comin' out from underneath. He had a nice head and everything…just a picture horse.

"The film was startin' the next week, and I was plannin' on goin' to the bull fights in Tijuana that next weekend. Well, just before the picture was due to start filming, that sucker throwed one of them fits of his. He hadn't done that in a long, long time, and he did it for no reason. I wasn't pushin' him hard, just goin' along with him good, you know?

120

"By that time I had him where I could ride him bareback, get on and off on either side, walk under his belly and between his hind legs. I honestly thought I had him good. He hadn't bucked in six months, hadn't done nothin' wrong. I'd roped on him and everything.

"I guess maybe that's what I did wrong, though. I was over at San Fernando Saddlery Arena, ropin' with Bob Burrows. The horse didn't like it when the cinch would come tight, but boy, even so, everybody had been braggin' on this horse. He scored good and gave me a good shot.

"Now, I rode out to heel one, and you know how you'll kind of set over on one of the stirrups? Well, I leaned out, and as soon as he felt me over there, oh man. I just went flyin' through the air! Then afterwards, when I was ridin' him back home, he just kept on tryin' me the whole way back. I was startin' the picture job on about Wednesday, but I knew I could never use him now.

"World's Fair had a wet brain, though. He must'a ate loco weed at some time or another, 'cause when he'd get a little bit stirred up, that's when it would hit him. But once again, he didn't buck for a long, long time. Then one day Ed Jauregui was over to Glenn's, and I was ridin' World's Fair. I was just workin' him in the indoor arena, a training hall made like a quonset hut. He threwed one of his fits for absolutely no reason. He'd already crippled me once when he tore my leg up so bad that it took me out of competition. He probably cost me thirty thousand dollars that year 'cause I couldn't ride.

"Well, he threwed this fit and he pawed the top of the damn roof of that building, so I just stepped off him and kicked him in the butt. I said to Ed, 'Tell Andy to come and get him.'" Andy Jauregui was Casey's friend and a rodeo stock contractor.

"See, after he'd crippled me, Glenn had told me, 'Oh, he'd never buck with you or me.' Junior, like a damn fool, came out here, and he got his kid on him. The boy used to clean stalls for Glenn and do chores so that he could ride Buttermilk, Dale Evans' horse. But he saddled up World's Fair, thinkin' that it was Buttermilk (also a buckskin) and rode him about ten steps when he broke in two, and like to throwed him over the roof!

"But Glenn had said, 'Oh, no, he'd never have bucked with you or me.' You see, my leg wasn't even healed up yet, so Glenn was workin' him.

121

Glenn, as you know, is a helluva horseman, and he was just spinnin' and slidin' him. He could really put the rein on a horse, and he's the absolute best. But he was ridin' World's Fair in a bronc saddle, 'cause I don't think Glenn really trusted him too much.

"I warned Glenn, 'Look out for him, that sucker ain't untracked yet!' I could see it in his ol' eye, and he had that tail of his, kind of set down. But Glenn said, 'Oh, hell. He'd never buck with you or me. No way!' Right then, as he turned him back, World's Fair felt him just ease out of the saddle a little bit as he was spinnin' him. And damn! You never seen a sucker blow any higher! He throwed Glenn off and tore his leg in exactly the same place as mine. He'd cripple ya! That son of a gun was a crippler!

"So anyway, I knew finally that there wasn't no use in messin' with him any longer. Andy took him, and he bucked riders off everywhere Andy took him.

"Then I took him to Europe in '58, and Bill Linderman would come into the arena and they'd bring World's Fair in. See, Bill and I used to work the wild horse race together in New York, so over in Brussels I had Bill work this with me. Bill would 'ear him down' while I'd climb on him. But as soon as Bill threw his arm up over the horse's neck, World's Fair would just go into the air pawin' and strikin'. I mean it was a helluva show, and Bill, he had the scar tissue over both eyes to prove it. And that horse bucked every time.

"But you know, if you just saddled him and rode him, and if you could take him plumb easy, he might go along okay. But if somethin' upset him, or if you tried to take captivity of him, he'd just come apart.

"But I bucked him over there in Brussels every day. He went to the National Finals three or four times, and I took him to Japan and bucked him every single performance. And he bucked just so good! He'd buck 'em off!

"We held contests over there in Japan some, and at the last performance we had quite a little bit of money up. I marked as high on that horse as I ever marked on any horse, even though he'd been bucked all that time.

"But gawd! I wish I hadn't spent so much time on him. He kept me crippled all of one year, same as Troubles. Troubles was that gray son of a buck that I had later."

Casey seemed to have had a penchant for ornery horses. Although some people might interpret this as just plain stubbornness, it went beyond this. Possibly he was so drawn to them because they reflected his own personality, in their determination, toughness, and tenacity.

***

The month of July is sometimes referred to as "Cowboy Christmas" because it's possible for a cowboy to compete in a different rodeo almost every day. It's hard to imagine, but during Casey's prime years, starting in 1953 and for seven consecutive years, he took a month off in the height of the rodeo season to organize, promote, and put on the Casey Tibbs 4-H Benefit.

Casey had participated in matched bronc riding events in other parts of the country, and he'd seen how well they were received. He was sure it would go over in his area and that it would be a good way to raise money. Casey wanted to build a youth center and 4-H building for the kids of Hughes and Stanley Counties.

"I came up with the idea myself," he said. "I thought we could make it an annual event. I figured eventually we could raise enough money to build both the youth center and a 4-H building at the fairgrounds. It would really help all of the kids in my home area.

"I mentioned the idea to Joe Schomer who was a rancher back there, and he liked it. He really put himself into the project. Later on, he and I and another fellow, Bill Sutton, got into the stock contracting business together. Joe donated the buckin' horses as well as his time, and was a huge pusher of the idea.

"It began as a matched bronc ridin' between Bill Linderman and me. The followin' year the match was between Deb Copenhaver and me. We made it a match-up of the top fifteen bronc riders later on. That was the real draw, and it went over really well. I remember one year we had eleven thousand people at one performance. We had people hangin' out of the tree tops. Along with it we held a team ropin' and, of course, the 4-H events.

"I owned some cattle back then, and I always donated a couple of calves each year for the 4-H calf scramble. A number of other ranchers also donated calves. We did it for over seven years, and lots of people donated their time and effort to make it work.

"Over that seven-year period, we raised over fifty thousand dollars clear. We bought the property, a corner lot across from the court house."

It's worth speculating about what all else Casey might have achieved in rodeo if he hadn't taken the month of July off for seven consecutive years. July should have been his best month, right during his most productive years, yet he gave it up to put on that 4-H event for the children of Hughes and Stanley Counties. He said, "It may have cost me the championship a year or two, because I would take off for approximately thirty days to go back there and set it all up and do it."

Casey did reap a tremendous reward from his years in rodeo, but it's certainly clear that he included in his goals ways to give back to the sport of rodeo, to the rodeo cowboys, and to the community from which he came.

***

It was on the famous One Shot Antelope Hunt, that Casey met and became friends with Joe Foss. Foss was a great World War II hero and flying ace. He'd joined the Marine Air Corps in 1940, and by 1942 he was the executive officer in a fighting squadron on Guadalcanal. During forty days of combat, he shot down twenty-six Japanese planes, five in one day, and he was shot down four times himself, winding up in the ocean three times. Foss was awarded the Congressional Medal of Honor.

At the Inaugural Ball for Joe Foss on January 4, 1955, Casey met and fell in love with Cleo Ann Harrington.

"I happened to be Miss South Dakota at the time," Cleo remembered, "and I was one of the hostesses at the Inaugural Ball. Casey was home for the holidays visiting his mother and was attending the Ball when a photographer introduced us.

"I was a freshman in college, and he began corresponding with me after that. He would call me from all these fabulous places, such as the Top Of

The Mark, or The Stork Club in New York, and of course, he was a very handsome young man. I was impressed.

"He always came home to visit his mother a couple of times a year, and at Christmas in 1956, he presented me with a lovely diamond ring. I was still in college, and I remember that the other girls at the Phi Beta Thi House were all duly impressed.

"My parents didn't approve of my becoming engaged to Casey," Cleo said. "My father, a South Dakotan, was a small-town banker, very well read and quite sophisticated. He tried to explain to me, in his wise way, his feelings that Casey and I were from different worlds. He wasn't sure that it would be in my best interest for me to marry him. I was a very naive girl, and although I loved my father very much, what he was telling me didn't matter to me at all.

"I'd seen Casey's picture on the front cover of *LIFE* magazine several years before. I remember saying, 'What a handsome man. Do you think I'll ever meet anybody like this?' A very sheltered girl, I didn't know much about the world of the West. It was my father who originally told me all about Casey. He admired him and liked him, but when we finally met, Dad wanted me to know that he felt our backgrounds were just too different for our own good.

"My parents were staunch Catholics, and although I told Casey it wasn't that important to me and not a prerequisite, he took instruction in Catholic doctrine. It may be that my father said something to him, I don't know, but it was Casey's idea and not mine that he took instructions."

During their engagement, Casey was asked to go to Brussels to star in a Rodeo and Wild West Show to be held in conjunction with the World's Fair. In preparation for what looked to be a long and lucrative engagement in Brussels, Casey had new clothes made costing over $4,500. He went to "Nudie, the Rodeo Tailor," who made costumes for various stars such as Roy Rogers, Rex Allen, Elvis Presley, and many others.

"I was going to be the star of this big extravaganza, and I wanted to dress the part," Casey reflected. "The wardrobe had to last two years, and they were paying for it. My contract with the Cremer Rodeo Company read $500 per week for six months, with a two-year option, plus all expenses paid."

One morning Casey went to the back lot at NBC to shoot some publicity photos for the upcoming trip. Galloping his horse toward the camera, dressed in his newly tailored clothes, he was suddenly intercepted by another rider dressed in a suit and carrying a book.

It was Ralph Edwards, asking, "Casey, do you remember me? I met you at Truth Or Consequences, New Mexico."

"Sure, I remember you, Ralph," Casey replied.

"Well," said Ralph, "I've been on your trail for quite a little while now, and I've got something here I'd like to show you. It's this book." He held up an album designed as a special gift from the program as he continued, "Tonight, Casey Tibbs, This Is Your Life!"

Casey did appear to be caught off guard, but the show turned out to be very special for him. He was not only honored by his family, but others who appeared included Lex Connelly, then secretary-treasurer of the RCA; Sioux Indian stock contractor Bud Annis; Jack Buschbom, Ken Roberts, Deb Copenhaver, Bill Linderman, Jim Shoulders, and Harry Nelson, who presented Casey with the Bill Linderman Award.

Ralph ended the show by saying, "Casey Tibbs, we know that you're off next week to the World's Fair in Brussels, Belgium, where you will be the featured star in the Wild West Show that America is presenting there. You'll be bringing rodeo to millions who don't yet know what the word means, and you'll be a great representative for us over there."

He presented Casey with a Bell and Howell movie camera and projector, an RCA Victor hi-fi record player, plus Casey's choice of a thousand dollars worth of RCA recordings. From Ivory Soap came a check for the 4-H project in Fort Pierre.

Florence was then presented with a beautiful gold charm bracelet. Each charm represented a special event in Casey's life. Ralph concluded the program by saying, "Casey, you've shown us what it takes to be a great champion, and your champion heart, as big as the West itself, we know will carry you on to ever greater triumphs! Good night, and God bless you."

The world must have seemed a rosy place to Casey about that time. First, he was engaged to the beautiful Cleo Ann Harrington, and although her parents disapproved, she had agreed to go to Europe with him. His future looked pretty secure right then. He was leaving for Europe as "America's Representative" and the featured star in a Wild West Show being presented in Brussels in conjunction with the World's Fair.

With his new clothes, the Bill Linderman Trophy, the surprise visit from his family and friends, plus being featured on *This Is Your Life,* things must have looked very good, indeed.

Casey Tibbs on Necktie, 1958. *(Photo Courtesy of The Donald C. and Elizabeth M. Dickinson Research Center Archives of the National Cowboy and Western Heritage Museum. Photo by DeVere)*

Casey Tibbs on Easy Money *(Photo Courtesy of the Donald C. and Elizabeth M. Dickinson Research Center Archives of the National Cowboy and Western Heritage Museum. Photo by DeVere)*

FIASCO IN A FAR-OFF LAND

With all the promise it had, the Wild West Show in Brussels turned into a complete fiasco. This huge extravaganza involved seventy-six cowboys and cowgirls and fifty-five Ogallala Sioux Indians. The producers flew them all over on two chartered planes, while a freighter loaded with fifty horses, fifteen buffaloes, forty steers and other livestock made landfall at Antwerp and finished the trip to Brussels by truck.

When Casey arrived in Brussels, he was disappointed to learn that the show grounds were a mile and a half from the World's Fair and a mile outside of Brussels. Casey complained, "It was an old gasoline dump that had been bombed during the war. As a matter of fact, Hank Fine helped bomb it. The water was contaminated, so most of the animals got sick. It was a mess!"

Even still, the opening went well with a near capacity crowd of ten thousand people, but it was one of the only evenings that it didn't rain. Huge neon signs had been erected all over Brussels advertising two performances daily, but the afternoon shows were cancelled due to foul weather, and Casey said, "We rode in the rain every night. It rains an average of 266 nights a year in Belgium, and we hit the rainy season."

The show's producer, G. Robert Flemming, had arranged a big cocktail party for the participants on their arrival. Casey said, "From there we were farmed out to various rooming houses and cold-water flats, which were equal to something on skid row. The only difference was that they were charging us each $200 a month, which was coming out of our wages. Most of the cowboys had lived under some pretty rough conditions, but it was so bad they wouldn't stand for it. In a couple of days they'd found better places on their own and were only paying something like fifty dollars a month."

Cleo was chaperoned by her friends, Dawn Denzer and Pudgey Randall. Together they rented a nice house, while Casey moved into the Plaza Hotel. As part of the promotion, the Indians were supposed to live in their teepees, but they were soon up to their hocks in water and had to be moved to a motel.

Flemming had gotten a company to build a red, white, and blue air tent that would seat ten thousand people. Casey said, "That tent was a pretty son of a buck. Too bad it didn't work. An air tent that big had never been made, and it had to be assembled in Europe. When they tried to inflate it, it got about half way up, then fluttered and flopped and came back down. Twenty extra-large generators failed to inflate the tent, and after their attempt to hold it up with tall poles failed, they rolled the expensive air tent up and pushed it to the side."

Casey had his own dressing room. He recalled, "Imagine a cowboy with his own dressing room! It was about the size of a two-seater outhouse, and built just as well. I had a helluva time finding a dry corner where my clothes wouldn't get rained on. This boudoir sat back of the arena near the shed row where they kept most of the livestock.

"Cremer Rodeo Company, owned by Gene Autry and operated by Harry Knight, furnished all the livestock. Since they already had a lot of contracts for rodeos in the United States, Harry Knight couldn't be spared to go to Europe, so they hired Vern Elliot to run the rodeo in Brussels. By using Vern's good name, along with Knight's and Autry's, Flemming had no trouble getting top cowboys, including myself and five other world champions, and I'm sure my name was used to entice others into going."

Casey said that one night after the show had run for about three weeks, things kinda came to a head. "A cold drizzle was coming down," he recalled. "The Indians were hungry and their blankets were all wet and there were only about three hundred people in the bleachers. The show started right. The covered wagons came into the arena where the Indians were supposed to ride in and circle them, then the cavalry was supposed to ride in and fight off the Indians. But the Indians didn't attack -- they just rode back and forth in front of their teepees and didn't even enter the arena. The cavalry finally rode in and shot one another while the assistant jumped up and down and yelled at Vern. He screamed, 'What happened to the Indians?' and Vern said, 'They struck!' The assistant howled, 'So help me, I'll dock them for this!'"

Casey laughed. "I wonder what he thought they had struck for, as they had not yet received a penny."

When things did get rough and the show started falling apart, the decision-making folks began to bail out. As Casey put it, "The wheels started leaving Brussels like mice quitting a sinking ship."

No one had been paid, and the feed bill for the livestock was huge. When the show folded after continuing to struggle in the rain and with all the other terrible conditions, it was Vern Elliot who finally closed the show. Belgium creditors immediately attached all the livestock and equipment, including Casey's three horses. He had taken his horse, World's Fair, along with the two blacks and nine of his trophy saddles and other trophies for display.

On the edge of Brussels there was a country club kind of place called Horse's Park. The people operating the park invited Casey and Cleo to stay with them and allowed Casey to bring his horses there.

"I knew it would be quite a feat just gettin' my horses off the grounds. I wouldn't stand a chance of gettin' them by van, so I buckled on my .45 that I used in the show, rode one black and led the other. The guard on the gate was talkin' one language, and I was talkin' another. I kept noddin' my head, but I rode out past him and six miles through town to Horse's Park. They treated us royally there, and when the attachment was lifted on my horses, I rode back to the show grounds the same way.

"There was no way of feedin' the livestock, the cowboys and cowgirls, or the Indians, because after the creditors attached all the livestock and equipment the show was shut down. I went to the creditors and made a deal with them. We would continue to operate and split the gate, 50/50, till some type of relief came. We ran this way for two weeks; one week the cowboys got paid $14 each, and the next week they got $15. They weren't too impressed with their one-dollar raise, but this was my entire salary for all the time I worked. Autry did loan me a hundred dollars before he took off for New York.

"I'd loaned out or spent nearly all of the $5,000 that I'd brought with me, so we were all cuttin' it pretty close. I'd brought over a trunk load of photographs to give away, but instead the cowgirls, Indians, and children sold them for fifteen francs each, or whatever they could get. I'd split it with them and would use my part of the money to buy that fine Rhine wine with which to keep everybody happy. The days of champagne and Scotch were gone.

"We had no means of transportation other than by tram or horseback, so we used horses. George Williams, a long, tall cowboy from Tulsa, Oklahoma, was usually the wine runner. He'd get on an old sorrel horse of Bill Linderman's and head up the street for the nearest saloon, which was about three quarters of a mile away. The old horse would hardly move going away; he looked just like an old picador horse in the bullring. George would kick him every step of the way to get up there, but when he'd get his tote sack filled with wine, you'd have thought he was Paul Revere headin' back. How he kept from gettin' involved in a wreck, I'll never know."

Casey continued, "I really should mention how great the Belgian people were to all of us cowboys and Indians. When the show folded people were bringin' carrot tops and garden greens in their wheelbarrows to help feed the livestock. A whorehouse stood near the grounds that treated the cowboys extra good, and the cowboys ate most of their meals there." When the money dried up, Vern asked Casey to go with him to pay a visit to Flemming at the Brussels Residence where he and Flynn were staying. Casey said it was one of the most expensive and finest lodging places in Brussels.

Of this meeting Casey remembered, "It was eleven in the mornin', but Vern and I had to get Flemming up out of bed to see us. He had to have a beer before he could talk to us, and from the look of his suite, I figured he'd had some kind of a party the night before. Flemming assured us that there just wasn't any money collected from the ticket sales as yet. He said that all the people who'd seen the show had bought their tickets in advance from ticket agencies, and the agencies had not turned in their receipts as yet.

"I unbuttoned my coat and let him see the handle of my Colt .45 stickin' out of my belt. I had only dummy bullets in it, but Flemming didn't know this. Flemming said, 'I've got $4,000 in francs and I'll let you have half of it.' I said, 'We'll take it all, and you'd better have some more the next time we come around. The Indians haven't been eating too well, and if I bring them up here you're gonna have some kind of hell. Besides,' I told him, 'the feed bill on the livestock hasn't been paid, and if the animals ain't fed, we're out of business.' Flemming turned to Vern and said, 'Well, Vern, you know we still have the credit with the Diners Card, so put it on the Diners.' This was the first time I ever heard of puttin' hay and oats on the Diners Card.

"I must have come on a little strong for G. Robert Flemming. It was only a matter of hours before he took off for New York City."

Casey did, indeed, have to sell some of his personal belongings, including one of his black horses, two saddles, and a pair of silver and gold .45s, all of which he sold to Western movie actor, Bobbejaan Schoepen. This got Casey enough money to return home with Cleo and see "Gay Paree" on their way.

Before they left Brussels, Casey saw the cowboys and Indians off for America. "It was a pretty sad affair -- but since they all got home safe I have to laugh. The Indians were all wearing Belgian-type tennis shoes, as they'd sold their moccasins to the tourists for eating money. Their drums were all warped out of shape from all the rain, and their feathers looked like they'd been sleepin' in 'em.

"Vern really tried his best to get everybody home. We made two or three trips daily to the American Embassy. The word finally came that the State Department was flyin' everyone home. They ended up backin' the show, whether they liked it or not. They did, however, require everyone to pay the government back their expenses.

"I had to sell one of my horses so I could afford to bring the other two home. Bobby Davenport, the horse trainer, and two cowboys, Buster Ivory and Bill Williams, came home by boat with the horses.

"Even the Russian Moscow Circus was generous. When our show was still operating, Vern Elliott received a call from the Russian Circus. He was pretty bitter by this time and didn't give them much time on the phone, so when he told me about it I called the Russian Circus back and invited them all to our show on their day off. A full busload came. The cowboys all packed flags of all the countries in the grand entry. We had never used the Russian flag, but I located one and put it right up front. Those Russian people really loved it.

"After the performance they stayed until 4:00 in the mornin', singin' cowboy songs and playin' guitars with the cowboys. Later, when our show folded, they offered to put on a benefit performance for us. No one could pay to see the Russian Circus from then on if they wore a cowboy hat.

"Cleo and I came home on our own via Paris and London. The Internal Revenue Service had attached my bank account in the States, on top of all the other hell I'd had. I figured we might as well see a little more of Europe and come home in style."

Cleo's memories of the Belgium tour involved mostly the fun and the positive side of things. "With Pudgy Randall and Dawn Denzer, I was well chaperoned," she recalled. "We had a great time together and enjoyed each other's company very much. We were involved in the show, but we weren't terribly Western. I rode a little, and I rode in one of the wagons. It was truly quite an education."

Upon returning home to the States, one newspaper ran a photograph of a lean Casey sporting a trim mustache. "The mustache and twenty-nine dollars is about all I got out of the trip to Europe," Casey was quoted in the column.

THE TWAIN MARRY

With the Brussels disaster over, Casey turned his attention to rodeo again. World titles were out of the question for 1958 since so much of the year had already gone by. With most of his own savings used up, Casey longed to immerse himself in something over which he had some measure of control. Bronc riding was something he could really get a handle on.

More than ever Casey's name and image appeared in the news. Walter Winchell announced in his column that Casey had been taking instruction in the Catholic faith in preparation for his upcoming marriage to Cleo Harrington. Other columnists speculated on whether they had, or had not, secretly married while in Europe. The Monday just before their planned wedding date, Cleo had announced to the press that she and Casey had postponed things again for a little while.

Casey said of this: "Mrs. Harrington was real happy when I was goin' with Cleo. I was the fair-haired boy of South Dakota and a good conversation piece, but when we became engaged in 1957, it was a different story. Cleo and her family were strong Catholics. I'd never been baptized, and I don't remember seeing the inside of a church except for a funeral or a wedding. So I studied catechism and joined the Catholic faith. Still, every time we announced our wedding date, her mother would arrange for a postponement. I can't say as I really blamed her. Cleo was her only daughter, and I had a pretty wild reputation.

"Cleo's father passed away during the fall in 1958, which caused yet another postponement. Cleo left home after the funeral and stayed with her friend Dawn Denzer, in Denver.

"We'd been split up for a short time, but I called her right before New Year's Eve to wish her a happy New Year. We decided to meet in the Black Hills of South Dakota and spend New Year's Eve together at Harley Roth's Ranch. Harley was a rodeo producer and rancher. He and I had been in business together, but he was later killed in a private plane crash.

"Cleo and I met at 5:00 P.M. in the airport at Rapid City, South Dakota, then drove out together to Harley's place at Nemo. We were married in a Catholic church by 10:20 that same evenin'.

"That wedding was some kind of an experience! First we had to find a Catholic couple to stand up with us. Our rings and wedding clothes were in Coleman, so they were out. Harley and his wife called a jeweler and had to reach him at a New Year's Eve party. I only remember him as 'Jerry the Jeweler.' But he left the party and opened up his store, and I bought Cleo another wedding band.

"Then we went to the nearest Catholic Church, which was in Sturgis, South Dakota. Mind you, this was all on New Year's Eve. I introduced myself to Monsignor Flulander. He informed me that I must be drinkin' to think that I could do this, and if I was a Catholic I should know better than to try such a thing.

"I put the rush act on him and asked him if he would make a conference call, provided I would pay for it. He finally agreed. I hooked Father Miller, Cleo's priest in Coleman, and Father O'Dougherty, my priest in Fort Pierre, up on the phone with the Monsignor. They were all for us gettin' married, knowing the hell I'd been through. They also assured Monsignor Flulander that the proper bans of marriage had been announced in the church. So we both said, 'I do.' Our marriage lasted about eight years, most of which we lived in Hollywood. This may be some sort of record."

Following the wedding, Casey and Cleo hit the rodeo trail in earnest. Casey frequently would stay with Happy Shahan between rodeos, and Cleo and he stayed there for a time shortly after their wedding. Happy was a Texas rancher involved with rodeo as well as making movies.

138

Married life was good for Casey as he and Cleo traveled about the country going from one rodeo to the next. Even though he turned thirty years old in March of that year, Casey rode well in 1959. Being admired by what may be described as two of South Dakota's most beautiful eyes, no doubt gave him great inspiration, because when 1959 ended, Casey was once more the world champion saddle bronc rider.

This was to be Casey's last championship. Although he still rode like a champion, he began to devote more time to the picture business and to the promotional end of rodeo.

As newlyweds, Casey and Cleo also lived with Glenn and Lynn Randall. Glenn was the great horse trainer mentioned earlier. The days spent at the Randalls' produced some wonderful memories, as well as deepening some very special friendships. Chuck Parkinson, a rodeo announcer, and his wife Sheila were the Tibbs' close friends, for example. As such, they were frequent targets for Casey's pranks. Chuck was one of the great rodeo announcers and was often seen in the movies portraying an announcer.

Casey played so many tricks on Glenn Randall, that Glenn once said, "I've probably got every right to hate him for the things he did to me, but I love him more than anyone in the world."

Glenn loved to smoke cigars, and Casey loved to load them. Once the prank turned out better than he'd hoped, and Casey giggled while telling about it. "I'd get every trick I could think of at the trick shops," he began. "I'd got Glenn so many times by loading his cigars, that I could hand him a brand new box with an unbroken seal and he wouldn't take one 'cause I'd just caught him so many times. He didn't trust me worth a darn!

"One day Glen had worked a deal with Leo Durocher to bring Trigger, Roy Rogers' horse, down to a ball field off Fairfax in Hollywood for some publicity pictures. He'd gotten some great shots of Trigger sittin' down on the mound and everything, with Leo Durocher going through his fit of rage. It turned out really good.

"Afterwards, we loaded Trigger into the trailer and started for home. Ol' Glenn felt for a cigar in his shirt pocket but didn't have one on him. So he absentmindedly said to me, 'Reach in that glove compartment and see if there's a cigar in there.' Well, I'd already been in that glove box, probably a couple of weeks before, and I'd loaded every cigar in there.

"Now, Glenn had gotten so paranoid he wouldn't even pick up a cigar around his house. You know, where he'd smoked maybe a third of it and then left it in the ash tray? 'Cause he knew I would already have loaded that one, too. I mean, he couldn't take any chances.

"This time, though, he never even hesitated. He just stuck his ol' elbow down in that steering wheel and lit up with one of those old, wooden, farmer matches. The cigar had laid in that glove compartment for probably two or maybe three weeks. There were five of them in a little old box, and they were all very dry. I'd put about four full loads in it, and when it went off, boy! It exploded, and tobacco flew everywhere. All that was left was just the wrappings in his mouth. Well, he never even flinched, never made a move -- just stared straight ahead, drove all the way home, and never said another word about it ever again."

Casey was shaking with laughter as he continued, "I was always playin' tricks on Lynn Randall, too. I had two horses that Glenn was training for me, so I stayed there quite a bit. I slept in the bunkhouse, which was just across from the porch entry to the house. I used to slip over in the mornings and scare the girls. I'd be hidin' under the bar-counter early in the mornin', and when Lynn would come out to make the coffee, I'd spook her.

"A lot of people in the rodeo business would stop by at the Randalls'. Glenn had trained a little red pony to fight with a man. It was a wild Shetland stallion, and he'd darn sure reach in and bite you. Buster Ivory had learned how to work him, and I had the new Bell and Howell movie camera that they gave me on *This Is Your Life*. I told Buster, 'I've gotta learn how to use this camera they gave me, so get in there and work the red pony, and I'll try and get some good shots.'

"Glenn had put a cue on him, and that pony would get with it. He would really fight you. He was an ornery little son of a gun, and he'd grab you if he could. Well, Buster gets in there with him, and he's really got him goin'. The pony did nip Buster a time or two, so after a while he said to me, 'Did you get that one? That ought to be a good one, did you get it?'

"I said, 'I think I got it, but let's do it again.' Well, I had him workin' that pony till finally he said, 'Damn, we can't work him much longer!'

"But I said, 'No, come on now. We've got to get this. Damn, this is good. I'm beginning to learn how to work this. Oh, man! That was a good one! Now get over there on the other side.' I was directin' him and the whole bit. 'Get in there now, a little closer, 'cause when I get him, I don't want to get you. Get in there! Work closer to him!' I was really puttin' ol' Buster on 'cause I had never even bought a roll of film for that camera. When Buster found out, he was hotter than hell! But we really did have fun around the Randalls."

SUCCESS IN THE FAR EAST &
AMERICA'S MOST BELOVED ROOSTER

A Japanese promoter contacted Casey in 1962 and asked him to take an American Wild West Show and Rodeo to Japan. The event turned out to be a huge success. He took with him many top cowboys; several of them were world champions, and in some cases, future world champions. Gerald Roberts, Eddy Akridge, Ray Honeycut, Clyde Vamvoras, Paul Mayo, and Gary Gardner were just a few of the top hands that went with Casey. George Williams and Eddie Little Sky were indispensable. World champion Ben Johnson went along, and while he was overseas working with Casey the offer came for him to do a role in a film called *The Last Picture Show.*

Rex Rossi, without question one of the top trick ropers of all time and a great showman, had this to say about the trip: "The show that Casey brought to Japan was a beautiful show. I'd never been in one that nice. We had a pageant in the opening that was outstanding. Everything went as smooth as clockwork. We were there a long time and Casey never missed a performance, and he rode three or four broncs in each show.

"We really had a good time, but it was a workhouse, with the two shows a day, six days a week, then three on Sunday. We had Monday off, but those three shows on Sunday would get you. We worked indoors, but without any air conditioning. Sometimes the dressing rooms got really hot, but the Japanese seemed to thrive on it. They'd get those little handheld fans going, and it seemed like all that did was stir up the hot air. But we did all right and we had a lot of fun.

"Casey was a real showman. He worked hard and never asked anyone to do anything that he wouldn't do himself. He was just great! I hate to repeat myself, but he was a credit to the rodeo business."

Casey's voice rang with pride when talking about the Japanese tour in 1963. "We were sold out in Nagoya for fifteen days," he said. All did not go as smoothly for Casey as it sounds, however, for he had to deal with numerous problems.

"One time, all my cowboys tied one on. I had it in their contracts that if they did anything like that I could withhold their pay -- and their airline tickets. Well, all my hands got drunk on me, so I just ran them off. I kept their tickets in a safe. They didn't think I'd stick to it 'cause it was gettin' on to production time. But the aircraft carrier *Midway* was in port, and many of the ship's crew was beggin' to ride. So, I put the wardrobe on the crew of the *Midway,* and the Japanese cowboys made better Indians than some of the Indians I brought with me.

"That sobered my cowboys up in a hurry. They'd go and talk to Cleo and say, 'Can't you talk to him?' and she'd say, 'I can't help you. He's set in his ways.' I laid off the whole crew except for Rossi and his wife, Joe Edwards, Gerald Roberts, and of course, Ben Johnson. Ben stayed with me right to the end. I made good hands out of some of the Japanese. They could really ride, and they made good Indians.

"We never could get any big trucks to ship our stock, so whenever we moved we'd have to use a whole fleet of little trucks. Some were little ol' short ones and we'd put stock racks on 'em and load those bulls and go. It was the damnedest looking caravan you've ever seen.

"It seems like everything was built smaller for the Japanese. Some of the entrances were so small, that we'd have to bring our bigger horses through them without a saddle. If we didn't, they would hang up. We kept the stock outside in pens and just ran the bulls and broncs up an alleyway into the chutes.

"There was a ballpark behind the Kanayama Gymnasium where we performed, and when we needed a little extra promotion, I'd let one of the bulls out. We'd take out after him and rope him on the ball field durin' a game." Casey laughed as he said, "People were climbin' trees and everything!

"Leonard Lancaster was over there with me, and he was a good hand. Clyde Vamvoras was really tough. Even when he broke his shoulder, he never slowed down. He had a steel pin stickin' up out of his shoulder, and he just tied a feather on the end of it and kept goin'."

Billy Hogue from Holtville, California, a rodeo cowboy with a great smile and an infectious laugh, told the following story of how Casey shared some of the benefits of his trip to Japan with his friends: "Casey would send these silk shirts over to us from Japan. They were tailor-made, real nice, and he'd have the tailor put our initials right here, over the pocket. He had them put 'B.H.' over the pocket on mine," Billy recalled.

"Well, he sent some to Lex Connelly, and his said 'Lex' just over the pocket. But on his, just above his name, there was a little Japanese insignia. It looked kinda nice, and I didn't think much about it until I saw Lex a couple of weeks later. When I looked close, I could see a kind of frayed spot where Lex had taken a razor blade and cut that embroidery out of it, so I asked Lex about it. At that time Lex was announcing the rodeo on *Wide World of Sports*. Lex took me aside and lowered his voice and said, 'Do you know what that damn Casey did? That monogram he had put on my shirt was Japanese for F-You!'"

Billy's great laugh pealed out for a few moments before he continued, "Poor Lex! Can you imagine? Fifty thousand Japanese-Americans watching *Wide World of Sports* on ABC, and them seein' that on TV?"

Casey loved Japan. He enjoyed the people and their culture, and as soon as he got back home he thought that someday he'd like to go back and do it all again. But it would be ten years before he finally returned with another show.

In the meantime, Casey got back into the picture business in various capacities. He worked not only as an actor, but also as a technical adviser, stunt man, stunt coordinator, second unit director, director, and producer.

He ran the stunts on the *Stony Burke* TV series, and even gave the show its name. Casey took the name Burke from the great Burk family of rodeo stars, Dee, Clyde, and Barry. Jack Lord was to star in the series, and before shooting began, Jack met with Casey to show him the character's costume he'd picked out to wear. Casey took one look at him and said, "Come with me."

Lord followed him into the men's room and was startled when Casey commanded, "Take off your clothes!" Casey then began to remove his own clothing. Next, Casey told Jack, "Hand me that costume," and Casey donned it. He finished dressing himself by placing the silly looking 'pork-pie' type hat upon his own head. Turning to face Lord, he remarked, "This is what you look like!" Jack and Casey both began to laugh. Finally, Casey threw his own clothes over to Jack. "Put these on," he directed him. Jack immediately put on Casey's western clothes, and when he looked in the mirror he was thrilled at what he saw. That's how the costume for *Stony Burke* was chosen for the series.

***

The Rounders was a humorous picture about two modern-day cowboys, starring Henry Fonda, Glen Ford, and Chill Wills. Some of the biggest laughs in the film centered around a cantankerous horse with a talent for making the wrong moves at the right time. This relationship between the two men and the horse had a real ring of truth about it, not just to the general audience, but especially to cowboys and horsemen.

The film was released in 1965. It was produced by Dick Lyons and directed by Burt Kennedy, another close friend of Casey's. Casey doubled both Fonda and Ford and did some excellent stunt work in the film, along with Buzz Henry and a number of other cowboys.

They did the location work in Sedona, Arizona, which is one of the state's most beautiful spots. It's filled with running streams, huge boulders, stately trees; it's mountainous and rugged with azure blue skies that, when seen in contrast behind a billowing thunderhead, give the impression that a talented artist has gone just a bit too far in selecting colors from his palette.

During the filming of the picture, the movie company stayed at Sedona's Oak Creek Inn, which was usually a very pleasant place to stay. This particular time, however, there happened to be a rooster living nearby who crowed at the very hour when most people would rather be asleep.

This annoying ruckus got so bad and so loud that actor Chill Wills, a country boy himself, had asked to be moved to other accommodations just so that he could get his much needed shut eye.

One morning Casey arose early and decided to see if he could catch the rooster. This proved to be far more difficult than he'd thought, because of the boulders and steep slopes surrounding the inn. Some of the other members of the crew had also risen early. They took great delight in watching Casey's stalking form, as the lively and uncooperative rooster repeatedly eluded him.

When at last Casey emerged from the bushes, tired and unsuccessful, the other guys took to razzing him about it. Quickly seeing this as an opportunity, he bet them that he could catch the bird. All of them wanted a piece of the action and bet two or three dollars each. Some of them bet as much as five dollars, until the pot had built up into quite a bit of money.

Much to the pleasure of the whole group, Casey's rooster chasing took on a greater intensity. Morning after morning Casey climbed up out of the rocks without the bird. Each time he had to take the full abuse of the entire company who'd been watching him.

Finally, Casey decided to do a little sleuthing. He'd noticed a few private homes nearby. By inquiring door to door, he learned that a family named Jones owned the rooster. He introduced himself to the Jones family, and they told him that they'd had a bunch of chickens, but they'd gotten rid of all of them except for the one rooster, which they'd never been able to catch.

Casey took the Jones kids aside and told them about the bet. He offered to split with them if they'd catch the rooster and keep it for him until the moment of truth. They agreed, and it wasn't long before the children caught the bird and showed him to Casey on their screened-in back porch.

"Man, he was a pretty thing. He was part fightin' rooster and part jungle cock, and damn, he could crow! Well, I gave the kids five dollars apiece for him, and I made 'em give me a bill of sale, so I don't get caught for stealin' a chicken. So I said, 'All right now, you keep him on the back porch and feed and water him and everything, but leave him out here where we can hear him crow.'

"By now I've got about three hundred dollars bet that me and the kids are gonna split, except that some of my bettors reneged on me. I'd go into the pool hall and I'd pull the old Harry Grib trick on 'em. I'd act like I was drinkin' twice as much as I really was, and they'd be makin' fun of me, kiddin' me and askin', 'When you gonna get that rooster?' And hell! I done already had that rooster in a box for three days, you know?

"And old Buzz, he'd be tryin' to get me to bet some more. He'd say, 'Come on, let's bet a twenty,' and then, 'let's bet another fifty!' So, hell! I was just bettin' with both hands, 'cause I done had the bird in a cage. Now, I brought the sucker up one mornin' and collected all my money -- except for Buzz. He welched on me, 'cause some of his was on credit.

"Then I took the rooster down to Dick Lyons' room. The fact that Dick was the producer didn't make no difference to me, and I opened the door and threw the rooster into the room. Well, Dick and his wife were just gettin' up and this wild thing just went crazy in there, squawkin' and a-flappin' and messin' on the carpet. Lyons was a yellin,' 'Get him outta here!' Oh, hell, he was really mad!

"Then I get him caught again, and I take him down to Burt Kennedy's room. I rap on the door and when Burt opens it, I throw the rooster in there. Old Burt, he just thought it was great, you know, 'cause he knew about the bets and he was sayin', 'Damn, ain't he pretty?' and he just loved it.

"So now I take this sucker with me on the set all the time, and I get him tame. He sets on my shoulder and nuzzles up against me. And I feed him a little bit, you know, and he loved it. He'd close his eyes and set there. But as soon as I'd leave him alone, he'd get lonesome and start to crow. And he'd just crow like hell.

"Now, it started costing me about two fifths of whiskey a day for the wranglers to wrangle this rooster while I was in a scene or something. And I had to keep him out there on the location site, 'cause when I took him to the inn, it was bad business. That sucker would crow all night. I'd never heard a rooster crow when it was rainin', so I put him into the shower and tried turnin' the shower on once. But that critter would crow all night in the shower. And it got to be a real problem.

"So I bribed the wranglers, Kenny Lee and them, into keepin' him. I figured if I could once get him established in a shot it would be worth it. So I kept on workin' on it. I'd say, 'Boy, wouldn't it look great, Burt, if you had a shot of old Hank [Fonda] takin' a bath in the horse trough and you had this rooster settin' on it?'

"And old Burt would laugh and say, 'Yeah, that would be good!' And I had the still photographer takin' pictures of him and everything, and I finally did get that rooster established in the picture. So now I got a rooster check comin' and the whole dang thing. After awhile it got to where the rooster was workin' more than I was, and I'm not likin' that too good, but he's bringin' home the money.

"Well, they finished up the location stuff, and they said they weren't gonna need the rooster anymore. I checked and found out that the rooster couldn't draw unemployment checks, so I gave him back to the Jones kids. Then the whole company headed back to Hollywood. When they went inside at MGM, they found out they had to match a shot. It's where these two cowboys decide that they should have a Christmas tree, even if there's no one there but them. So they fix up a tree, and in this one scene the rooster crows, and Fonda says, 'What in hell are you crowin' about? There ain't a hen within twenty miles!'

"Then they discover that they had no rooster. So they call me up at home, 'cause now I'm all through with my stuff. So I told 'em where the rooster was and that they had to send a limo all the way back to Sedona to pick him up. I told 'em, 'If you can't fly him, make sure you send an air conditioned limo.'

"Well, they got him back on the set, but now they can't make him crow. So they call me again. And I'm a little mad 'cause this rooster is workin' and I'm not. Burt Kennedy and Dick Lyons tell me they worked all mornin' settin' up this shot, but now they can't make the rooster crow.

"So I milked it a little bit, and I told 'em, 'Oh, you don't need me. You've got my rooster, what the hell! Nobody even invited me over for lunch.' And they're sayin', 'Damn it, Casey, he won't crow! You've got to come over.' So I tell 'em, 'Well, put me on a rooster trainer check and I'll come over and make him do it.'

"I hurry on over to the studio and I just take over 'cause Burt and I are good buddies, and he lets me get away with anything. So now I'm the director. So I get everything all set, and I tell 'em, 'I know what's the matter. You guys are all talkin' and sayin' your lines, and you won't give him a chance to say his.' I'm really milkin' it, sayin', 'All right! Be quiet! No walkin'! No talkin'! Quiet on the set! Roll 'em! Action!'

"And damn! Just that quick, he crowed! I couldn't stop him. I hollered, 'Cut!' And I picked him up and I said, 'Will that do it for you, Burt?' and I took my rooster and left 'em all there laughing."

Casey took his trained rooster to the El Morocco Apartments on Holloway Drive just off Sunset Strip where he and Cleo were living. Cleo was delighted with what she saw. A genuine bond of affection had developed between Casey and the rooster and she thought that was real cute.

Apartment living has its major drawbacks for a rooster, however, and most especially this "Caruso." But Casey couldn't resist the opportunity to give the other apartment dwellers a little taste of farm life. There was a small balcony at the back of the apartment and Casey tethered the bird there. The bird couldn't fly off and get lost, but he could entertain his neighbors to the maximum. This worked out pretty well until Casey noticed his pet's crowing sounded a little funny. When he went to look, he found the rooster over the side hanging by one foot. He'd been crowing upside down.

Casey's rooster had made a real hit during the making of *The Rounders*. Henry Fonda even did a painting of the bird, but apartment living didn't agree with him somehow. Casey figured that since the bird's movie star days were over, it was time for him to retire to a quiet home in the country. He took him out to Newhall, California, to Glenn Randall's training stables, and turned him loose. There was, after all, plenty of room there for him, with no need for the "balcony tethers."

Not satisfied with the action there, however, the rooster went down the road to the home of Ed Jauregui, brother of Andy Jauregui, the rodeo stock contractor. At Ed's place, the "Pride of Sedona" found what he'd been looking for: a dozen hens with combs as red as his. When his lust was at last satisfied, he strutted back over to Randall's with his whole harem happily clucking along behind. He was possibly "America's most beloved rooster."

A NEW DIRECTION

Unfortunately, the marriage that had looked as if it were made in heaven began to weaken until finally Casey and Cleo separated, then later divorced. "It was quite bitter at the time," Cleo remembered with a sigh. "At least, on Casey's part. I guess divorces are never easy.

"We were both young, with different backgrounds, even though we were both from South Dakota. Casey traveled a lot when we lived in Hollywood. I don't really know how those things happen. I'd gotten a little bit interested in trying for a career. Also, we didn't have any children. We didn't buy a home, and maybe not having roots was something that sort of added to our troubles.

"When I married Casey I was emotionally quite young. During the course of our marriage I suppose I grew up somewhat. I guess it was mainly that we just had different interests, like the racetrack and gambling. I didn't like that too much. But the breakup was certainly not all Casey's fault. It was partially mine, too. I try to be fair about it."

Bob O'Donald recalled that Casey's pal, Arthur O'Connell, had told him the following story, which does shed some light on the breakup of Casey and Cleo's marriage. He said, "Casey would bring all his winnings from the track for Arthur to hold for safe keeping. Casey'd told Arthur, 'Don't give me any of my money till I go to South Dakota this Christmas, no matter what. Even if I beg you for it, don't let me have it till then.'

"One day Casey received a call from Burt Kennedy who asked him if he would pick up some prop he needed and bring it over to the set. Casey said, 'Don't worry, Burt, I'll take care of it.' With that he called Cleo, who was working at the time. He told her he needed three hundred dollars for a little while and that he'd give it back right away."

As Cleo said, she really disapproved of Casey's gambling at the racetrack. Bob continued, "According to O'Connell, she'd told Casey, 'You lose our money once more, and I'm going to leave you.' Casey took the three hundred to get the prop for Burt and went straight to the racetrack with it. Casey could go right in and talk to the jockeys, which was a no-no for the rest of us. O'Connell told me that one of the jockeys who was just walking by said to Casey, 'Bet the long shot in the last race,' and then continued walking right on past him.

"Casey'd been betting all the races, and had run the three hundred up to twelve hundred by the time the last race posted. So he thought, 'I'd better save back three hundred so Cleo won't leave me,' and he bet the rest on the long shot on the nose. That horse paid him thirty-eight thousand dollars. He got the prop for Burt, gave Cleo back her three hundred, and gave the rest to Arthur to save for him.

"When Christmastime came, Casey and Cleo headed for South Dakota, so Arthur handed him seventy-two thousand dollars in cash. Driving back to South Dakota, Casey and Cleo stopped in that little city called Las Vegas, and Casey lost it all -- and Cleo."

There is no doubt that Casey was a compulsive gambler. He said, "I used to pull stuff at the quarter horse track, but they knew me and would cover my bet, and the next day I'd go back and pay 'em. I'd bet $200 across the board, or whatever, but it was a little different at Santa Anita.

"I'd been betting in the Turf Club at the hundred dollar window, and I was hanging out with C.W. Smith, the ex-football player who owned Hillsdale, the Kentucky Derby winner. We were running around together, and both of us playin' pretty heavy. I had credit at the track then, but I'd already used it up. They'd give me credit up to ten thousand and I'd go over and then have to make it up.

"Well, I just had to bet this one horse and I didn't have any money. It was do or die. I could go without food or anything else, if I could just get this bet down. It's the same addiction as alcoholism.

"So, I waited till the bell was about to go off, and I said to the clerk, 'Give me the seven horse ten times.' Remember, this was the hundred dollar window. I got the tickets and then said, 'Oh my gawd! I've been robbed! I don't have but three dollars on me!' I really played the act, lookin' around and I said, 'Wait a minute! Don't worry. I'll go get Smitty.'

"Well, the pari-mutuel clerk has gotta make it up, just as soon as the race is over -- he's gotta account for it. But he didn't press the bell on me -- he didn't call the fuzz. So I ran out to the rail and I said, 'Smitty, go cool the old boy off at the window. I got a grand on this horse, and I don't have a dime.' Smitty said, 'Why, you crazy s.o.b. I don't have a grand on me. Hell, I'm busted, too!'

"Well, the horse is laying about third, and he moves up, and dang! He turns for home and he's five in front. So I ran back to the window and tell ol' Bill, 'Hey, don't worry, I told you not to worry. It's okay!' When it was all over, I laid three hundred on him. He's retired now, but he swears it was the most nervous he'd ever been."

It's a certainty that Casey had his share of great times at the track; still, it was always a roller coaster ride, because he never did anything in a small way. His gambling had really gotten out of hand. He began attending Gamblers Anonymous meetings.

Casey admitted, "I look back and feel ashamed of what I did when I went to Gamblers Anonymous. I feel guilty that I didn't take it more seriously. I knew I had a real problem with gambling. I'd almost beg, borrow, or steal in order to gamble, the same way an alcoholic will do for a drink.

"Hell! You'll lie for it. You'll do anything just to get another bet down. And when you've got a drinkin' problem along with a gamblin' problem, it's a hell of a parlay. I was givin' up picture work and everything else to go down to the racetrack.

"I enjoyed seeing my friends, and I enjoyed mornin' workouts more than anything else. It used to be that I'd have to stay there. I used to have to bet everything I had on the last race, and many times I'd blow myself out.

"Like I said, I'd even stiff the guys at the windows and come back and pay 'em the next day. The guy that I stiffed that one day, for the grand, wasn't goin' to be stiffed. They'd have probably run me off the track if that horse hadn't won.

"I'd heard about Gamblers Anonymous, so I just started goin' to the meetings on my own, lookin' for help. Once I started goin' to meetings they started callin' me, the same way they do in A.A. You know, if there's someone you haven't seen at a meeting for awhile, you call him up and see if you can help him. I hadn't been goin' to the meetings all that long, and I'd never gotten up and talked and copped out on myself. I didn't do that at first at the A.A. meetings either, 'cause I never knew what the A.A. was really about back then. I thought it was just a bunch of people who got together to hustle books or something.

"I'd been goin' to Gamblers Anonymous [in Beverly Hills] fairly regularly, six weeks, maybe. Bankers and lawyers and business people of all kinds attended, and they'd get up and tell the damndest stories about how they almost swindled money in order to have funds to gamble with. After the meetings we'd go out for coffee and so forth, if some of them were in A.A., too. Most of 'em were just in Gamblers Anonymous, so sometimes we'd go out and have a drink.

"This one evenin', just after we left the meetin', I got about six of them into a crap game. I had a set of dice in my pocket -- a lot of cowboys used to pack dice. As soon as they bet their first dollar I brought them to their knees. I didn't have phony dice or anything, but I rolled a seven and I rolled another natural, and one of them said, 'I'll bet you can't do that again,' and I said, 'Get your dollar down there!' He tossed it down and I busted every one of them in that damn game. They had their tongues hangin' out, so I said, 'You guys need help!' That was the last Gamblers Anonymous meeting I went to.

"But after I really got into A.A., I was ashamed. It's like draggin' a bottle of whiskey out around a bunch of alcoholics and offerin' 'em a drink. They just couldn't resist, you know? After they covered that first dollar, why there was no lettin' up on it."

A New Direction

***

In 1967 Casey was devoting full time to the picture business. As with all actors and stuntmen, sometimes he worked and sometimes he didn't. One day he received a call from his agent. "I've got an interview for a commercial set up for you, and it should be a good one. They're looking for a cowboy. Take along some good rodeo pictures and be sure to take the *LIFE* magazine cover."

When Casey arrived they told him they wanted a nondescript cowboy, therefore his name wasn't necessary. They also said he wasn't old enough and didn't look the part. Casey wasn't too pleased, to say the least. He handled the rejection by going to the phone and entering the bronc riding at the upcoming rodeo in San Bernardino, California. He placed second and then entered nine more rodeos and won them all.

Casey felt that the general public had a distorted view of what the real West was like. What he'd seen in the movies didn't seem to reflect the world of broncs, cattle, Indians, or the rugged pioneer people he knew in South Dakota, Kansas, or anywhere else he'd been in the West. He felt that if you showed people the real West as he knew it, they'd be entertained and educated at the same time.

For a number of years he'd been amassing a large herd of horses on the Lower Brule Indian Reservation in South Dakota, the land of the Teton Sioux. Casey believed that good bucking horses are born and not made. He'd selected mares and stallions for his herd that he felt had the right temperament and constitution to make good broncs. Knowing that horses in the wild tend to breed down in size, Casey not only used the rugged South Dakota horses, but added to the herd Spanish Bloods, Kentucky Thoroughbreds, and even a Clydesdale stallion to contribute size and bone.

Bronc riders tend to like the big, tough-type horses the best. Casey referred to the smaller horses as "little rats." Little horses, although they can be hard to ride, are difficult to score on. They don't allow the bronc rider to show off that picture-perfect form so pleasing to the judge's eye.

Casey allowed these horses to breed freely on the Lower Brule. His plan worked well, or perhaps too well, because the deal that Casey had made with the Indian agent was for no more than a hundred head on the reservation at any one time. Because he had so many irons in the fire, time had just gotten away from him and the herd had grown to four hundred head.

The Indian agent ran out of patience and gave Casey thirty days to move them. Casey saw it as the perfect way to show people the West he knew and loved. He decided he should make a documentary film that would show the actual roundup, the drive, the trying out of the broncs, and the sale. The film would also showcase the beautiful South Dakota country he knew and loved. But when he took the idea around to his various contacts in the movie business he ran into a problem.

Using ten thousand dollars of his own money, he shot the film as a semi-documentary. All he needed for a script was the simple truth: he actually was raising horses to buck, and the herd had grown in numbers beyond his agreement with the Indian agency. He'd arranged to hold a rodeo and auction in Fort Pierre, but the safest way to get the horses there was to drive them. He felt that trucking them could prove too dangerous, especially for the foals.

Casey said, "Everyone kept telling me that I couldn't make and distribute my own picture, but the more they told me, the more I knew I could do it. I made the film, *Born to Buck*, with the same horses I believed in, and with the same people who believed in me."

The cast featured Casey and a roster of cowboys that he had called on to gather the herd and make the drive. These top hands included his old friend Albert Lopez and ninety-six-year-old Jack Hart. Jack lived to be nearly a hundred and five and worked as a cowboy, in one capacity or another, the entire time.

It should be pointed out that Casey had great respect for some of the Western films that had been produced in Hollywood in the past. In fact, he loved the work of Gary Cooper and Joel McCrea especially, as well as the great films of John Ford and many others. At the time he made *Born to Buck*, however, Hollywood was just emerging from the boom of the TV Western. During the late fifties and early sixties it was impossible to turn the dial on a TV set without being offered a thirty-minute or hour-long Western.

These shows, often filmed with low budgets, were cranked out week after week. The star often wore the exact same costume every episode and was viewed against the same familiar sets which were built on sound stages. Rarely if ever, were they filmed in a setting that even came close to the real West that Casey knew existed.

Casey chose a place called Ambush Creek for the base camp for the roundup and drive. The remarkable crew of technicians, cameramen, sound men, lighting crews, and everyone else it takes to make a film, slept on the ground in bedrolls. They ate from the chuck wagon just like the cowboys and bronc men who handled the herd. The weather had no respect for their comfort, either. It rained over ten inches during the drive.

South Dakota sported lush green hills, blue skies, and billowing clouds of white or gray. During electrical storms, huge bolts of lightning bored into the earth. Add to this scene four hundred horses of every color imaginable: bays and grays, chestnuts and blacks, sorrels, browns, pintos, both overo and tobiano types, grullas, buckskins, whites, palominos, albinos, strawberry roans, red roans, canellos, blue roans, and savinos. All of them were slick, fat, and shiny from their diet of rich South Dakota grass. All these elements combined to make this a magnificent piece of film.

They photographed the horses as they were being gathered and driven, with all the spectacle that such a drive creates. They showed horses jumping gullies, sliding down embankments, and running at full speed with manes and tails flying. A kaleidoscope of equine colors and shapes resulted. Cameramen filmed from other perspectives as well. They showed a frolicking foal, a nipping mare being saddled and ridden, and horses bucking and bucking and bucking. Many of the scenes have the look of a Charles Russell painting about them, especially his famous *Bronc for Breakfast.*

When they arrived at the Missouri River, they found it in a rolling, swirling rampage. Even so, the Highway Department would not give permission for the horses to cross the bridge, so Casey made the decision to swim the herd across. The plan was for Casey to enter the river well ahead of the herd. On a trail drive this is called "riding point."

The crossing began smoothly, with all hands crowding the horses into the river. The herd entered the water then began to follow Casey across. The weather soon turned violent, and the black sky released its fury. Rain, wind, and lightning bolts thundered disapproval of the venture. Even a full-blown tornado augered down into the earth, black and screaming, while the cameras ground away. The crew captured the whole frightening scene in a way that Hollywood could not have staged.

When the herd had gotten about two hundred feet out into the river, they had taken all they could stand and began to circle back to shore. Casey, the nonswimmer, kept his horse from turning back. Using his hand, he splashed water into his horse's face on whichever side the horse tried to turn. Out near the middle of the river, it became clear that Casey's horse was nearing complete exhaustion.

Casey slipped off him, holding only to his rope, praying that it wouldn't come loose. The horse thrashed in the water, his head at times slipping completely under, but the gallant horse blew the water from his nostrils and struggled on toward the far shore. At last he emerged with Casey in tow.

The lens of the waiting camera, set up to film the arriving herd, showed an exhausted Casey. He flopped down in the mud, totally spent. When he finally looked back at the river for the first time, he was relieved, for he saw the herd still on the far shore. All the hands were safe over there, too, staring anxiously across at him. It was another example of Casey's daring. He was lucky to be alive, and he knew it.

It took him two days to talk the Highway Department into letting him cross the bridge with his herd, but it worked out well. Everyone, including the herd of horses, was tired and in need of a rest. The bridge crossing caused a sizable traffic jam, but that was the least of Casey's worries. As they approached the gates of the Stanley County Arena at Fort Pierre, the main thing on his mind was, *How well will they buck?*

When they got to the arena it was a sea of mud, disliked by horses and riders alike, and still it continued to rain. When showtime came, however, Casey's concerns diminished. A sizable crowd arrived, and when the chute gates flew open, it also rained cowboys.

A New Direction

The film develops into a series of bronc rides, each of which ends with a cowboy disappearing in the mud. A whole section of bronc riding featured ten-year-old boys riding yearling colts. They didn't fare too well, but no worse than the older cowboys on the older broncs. One of the better rides came from none other than Mark Reed, the gunslinger, who whipped and fanned his bronc with his hat all the way through the ride.

Last, there came a string of saddle bronc rides, including Casey and world champion cowboy Dennis Reiners. The film ends as a bucked off but very happy Casey rises from the mud.

When Casey returned with the footage, he had no trouble finding the backing to complete the project. He raised the money from business acquaintances who were not connected with the movie industry. The cost of the finished project totaled two hundred thousand dollars.

Henry Fonda narrated *Born to Buck*, and Rex Allen announced the bronc sequence in Fort Pierre. Dick Stabile wrote and conducted the excellent musical score. Casey distributed the film himself, releasing it in the fall of 1968. He felt that Fort Pierre was the natural starting point, and he leased the theater there for four days. The film grossed what then was a whopping $6,190. After a successful test run in a few other selected cities, one hundred and four theaters throughout South Dakota, North Dakota, Minnesota, and Iowa booked the film.

From the beginning, Casey knew he had bought way more film than he would ever need for the making of the picture. He wanted to ensure that no opportunity would be missed during the filming of the drive, rodeo, and sale. Knowing that he had all this extra film, he came up with a unique plan for a future project.

He selected a young, very appealing palomino colt and called it Big Enough. He also found an orphan buffalo calf that a little girl, Terry Ann Valberg, had been bottle raising. Casey decided to use Terry Ann and two young boys, Jeff Jones and Jimmy Hunt. They had not only exhibited considerable riding skills in the making of *Born to Buck*, but had an appeal that Casey thought was just right.

Casey filmed the opening scenes featuring the palomino colt, the buffalo calf, the three youngsters, and their dog Silver. He did this over two years before he announced the start of production of the film he called *The Young Rounders.*

Casey cast Joel McCrea as the lead in *The Young Rounders*, whom he considered the most natural actor he had ever seen in a movie. McCrea had not done a film since *Ride the High Country* for MGM back in 1962.

Joel McCrea was already a millionaire. His more than a hundred major screen rolls and his vast cattle ranch interests had put him beyond the necessity of working in films, but McCrea came out of retirement to star in Casey Tibbs' outdoor adventure drama. *The Young Rounders* was shot in the fall of 1969.

McCrea himself explained the reason he singled out *The Young Rounders* for his return to motion pictures. He said, "I'm doing the picture because Casey Tibbs asked me to do it. Casey is a great friend, and a most sensitive film maker." He continued, "I'd just seen his fantastic *Born to Buck*, and it convinced me that if things go right for him, Casey can very well become the Disney of the Westerns."

McCrea also said that he was influenced by the Fort Pierre location site. "I'd been to that South Dakota area before, and never had I seen such raw, untouched beauty."

Slim Pickens, veteran character actor, was also featured in the film. Casey cast him to play a shady horse buyer who haunts the horse auctions looking for stock for his "horse meat" business. After he wrangles the purchase of the kids' beautiful palomino, he heads for the "glue factory" with the horse. However, little Terry Ann, Jeff, and Jimmy come to the rescue, assisted by their dog.

Casey not only produced and directed the film, he also played a featured role. Trick roping legend Montie Montana was also featured. Songs for the movie were specially written and performed by the great Marty Robbins.

The little orphan buffalo calf had grown into a huge animal. Terry Ann Valberg trained him to the bridle and rode him in the picture. Casey often remarked with pride that Jay Sisler trained the dog Silver. Jay later used Silver in his act, "Jay Sisler and His Dogs."

Joel McCrea had indeed "been to that South Dakota Country before." It had not been that long before, either. Following the completion of *Born To*

Buck and the first shooting of the early segment of the *The Young Rounders*, Casey shot an award-winning documentary film in the spring of 1969. This documentary, *Sioux Nation*, also featured McCrea.

Casey said, "It was the first time that the Indians ever let anyone film the sun dance, the rite where they dance with rawhide thongs tied through slits they cut in their chests. They never bleed, even though they push the knife right through the pectoral muscle. They go into the sweat lodge first, and they have a whole ceremony they go through. It's real interesting, and I got my money back on the film just showing it around the country."

The U.S. Government banned the sun dance ceremony in 1883. In some cases the army had to be called in to enforce the ban. At Pine Ridge, the rite was stopped by a show of force and the threat of bloodshed by fifty Indian police. A few Indians managed secretly to keep it alive, and in 1933 it was revived, without the torture. The self-torture was openly restored by a Sioux named Eagle Feather. He did this only ten years before Casey captured the sun dance ceremony on film, and Eagle Feather is one of the dancers shown in the film. A great many Indian customs and rituals are explained during this film.

Casey himself is seen briefly only twice in the movie: once as he danced in full headdress, and again as he shared the peace pipe. It was one of the few times Casey ever smoked.

That Casey, Joel McCrea, and the crew counted the making of this movie a privilege is obvious. The privilege is also obvious in that they were allowed to photograph this sacred Indian ceremony at all.

MORE LOVES...AND TOURS

Rodeo stars attract women like magnets. In general, men who live on the edge and flirt with danger seem to have a certain sex appeal. Rodeo cowboys, racecar drivers, and matadors all enjoy this magnetism, and Casey was certainly no exception. Unquestionably, his handsome appearance added to his appeal. He dated some of the most beautiful and glamorous women in the world. The younger debutantes swarmed around Casey like bees to honey.

When Casey worked in *Bus Stop* in 1965, he got to be friends with Marilyn Monroe. One evening after work she invited Casey to her dressing room. Naturally, the other cowboys were dying to know how it went and pressed Casey to tell them all about it. "She fixed us a couple of drinks," he told them, "and she told me to sit down on the couch while she changed into something more comfortable."

Casey said, "They were just like a pack of ol' hotdogs; they were leanin' in real close to listen. I told them, 'She came back in a sheer negligee and sat down beside me and started blowing in my ear. I took the straps off her shoulders and she stood up, and her gown slipped down to the floor.' The cowboys were hanging all over me when I looked at them and said, 'That's when I woke up!'

"They pounded on me and like to have beat me to death with their hats. She'd invited me up to her room, but it was for a press party. I got to know her pretty well, though, and she was a neat person; she just wanted to be one of the people. She just wanted to be accepted. I liked her."

One of Casey's more serious affairs occurred with the stunning Katherine Ross. At the time Casey met Katherine, her career was soaring from her performance in the movie *The Graduate*. It was during the filming of *The Hellfighters* at Universal Studios that Casey loaned Katherine a paint horse named K.C. "I was on one picture and she was on another when we met," Casey reflected. "I went with her a long time -- two years, maybe two and a half. She was a beautiful gal." Casey was thirty-eight and Katherine was twenty-five at the time of their love affair. One can only guess why things went wrong, as Casey's only remark after a long silence was, "I can't go into that right now."

Christmas of 1970 proved to be a tragic time for Casey and his family, as they were jolted by the sudden death of Casey's brother, Johnny Tibbs. Johnny was only 54 years old, and Casey was not aware of his brother having any health problems. He said, "Johnny's death was a shocker. Johnny and I were real close. If he knew of anything wrong with his health, he never told us. But then Dad had several strokes that he never told anyone about, so I don't know. He went out with a friend, Potty Hanson, in the early mornin' to break the ice out of the waterin' holes for his cattle. When he was through, he threw the axe in the back of his pickup, and when he got behind the wheel he keeled over. Poor old Potty nearly had a heart attack himself tryin' to get Johnny in for help. He couldn't get him out from behind the wheel, and then the truck got stuck, and it was a mess. They revived Johnny briefly at the hospital, but in the end he didn't make it."

***

At the famous Schwabs Drug Store on Sunset Boulevard in Beverly Hills -- the same Schwabs Drug Store where Lana Turner was said to have been discovered -- Casey met Renee D'Balsac. Renee was working behind the cosmetic counter when Casey and Joel McCrea walked in. "I didn't know either one of them," Renee said as she reminisced about their first meeting, "but Mr. Schwabs knew them. Casey gave me a hard time, pretending that he was going to buy some perfume, but he was really just checking me out. I asked him if he was the 'Midnight Cowboy,' because the movie had just come out. He said, 'No, I'm the "High Noon" Cowboy!' I laughed, and that was how we met.

"When I first met him," she continued, "his affair with Katherine Ross had just ended. It was not an easy thing at first. Casey was not that trusting with women at that time. Once he knew you and was committed, he was a great guy, but until then he would just fool around. But when there was commitment, he was very loyal. We started living together, and it lasted over seven years.

"There was a Hamburger Hamlet right next door to Schwabs and I used to meet Casey there for lunch. He was never alone. He was always with somebody and I never knew from one day to the next who he might have with him. Sometimes it would be Pat Butram, or Robert Mitchum, Steve McQueen, Frank Sinatra, or John Wayne. It could be just anybody you've ever heard of. He seemed to know everybody.

"I remember a lot of funny things that happened. Casey threw a big surprise party for me on my thirtieth birthday at the Playboy Club. A lot of people came, including my mother, my sister, and her husband. I had on this long, glamorous, green gown, and as we were being introduced, Casey pulled the chair out from under me. Can you imagine that? When I went to sit down, I dropped clear down on the floor, and everybody stared at me. I was so embarrassed, but Casey just looked down at me with those big, blue, innocent eyes. Still, I wanted to kill him! But you couldn't stay mad at him.

"He did all sorts of things. Once we went to eat at a Japanese restaurant for a business meeting. The stairs into the dining area stretched down two long flights. He did a stunt fall and tumbled all the way down those two flights. People panicked, and he convincingly played dead at the bottom. People really bought it, and then he got up and laughed.

"Then, of course, there was 'eating the glass.' He was always doing that. He even ate the best crystal at a party one time. The hostess said, 'That's my good crystal, Casey!' but then she couldn't get mad, of course. That's the kind of things he used to do, but you just couldn't get mad at Casey.

"One time he won sixty thousand dollars at the track. I hadn't seen him all day. He came home and threw the bills all over the room and said, 'You've got five minutes to pick them up, and if you do, you can have it – it's all yours!'" Renee continued, "He clocked me. He just threw it all around, but after five minutes, I couldn't get it all. That didn't happen too often, but he was very generous.

"Mostly he would never tell me how he did at the track. I didn't care about racing. Oh! Another thing, if he went to the track during the week and I couldn't go, he would always bring me these big, beautiful flowers. He'd steal them from the Turf Club! They were great arrangements, these big tropical flowers that cost a fortune. He just put some newspapers on the floor of the car and at the end of the day he'd put those huge, beautiful flowers in there, and he'd bring them home to me so I wouldn't get mad, you know? He'd say, 'Look at these! I brought you these flowers.' I was a lucky girl, I tell you. I feel very privileged."

***

After Casey had finished his third picture, he still had enough horses running loose on the Indian Reservation to require two more roundups. It was not so much the Indians that wanted the horses out as it was the Bureau of Indian Affairs. The Sioux were all great horsemen themselves, and many were real rodeo fans. Casey's relationship with them was quite good. Throughout his life he'd known, respected, and traded with the Indians. He considered himself fortunate to have so many Indian friends from tribes all over the United States and Canada.

To finance these roundups, Casey decided to advertize for a few paying customers who might want an escape from high-rise buildings, smog, and traffic snarls. The plan worked well enough to merit a second Casey Tibbs Roundup.

The printed application form included a map of the area showing the three main camps and their relationship to the Cheyenne and Missouri Rivers. The form also stated that for seven hundred fifty dollars, each guest wrangler would receive a gold and silver buckle with his name engraved on it. Top horses were guaranteed for each rider, as well as the

168

finest cowboy grub and spirits at the end of each day. Each rider was to bring his own bedroll and would sleep in roundup tents equipped with cots.

Two days of horse roundup and branding would be held at Main Camp #1. This event was to be followed by two days of gathering and branding cattle on the open range between Camp #1 and Camp #2 at Whitehorse. The form promised that horse breaking would start the first day and continue through the final day. Roping and horse breaking lessons were to be given by Casey and other "sons of the western range" each day. Good fishing was promised along the way also. No women were allowed in camp until the final day at Timberlake, and no spirits until after evening camp was set up.

The second Casey Tibbs Roundup took place June 11 through June 18, 1972. *Playboy* magazine saw the advertisement and sent along writer Bil Gilbert to cover the event. Bil's feature article ran in the June 1973 issue under "Personality." It was titled, "Where the West Has Gone" and took up nearly nine full pages. Gilbert began by saying, "I had a hell of a time, I really did." He also said, "Casey's an appealing guy. I like him a lot."

***

Rick Le Fevour is from Chicago, and his love for horses took him to a boarding stable in the northern suburbs. There he met Al Rosin and earned extra money by working Al's horses for him. Rosin was a representative for a big agency that handled the model used as the "Marlborough Man" in the advertising campaign for Marlborough cigarettes. Through Rosin the agency learned of the Casey Tibbs Wild Horse Roundup. Rosin and his brother decided to go, and they took young Rick Le Fevour along for company.

"That's how I met Casey," Rick stated as he began telling of the experience. "We hit it off pretty good and became friends. I was only about fifteen or sixteen years old at the time. I went out to South Dakota with Al Rosin again in 1972, for Casey's next roundup. Then in 1973, Casey was taking a show to Japan and asked me if I wanted to go along with him, and that's how I really got into stunt work."

Rick continued, "In Japan, every day we'd start out by riding a buffalo and later a bareback horse, and a bull. Every performance we'd do live stunt shows, robbing banks, rolling wagons, etc. At first, Casey merely turned the buffaloes out and ran them around the arena, just so the audience could get a look at them. But right away he thought that was too tame, so he decided that some of us should ride them out of the chutes. They were young buffaloes and were jumping out of the chutes and tearing down boards. None of us wanted any part of getting on them.

"But the first day Casey looked around behind the chutes and said, 'Okay, we need some buffalo riders here.' Everybody kind of hid a little bit. Then he said to me, 'Here! Come here! Get over here!' So I said, 'What do I do?' And he said, 'Just get on him. Any city kid can learn to do this, and you kinda look like a good candidate for buffalo ridin'.' And he just put me down on one and told me to grab hold of the mane, and then he opened the gate on me. That's how I started out buffalo riding.

"We rode them like that for the first month and a half, but then some of the cowboys were starting to get hurt. We didn't want to be riding the buffaloes anymore, so Casey started giving us an option. He told us that if we could get volunteers out of the crowd, we wouldn't have to do it.

"We were really motivated then. We'd go up into the crowd, and of course none of the spectators spoke English, so we'd say, 'Would you like to ride the buffalo?' We'd ask them, but they didn't know a word of what we were saying or where we were taking them, but some of them just followed us down to the chutes. Others would hang onto their seats with their wives or girlfriends screaming, but it was either them or us, so we took them down anyway and put them on the buffaloes.

"Once in an outdoor show, we took a Japanese guy out of the stands who really didn't want to go. It'd been raining and he left big, long, finger marks in the mud where he tried to resist. But if we didn't come up with at least three or four 'volunteers,' *we* had to ride those buffaloes.

"Up in the stands, their wives would be screaming and crying, but we put them on anyway. There were injuries, too. We tried to put them on way back toward the back end of the buffalo. That way, just as soon as the gate opened they'd sort of quickly fall to the ground. But one guy tried to grab the buffalo around the neck just as we were opening the gate and he got a horn right through his cheek. Right away, Casey said, 'Okay, you guys get on them and show them how it's done.' And we were back to riding them again.

"We did a lot of promotional things like TV shows and interviews, and Casey was always coming up with ways to promote the show. We played an amusement park once. The show was set up a long way from the main part of the park, so Casey had a bunch of us dress up in cavalry uniforms and all that, and we rode down through the parking lot chasing each other and shooting. There was a giant pool there that tapered in and out and made four-foot waves, like on a beach at the ocean. Casey rode in and scattered people everywhere. The rest of us were doing our thing when we saw what Casey was doing, so we all raced down and rode into the pool on our horses, too. It made the news, and it did generate some interest in the show.

"Once in awhile Casey would hold a big press conference to promote the show. I remember one time about thirty or forty people from the Japanese press came, as well as some of the International press headquartered in Tokyo. We had a bar/restaurant in the Western town. We actually used it to serve food to the people who came to the show. Casey had about four or five of the stunt guys come up there to stage a fight for the press. We thought we were going to use one of the routines that we used every day during the show. We'd talked it over among ourselves, but Casey had other ideas. He took out his gun and started shooting and yelling at me, 'You can't get no good help anymore, damn it!' And he just hauls off and smacks me right in the forehead. A goose egg rose up. It looked like something out of a cartoon, and the blow practically knocked me out. He wheeled around and threw me in the middle of a table, right in front of the reporters.

"Another stunt guy was there and Casey kicked him in the stomach. Taking him down, he yelled, 'Come on! Go on with it!' He got everybody fighting. It got pretty wild, throwing guys out windows and everything, and the press was right there in the middle of it. They thought he was really mad and firing us!

"He finally threw us all out the doors of the bar. Turning to the press he said, 'You can't get good help over here and put on a good show!' He said it just like he was still mad. The ruse made all of the papers the next day.

"When I first got there, I was just starting out and I thought, boy! This is great! I'll really get some pointers, you know, with him being the saddle bronc champion six times over and all that. Here's a guy who knows it all.

"One day Casey brought us down to the arena to start us out, and he put me on about eight bareback horses in one afternoon. Every time I'd get bucked off or just about get one ridden, I'd go back and ask him, 'What am I doing wrong?' or, 'What should I do different?' And he'd say, 'Oh, don't worry, you look great. Just get on another one. You're doin' good!'

"I figured out later that he was just checking out the horses to see how well they were bucking. He didn't care what I was doing at all. He'd just say, 'Don't worry, you'll know when you're doin' somethin' wrong -- it'll hurt. If it doesn't hurt, you're doin' it right.' Here's the great world champion cowboy, and that's all the pointers he gave me the whole time I was there.

"It was a thrill for me to see Casey ride. I'd only seen movies and still pictures of him. He hadn't been riding for awhile, but one day we had an extra big crowd and the press all wanted to see the great champion ride, so he decided to get on a bronc. I've still got pictures of it."

There was a tremendous difference between the first Japanese tour that Rex Rossi described and the second one in 1973. It was a difficult and trying time for Casey, as he was caught between the broken promises made to him by the Japanese promoters and his own troop of unhappy cowboys and Indians.

Neither the money nor the shows worked out as anticipated. The Japanese backers broke their word and their contracts with Casey. Of that miserable experience he said, "The Japanese had changed completely in the ten years since I'd first gone there. In '62 they'd do anything they told you they'd do, but in '72 they'd just promise but not deliver."

Renee confided, "I had my bags packed for the airport twice. I was ready to go! I couldn't take the pressure. It was hard times, and Casey had to send a lot of the people home. Then again, some stayed with Casey for the whole tour, even without pay."

Renee pointed out, "If there was an upside to this, it was that Casey gained some very close friends. Those folks went sometimes two or three months without any pay. He kept that show going. He was a trooper. Any other guy would have just said, 'Let's go.' But he kept that show together."

A NEW CAREER

When Casey and Renee flew back to California from Japan, their place just off Sunset on Holloway Drive had been leased. "We didn't have a place to stay," Renee recalled, "but my sister and brother-in-law had a plush apartment on the sixteenth floor of the Champagne Towers in Santa Monica overlooking the ocean. They'd bought a new home in La Costa, so we subleased the apartment from them.

"We'd lived there about a year when Casey received a call from the Watts Brothers, the developers who built San Diego Country Estates. They flew us to Ramona and asked Casey if he wanted a job."

It was actually Don McAdams who offered Casey the job. The two had first met when Don was a teenager. Don was the young man who worked for Glenn Randall, mucking out stalls for the privilege of riding some of the horses kept there. He was also the same young man who confused the two beautiful buckskin horses, climbing on Casey's World's Fair, thinking it was Dale Evans' Buttermilk, and was launched into orbit by the outlaw.

Having survived the ride and the fall, McAdams had grown up to become one of the developers involved with San Diego Country Estates and American Land Systems. He still loved horses and thought Casey would be the perfect person to serve as the Director of Western Activities for the Estates.

"I wasn't keen on going there," Renee remembered, "because when we first flew over the place, there was hardly anything there, just a clubhouse and a few condos. There weren't even any roads. I told Casey I didn't want to live way up there. But Casey said that after six months in the sticks in Japan this was paradise. And they did give us a beautiful model home, all furnished.

"Part of the deal that Casey made with the Watts was that he could graze his cattle wherever he wanted on the Estates as long as they didn't cause any damage. Oh, there were damages! I don't think I had a good night's sleep the whole time we were there. We were constantly being awakened by people telling us that our cows were grazing on the golf course. We'd have to get up in the middle of the night and go move them.

"Casey had five hundred head of cattle, and there were no fences. He would leave me out in the sun with one horse to watch them while he went to the clubhouse. There I was with five hundred cattle and a golf fairway on each side. He'd be having martinis at the club saying, 'Everything's all right – Renee's keeping the cattle.'

"I finally had enough and I let them all loose. They went all over the place. I stormed to the clubhouse and announced, 'Your cattle are having a feast on the fairway!' And he couldn't believe it. He was just taking advantage of me." Renee laughed as she related this story, and then she sighed as she continued, "I can't believe what I did for this man!

"Casey loved it there. I'd never seen him so happy as when we moved. You know, he'd been hired to bring people up there, and he really knew a lot of people. Every weekend he'd bring in different celebrities and so forth, and it was fun for him. The money was good and we didn't have any rent to pay, so we didn't have to worry about that. But that's when Casey's heavy drinking started, though, because he was meeting people for lunch and for dinner every day. He had to do a lot of socializing.

"Remember the first big tennis match they held there with Bobby Riggs and Billy Jean King? That's what really put San Diego Country Estates on the map, because Riggs was such a cocky little guy and Billy Jean beat him. It was a big thing, and Casey brought in a lot of celebrities for the event. Before that, nobody knew about the Estates."

As Director of Western Activities, Casey managed the Equestrian Center. He organized rides, put on rodeo schools, held team ropings, and even had a mechanical bucking machine. Ben Johnson's nephew, John

Miller, a world champion team roper, put on roping clinics for Casey. Ben often came to help Casey, too.

San Diego Country Estates lies about seven miles beyond the small town of Ramona, which is near the top of rugged mountains in San Diego County, California. The picturesque area is covered with small farms and ranches. It's a mixture of homes which range from the very fancy to the very modest. Pastures laced with live oak trees can be found there, some of which are several hundred years old, and the whole country is strewn with huge boulders.

In contrast to Ramona, the Estates is more of a planned community, rather posh looking, built around golf courses and tennis courts, and of course the Equestrian Center. The whole thing is nestled up against the Barona Indian reservation, and it didn't take Casey long to make friends with the Indians. They were very generous in letting him lease their lands to graze his animals.

***

Pete and Olive Dunsmore also had leased their home out when they left for Japan with Casey, but they had a motorhome and lived in that until their home was available again. When they went to visit Casey at the Estates, he set them up among some beautiful old olive trees out at what they called "The Old Ranch."

Olive Dunsmore told Casey that she'd read that President Ford's son, Steve, was working as a cowboy on a ranch in Montana. "Casey was starting his rodeo school when I read of young Steve Ford's interest in rodeo and horses. I asked Casey, 'Why don't you send him an invitation to your rodeo school?' 'Olive,' he said, that's a great idea! I'll do it.'"

"The whole thing started just after my dad became president," Steve Ford said, "in the summer of 1974. I'd been accepted at Duke University and was supposed to go there and study oceanography. About three weeks before I was to begin at Duke, I walked into the Oval Office and told Dad I wanted to go out West and be a cowboy.

"I'd always had this dream, this romantic idea of doing it. Heck, I'd never even been on a horse. I didn't even know which end to feed, let alone know how to ride 'em, but I'd always wanted to go out West and try it. Well, to say the least, Dad wasn't too impressed with the idea. I've often told people that you sure take notice when your dad shakes his finger at you and starts telling you something, but it's even more impressive when he's standing in the Oval Office with all those flags and the President's Seal behind him!

"Obviously, his lecture didn't work, though, and I actually got his blessing before I left. Mom and Dad were both the kind of parents who were understanding enough to let their kids go out and make their own mistakes or their own successes.

"Dad let me go, and I headed west that fall. I had some contacts in Utah, so I went there first. I drove across the country to Logan, Utah, where some friends introduced me around and helped me get settled. I finally got a job on a cattle ranch in Montana. I worked there through the winter feeding cattle, learning to ride, doctoring calves, and doing all the things I'd always dreamed about doing.

"While I was there, I got a letter from Casey. He told me he was putting on a celebrity trail ride at the San Diego Country Estates with Slim Pickens, Ben Johnson, and a lot of other guys of that type. He said he'd like to have me come out for it. At that time, I wasn't familiar with Casey Tibbs. I'd grown up in the East and hadn't been around rodeo, so I didn't know anything about him. It didn't take the other cowboys around the ranch long to explain who he was, though. They filled me in on what all he'd done and were saying things like, 'My God! You got a letter from Casey Tibbs!' And so on.

"Well, then I was impressed and just tickled to death. So I wrote back to him saying something like, 'Dear Mr. Tibbs, I'm up here working for cowboy wages, two [dollars] an hour and room and board, so I can't afford the plane fare to come down to San Diego, but if you can arrange to take care of my ticket, I would be more than happy to come.'

"He sent me a ticket and I flew out and met him for the first time. Right off, he treated me like a million bucks. He was the kind of guy that you liked from the word go. There was nothing pretentious about him. He was a first-class guy from the moment I stepped off the plane. We had our ups and downs, but our friendship continued from that day.

A New Career

"On that first trip out, I stayed about a week. Soon I got to pushing Casey to get me on a bucking horse. I'd always wanted to ride one. I didn't really know what it was all about, but I figured if you're going out West to be a cowboy, you'd better try to ride a bucking horse. I figured if I was ever going to get someone to put me on one, Casey Tibbs would be the guy to do it.

"Casey didn't think that it was such a good idea, and he tried to talk me out of it. He looked at those secret service guys with their guns and all, and probably figured that if anything happened to the president's son, he was gonna get audited for sure.

"I was young and dumb and kept insisting. He kept some broncs around that he used in his bronc riding school. Finally, after a lot of hemming and hawing and my persisting, he let me get on one. The ride didn't last very long. I saw dirt pretty quick, but it was probably one of the most memorable events of my whole life.

"I was so honored that someone of his stature would do that for me. *Western Horseman* magazine got some great shots of it, with the secret service guys standing there, and it looks like a pretty tense moment. I got a couple of pictures of it, with me heading for the ground and Casey is in the background closing his eyes. He was probably thinking, 'What if I've killed the president's kid!'"

Steve continued, "As you go through life and look back, there are certain events that stand out. I've got those pictures on my wall to remind me that experience was one of the highlights of my life. All the cowboys back on the ranch wanted to know about Casey Tibbs. They saw the pictures, and to those cowboys, Casey was a living legend.

"Eventually, I moved to California and Casey and I saw a lot of each other. I'd go down to San Diego Country Estates where he was working, and I'd go to roping schools, or sometimes we'd go out and gather cattle. He was just a lot of fun to be around.

"He was always pulling some kind of prank on me. One time I went to one of his rodeo schools and he had one of those bucking machines. A couple of us kids had been riding it all morning, kind of practicing. When I got on it, Casey just walked over to the controls and turned it up full blast. Then he and the other guys that were there piled into the pickup and left for lunch. They just left me there on that thing! I knew I had to get myself loose and take a whipping on the way down, and that's what I did. But he was always pulling that kind of stuff.

"He used to call all his buddies to come and help him round up his cattle, down in the El Capitan. It was a hot, miserable ride getting down in there, and we'd take bedrolls and sleep over. The mosquitoes would eat us up at night. We'd be getting his cattle out of those thickets and stickers, and it was always hot. Casey always rode his gray horse, Troubles, who was about half bronc, and at night he'd just cut Troubles loose. He knew that ol' Troubles would head for home, and that's the way he would get out of gathering the next day. That way, we'd have to do all his work for him."

The gray horse that Steve mentioned was one of those good-looking, bad actors, mentioned earlier -- the type that Casey couldn't seem to resist. Just like World's Fair, Troubles was the kind of horse that seemed to be merely waiting for the right moment.

While Casey was managing the San Diego Country Estates he was severely injured in a roping accident while riding Troubles. He went on to tell about it: "Why I kept that sucker, I really don't know. He was twenty years old when he crippled me so bad that I dang near died. I was workin' at the Estates and I brought some horses out from South Dakota, and Troubles was one of those.

"I was ropin' on him and he got a little mad, and he didn't follow the steer. I had the steer roped and I didn't take my dallies off, and as soon as he felt things go a little haywire, he blowed up and bucked. I broke one rein and I hit the ground. I hit real easy. It didn't look that bad, but I hit just right and broke my ribs.

"I've got a video tape of it. In the video, Ben [Johnson] rides over, and he's just a slappin' his leg and throwin' back his head laughin'. I don't even think I'm hurt, but I've got one rib through my lung and four more broke.

"I went to the doctor and he said I 'possibly' had a cracked rib, so I was right back up on a horse the next day ridin' -- coughin' up blood and everything. I wound up in the hospital eventually, and it was a pretty bad deal.

"Ben used to come down quite a bit and rope, and John Miller, his nephew, used to come down and put on some schools with me. John asked me one time what I'd take for that Troubles. I said, 'Hell, you've been a good friend of mine for a long time -- I'll just give him to you.'"

"No," he said. "What I was gonna do was take up a collection from all these other guys around here, so that you can get some money for him. I know they'd pay at least a hundred dollars apiece just to get rid of him."

Laughing, Casey continued, "'Cause they had to ride him once in a while, too. Ben Johnson would just shake his head and ask me, 'Why do you keep that horse?'"

When asked what he kept him for, Casey thought for a long minute then said, "I don't know. I didn't need him. I had a whole bunch of good horses I was breakin'. But he had a lot of heart. He was just a tough ol' horse. I guess that was the reason I hated to see him go. He'd never quit you.

"He was a good, good, brush horse, and he was good with them motorcycles. They'd come into the Estates there, and there were signs posted all over, NO MOTORCYCLES, but they'd come a chug chugging in real quiet like, then they'd just gun 'er and take off down behind. They'd try to go around, but I'd just cut down through this gap, a ridin' Troubles, and boy! He'd just lay his head right up on 'em. You had to rope 'em, and I'd just rope them suckers! He hated them as much as I did. Ridin' him, I could chase them motorcycle guys down real easy. He'd track 'em better than he'd follow a cow.

"I always was bad about stickin' with a horse that I should have gotten rid of, but he was a horse that I could go almost anywhere on. Everybody else might go afoot, but I'd come back, and there would be a horse under me."

***

In April of 1974, Casey accepted a part in the film *Breakheart Pass,* with Charles Bronson, Jill Ireland, Richard Crenna, Ben Johnson, and Charles Durning. Casey played the role of Jackson, the train fireman. The film had been set to go when Casey's accident on Troubles occurred. With those five broken ribs and a punctured lung, he wasn't in any shape to ride a horse in the picture, hence, the role of the fireman. Nevertheless, before the filming ended, Jackson was thrown from a wooden trestle in the picture, and Casey did the stunt himself.

Unfortunately, it was also in 1974 that a major tragedy occurred in Casey's life: the family was forced to move Casey's mother, Florence, to a nursing home. She was failing fast and they knew that she would never again return to the home that Casey had bought for her.

Casey's sister, Katie Hannum's, voice trembled with emotion as she remembered those sad days. "Casey went through his things that Mother had kept for him at her house, clippings and memorabilia he'd sent her over the years. He stored them in big trunks in our garage. He'd quit right in the middle of doing his sorting and all, and go over and see her every day. After each visit, he'd go out back of the nursing home and lean up against the wall and cry like a baby.

"Mother recognized Casey, most of the time, but sometimes she didn't. We knew it wouldn't be long, so I told him, 'Casey, it's too expensive for you to come back and forth, and you came back now, so don't think that you have to come back again.' But he said, 'I'll be back!' and he did come back. He did so love Mother." Casey's mother, Florence Leggett Tibbs, died on July 17, 1974.

***

San Louis Rey Downs is a race horse training facility only about a thirty-five minute drive from the San Diego Country Estates. Casey kept horses of his own in training there, and he loved to go down for the morning workouts whenever possible. It was a great place to meet other horse owners and trainers, watch the horses work, and occasionally get a hot tip.

Del Mar Racetrack was not too far away, either, and Casey went there whenever he got the chance during racing season. Gambling fever never completely let go of Casey, although for periods of time he thought he had a handle on it.

He loved to get up a bet with various folks among the regular customers, but he truly had the most fun betting with the golfers, tennis

182

jocks, and businessmen at the Estates clubhouse. Every day, during the evening news hour on television, a spot featuring Joe Carcione called *The Greengrocer* ran. Each day Carcione featured one vegetable as the "vegetable of the day." He always told some interesting facts about that particular "veggie" as well as its food value, and he offered ways to prepare it. Carcione based the vegetable choice on its availability, and if it was a "good buy" because of the season, abundance of the crop, etc.

Casey began getting up bets as to which vegetable Carcione was going to choose as "the vegetable of the day" for the following day. "Tomorrow will be rutabagas, or tomorrow it'll be turnips," he'd taunt them until they covered his bet. The next day he was right, more often than not.

"Casey, how in the hell did you guess that?" they'd want to know.

"Hell! I'm a country boy," he told them. "Don't you know nothin'?"

Then he would launch into the most lengthy and detailed explanation on the planting, growing, and harvesting of the vegetable in question.

"I had to let them win once in a while, just so they wouldn't get suspicious," he admitted. "Actually, every day I was calling a friend who lived up in San Francisco, and he'd tell me what the 'vegetable of the day,' was up there. *The Greengrocer* was taped and always ran a day earlier up there. They never knew how I did it!"

Casey also took their money by betting on the soap operas. He confessed, "All I had to do was call Steve Ford and he'd tell me what was gonna happen next, 'cause he had the script -- only Steve never knew that I was bettin' on it."

***

Casey received what might well have been the biggest surprise of his life in the latter part of 1975. It came in the form of a letter from twenty-one-year-old Beth Meigs. In the letter, Beth told Casey that growing up she had not known who her biological father was. Her mother had informed her when she was sixteen years old that he, Casey Tibbs, was her father.

"I started gettin' letters from her," Casey remembered. "In part of 'em she'd be mad, and in other parts she'd be like sympathetic and almost beggin' to meet me. She said she knew I was her father because she'd won all these things in 4-H, and she knew she didn't get that ability from her mother's side of the family. She said her maiden name was Tibbs, and she just wanted to be able to say that she'd met her real father.

"About the third or fourth letter I got from her came just before I left to go to Pueblo, Colorado. I was goin' there for the opening of the development of Pueblo West. She said she was gonna be down in Southern California toward Laguna Beach, and she would meet me half way.

"When I got up in the mornin' in Colorado, I thought, 'What the hell. I'm gonna call her.'

"So I called her and I said, 'Why meet half way? Why don't you come on down to the Estates? I told her when I'd be back and that the French Connection [Renee] was with me, and so forth. Renee and I weren't married, although we were -- in a common-law sense. So I said, 'Come on down, and we can at least meet.'

"Beth had a baby daughter, Kristen, that was about two or three months old, and I'd made reservations for them at the clubhouse. I thought at least for the first night or two it would be better for them to stay there, even though we had a three-bedroom condo. I was expecting her and Kristen, so when she called and said they'd arrived, I went up to the clubhouse to get them, and there standing beside her was her mother! She'd brought her mother along for protection, I guess. It was just like a soap opera. Renee was really great about it. I'd told her the story, and she'd fixed a special dinner, but Beth's mother was very uneasy. She got sick that night and had to leave the next day.

"The next day Beth moved in with us and stayed about a week. The next time she came she brought her husband, Nick. She came several more times and then she and Nick got divorced. Later, she married Butch, who's a nice guy."

Beth's features show some resemblance to Casey's, but her strongest similarity is in her walk. Anyone who has ever seen Casey's walk, especially from the rear, will attest to its uniqueness.

***

A New Career

Wag and Faye Blesings, who also lived in Ramona, were two of Casey's good friends. Wag was one of the great rodeo cowboys, having won bareback bronc and all-around in 1946. Faye was one of the top trick riders in the profession. They'd been friends of Casey's for many, many years, and he did dearly love to find ways to pull pranks on his old friends, especially Wag. Casey loved to laugh at some of the funny things that happened with them.

One of Casey's favorite laughs on the Blesings involved a product called Willard's Water. "I don't know if you've heard about it before or not, but it came out of South Dakota," Casey began. "Some old boy came up with it. I think he just had a scam goin'. They were sellin' this water for $19.90 a pint. You take it and it's supposed to help your arthritis, and do everything else. It's supposed to be a sort of miracle cure-all. They even featured it on *20-20* and the news.

"I told Wag about it, and Wag wanted to obtain the franchise in California. So I was gonna get Wag in touch with the guy who formulated it. I finally told Wag, 'I'll get some and I'll split with you, but you've gotta mix it with distilled water. It looks like black sap in the pint bottle, but you just add a little bit to a gallon of distilled water. It won't work any other way.'

"Well, I'd taken a gallon of ol' well water from the well right out there at ol' Dale's, and put it in a distilled water jug. I didn't put even one drop of that Willard's Water stuff in it, but I took it over and gave it to ol' Wag.

"He said, 'How much of this am I supposed to drink?' So I wrote on the jug so many glasses the first thing in the morning. I put a label on it, and everything." At this point, Casey could hardly talk as he chuckled his way through the rest of the story. "Wag called me on the phone and said, 'Man! I'm feelin' better!' Yes, he was feelin' better, 'cause he didn't have nowhere to put any of that ol' beer after drinkin' all those gallons of that dad-gum water by noon time."

Casey was laughing so hard, it took him two or three tries to get out the next sentence. "Then Wag said, 'But it seems to give me a lot of gas.' He was really thinkin' the stuff was good, but all it was just that ol' well water.

"I did feel bad then, 'cause I never let Faye in on the prank. Faye's a really sharp gal. But then she told me, 'That stuff is the greatest. I can't believe how many uses there are for it. My plants have never done so good.' Well, they'd never had such good care before, either, 'cause she was sprayin' 'em with that ol' well water all the time." Casey's laughter was reaching a crescendo as he continued, "Then she said, 'I'll never buy Windex again, 'cause if you don't get the grime off the first time using this Willard's Water, the second time it just wipes right off!'"

ALCOHOL RELATED

Stu Carnall was a booking agent and personal manager who handled some of the biggest stars of country music. Over the years, Casey and Stu became close friends. Stu had a fascination with Casey's love of practical jokes, to the point of encouraging these pranks and even participating in some of them himself.

Each year, for several years during the rodeo at Reno, Stu would book Casey at the Shy Clown, a casino that catered to cowboys, and where the world champion cowboy Larry Mahan performed with his own Western band. Mahan had quite a professional outfit, and he did a fine job not only singing, but as a great ambassador of goodwill for rodeo. The Shy Clown frequently booked Red Steagall and his band also. Red became very popular in the cowboy entertainment field as well.

"I always made Stu get me top billing, even though I didn't perform at all," Casey said, chuckling as he continued. "I just gambled a little and signed autographs -- I just did it as a joke. They paid me top money just to be there, so I insisted on the top billing. People would call up and want to know, 'What time does Tibbs go on?' Well, they had my name up on top of the marquee even though it was Larry and Red who were actually playin' there. I was just havin' fun with it. Sometimes people would page me in the club and I'd get on the phone and pull a 'Gene Autry.'"

Casey put on a husky voice then said, "I'd say, 'I have laryngitis pretty bad -- I don't know if I can sing tonight or not, heh...heh...heh...' I went on like that for four years. It took me that long to put the Shy Clown out of business. But they did get packed houses during Rodeo Week.

"Well, the Shy Clown didn't have rooms, bein' just a casino and not a hotel, so I'd book a suite of rooms down at the Holiday. One night Stu and I were leavin' the casino about three o'clock in the mornin'. Right in front of the Shy Clown, all lit up, is this beautiful two-horse trailer that's to be given away as one of their jackpots. It's got every extra you could put on one. I mean, it looked like it was worth about twenty thousand dollars. So I said to Stu, 'I sure wish I'd have brought my car up here. If we had a trailer hitch, I'd take that trailer with me.' Well, Stu loved the idea and asked, 'Who do we know who's got a trailer hitch?' I said, 'C.R.'s got one, let's go get him.' C.R. Jones had this beautiful truck all covered with Winston advertising that he used to pull the Winston Scoreboard with.

"'I won this trailer and I've got to get it outta here. Can you give us a pull?' I asked him. Well, ol' C.R. goes for it. We backed old C.R.'s pickup up to the trailer and hitched it up. Now, it's three o'clock in the mornin' and we've got no lights hooked up on it or anything, but as we started to pull out, I noticed that the dressin' compartment door was floppin' open, so I had C.R. stop. I got out and went back to close it. I figured out later, that must've been when somebody spotted me. But nobody said anything about it until the next mornin' when they started missin' the trailer.

"By that time of night the valets had gone home, so we just picked a nice spot for the trailer and parked it right in front of the Holiday Hotel where everyone could see it."

Casey continued, "I had my daughter and my granddaughter with me, so I had three adjoining rooms. Beth and I were just gettin' acquainted and she didn't quite know what to make of me. Stu, as usual, hadn't brought a suitcase or anything, and he started to stretch out on top of the bed in my room, but I made him get up and go to bed in the other room because he didn't have any pajamas, and Beth and Kristen were in the next room. If I hadn't made him move to the other room, things might have turned out different.

"All three rooms were in my name, but the police came to the middle room and knocked on that door. If I had just left Stu there in that middle room, they would have arrested him instead of me. Luckily I had pajamas on, which I hardly ever wear, but I brought them this trip because my daughter and granddaughter were next door. The police wouldn't even let me change -- just handcuffed me and took me downstairs, questioning me in front of everybody."

At the jailhouse, Casey was having his problems: the policeman who'd arrested him failed to see the humor in the incident. He was not going for Casey's line when Casey told him, "I'm as innocent as a baby. I just flew into town -- how do you put a trailer hitch on an airplane?" But, of course, he'd been seen by that security guard when he got out to close the compartment door.

"Finally, the smart young cop who'd arrested me stepped out of the room for a minute," Casey went on. "The desk sergeant knew me from previous rodeos, and he came around the desk and said that as soon as they got rid of the arresting officer, they'd put me in the visitin' room, but I'd have to go through the formalities and be fingerprinted and so forth. I thought that the visitin' room sounded pretty good, but it turned out to be just another room with bare cement walls, except it had a phone in it.

"I phoned Jim Beaver, who was the manager of the Shy Clown, an ex-football player and a real good guy. But he'd put up with so much b.s. from Stu and me both, and cowboys in general, that he didn't want to hear it. I'd called him at home, but I caught him at a bad time, 'cause he was asleep."

Casey's voice rose with excitement to demonstrate the desperation he'd felt when he talked to Jim. Casey said, "'Hell, Jim, you think I'm kiddin' you, but this is really happenin'. I'm in jail! For God's sake, come and get me out! Hang on, let me put the desk sergeant on, I want you to talk to him!'

"I put the desk sergeant on and he talked to Jim awhile, and I hear him sayin, 'Uh huh, uh huh, yea... uh huh,' and finally he hung up. 'What did he say?' I asked him. The sergeant turned around and looked at me and said, 'Well, he acted like he just didn't give a damn.'"

Having struck out with Jim Beaver, Casey next thought of Sharkey, another old friend in the area. He continued, "I told the desk sergeant, 'I'll just call Sharkey to come and get me.' The sergeant looked kinda impressed, and he said, 'You know Sharkey?' I said, 'Hell yes I know

Sharkey!' Sharkey was a pretty heavy-duty name in Nevada, especially around Reno. So I called Sharkey, but he just said, 'Get a name off the wall. There has to be a bail bondsman who can get you out.' But I told him, 'Bullshit! I'm not goin' to blow two hundred dollars on bond. It was a joke! I didn't steal the trailer!' Sharkey didn't know what to think at first, but finally he called Jim Beaver at home and put the heat on him to get me out. Jim came down to the jail, and he's tired and beat. He looked at me and just scowled.

"So I signed the papers and I said to Jim, 'Mr. Beaver, I'm really sorry if this has inconvenienced you, but I did hit a couple of slot machines and I thought I might have won it.' He finally broke down and laughed."

There is a phenomenon that occurs whenever someone shows pleasure or takes delight in observing the results of a practical joke. If they keep it up, it's a near certainty that they will one day become the victim of a joke themselves. Those who take great pleasure in this kind of humor become walking targets.

Casey, of course, knew this only too well. Stu Carnall repeatedly found it out the hard way, for whenever he booked Casey anywhere in the Reno area, he usually "got had." Casey loved to tell this story: "I probably shouldn't tell this, but since I wasn't married at the time and Stu's divorced, I guess I can. We were in Reno and booked into the Shy Clown, and we've got a suite of rooms there at the Mapes. Stu always came up, and he'd never bring a suitcase or a damn thing, and then he'd decide to stay over a night -- or even two or three.

"Well, we'd been partying pretty good up in my hotel suite. We had some gals up there and we'd really been havin' a good time. Next mornin' I'm checkin' out, so I take a shower and get my suitcase all packed, and then old Stu goes in and gets in the shower. When he gets out of the shower everybody's gone but him. I left him his boots and hat...nothin' else!

"I took his clothes and sent them out to the laundry. Now he can't go home, and he's afraid he's gonna get caught. He's stuck good, and he doesn't know what to do or who to call without bein' embarrassed."

Stu remembered the feeling as he emerged from the shower. "I come out of the bathroom and look around, and all my stuff is gone. All that's left is a pair of boots and that's it! I thought, 'Well, Casey'll be back in a minute, and I turned on the TV, and I waited about an hour. It finally came to my damn head -- this sumbitch is never comin' back and I'm gonna have to call someone if I'm ever gonna get home.

"So I called Jim Beaver, the guy who owns the club, and I said, 'That son of a bitchin' Casey's done it again!' Well, Jim brings me over a pair of pants and a shirt. I get dressed and go down to the club, and there's Casey sittin' there playin' twenty-one with that damned ol' silly grin that he gets. He's lookin' over at me, you know, kinda duckin' down and everything. He'd have left me there for life!

"And one time during Rodeo Week, we were at the Peppermill, in Reno. This was after he'd busted the Shy Clown. We were playin' twenty-one, and we were actin' like we weren't together. And we started in, like we're arguing, and then get into a big fight. You know, we staged it. It's a real knock-down, drag-out thing. He picked me up and knocked the chairs over, and over the table I went. I had my hand out and I knocked those hundred dollar and twenty-five dollar chips all over the damned casino. Well, I get up and do another dive on the table, and the whole thing goes down, and here come the security.

"Casey had staged the fight so that he'd look guilty, so the security guy comes up to me and asks if I'm all right. And I said, 'Oops, my back! Don't lift me!' Casey had run out the door, and they get me up and I tell them, 'I think I'm all right, I just have some sprains -- bad sprains.'

"Well, Casey comes back in the casino right then with a shotgun, comin' after me. And here come the security guards and they're not in on this at all. He's lucky they didn't shoot him, but he's been lucky all his life. He's the luckiest son of a bitch alive, to still be alive. One of the casino managers jumped in and stopped the security guards. 'They're all right! It's a gag! It's all a gag!' But it was the talk of the town for a long time."

Eddie Nordquist was another old friend of Casey's. Their friendship went back to the days when Eddie owned the Plaza Hotel in Thermopolis, Wyoming. Eddie's own colorful past included the twenty-five years he spent as trainer for the San Francisco Giants. "I used to throw baseballs up into the crowds for them to keep as souvenirs," Eddie told me. "I remember Casey at Deadwood, South Dakota, throwing the buckles he'd won up into the crowd, just to be a showman. He threw his own buckles the way I used to throw baseballs.

"Casey and Cleo used to stay at my hotel in Thermopolis before they were married. They had to have separate rooms because she was a good Catholic. Years later I owned a bar called The Flame up on the road to Mount Rose just outside of Reno. Casey used to come up and see me when he was working at the Shy Clown. I remember I had to leave the bar one day to run down to the grocery store to get some supplies. Mine was just a small bar, and I was low on juices or some damn thing, so I left Casey there to tend bar for me. Well, hell! I came back, and there was no bartender. The money was gone, but there was a note in the till that read, 'To hell with it! I quit! Casey Tibbs.'

"Oh gawd, I could tell you stories. When I first met Casey in 1950 he was so thin that Bill Linderman said he had to wear padded sport coats so he'd look like a cowboy. I used to tease him about that a lot. I owned the Plaza Hotel there, and I was also a masseur. When Casey first came in there, he ran and jumped into the mineral baths with all his clothes on, hat, boots, and all. I've got a picture of it someplace.

"One day Casey took my station wagon and parked it in front of the whorehouse there in Thermopolis. It was a very small town, so when my wife drove past and saw it, she thought I was in there. I was working, giving treatments, but she left me after that and went to Arizona. That incident caused my divorce.

"Casey used to make movies over in Arizona at Apache Junction. I was working there at the Buckhorn Mineral Wells Resort, and he used to come by and see me. He was always pulling something on me. He put on some shows down there, too. It was crazy! He'd played so damned many jokes on me that once, when I was living with a little gal here in Reno, I wouldn't give Casey my home phone number. I was afraid of him -- he'd already wrecked my marriage. Anyway, we both knew a guy up here who got put in the penitentiary. Casey wanted my phone number, so he broke into the pen to see the guy by posing as an attorney. And by God, the cops let him in and he got the guy to give him my number."

Alcohol Related

While Casey worked at the Shy Clown in Reno, Arlo Curtis talked to him about seeking help from Alcoholics Anonymous. Arlo said, "I hadn't seen Casey in twenty-five years. When I went to see him at the Shy Clown, I asked one of the cocktail waitresses if he was there, and she told me he was back in the cafe. I looked for him but couldn't find him. Finally the waitress took me up to his table. He was having dinner with a woman and her daughter. He was drinking heavily, and he'd put on a lot of weight. I didn't even recognize him.

"I stayed around there with him for about a week, and during that time I told him about my experience with A.A. He kept asking me if I thought he was an alcoholic. I told him, 'Hell, I don't know. You'll have to answer that one yourself.' I know he had it on his mind a lot though, 'cause he kept bringin' it up and askin' me questions. I'd been the same way when I first got into A.A. I'd had it on my mind for at least seven or eight years before I ever got into it.

"I had to go take treatments before I could make it work. I'd gone to meetings before the treatments, but I didn't like 'em, and I told them so. I didn't understand them, and I don't think they would have ever helped me at all until I went to that treatment center. Till then, I was pretty green and resentful, but afterwards they made all the difference to me.

"I hope I had some influence on Casey. He at least started thinking about maybe trying A.A. out. Seeing what other people had done through the program made him believe in it, anyway. Some of those 'un-practical jokes' that he thought were funny were just miserable for everybody else. He became a real human being again, but for awhile there he sure wasn't."

Alcohol eventually became a major problem for Casey. He said that he didn't realize he was having a problem until it had gotten completely out of hand and he was forced to seek help, ultimately joining Alcoholics Anonymous.

On the other hand, he knew that his gambling was compulsive. Also, throughout his career, Casey was always inclined to give away both his money and his time. Casey visited hospitals and involved himself in charitable functions throughout his entire life. He shared the following: "If you work for nothing...you'll never be out of work."

Casey Tibbs

***

Lorrie Carnall, formerly married to Stu Carnall, also fell victim to Casey's pranks. Country music fans will remember her as Lorrie Collins of the famous Collins Kids.

Lorrie often laughed uproariously at the memories she shared. Sometimes, though, frustration was clearly evident in her voice. "Oh, what a miserable experience! It was probably the worst thing that anybody has ever done to me! And you know, he always seemed so sweet and innocent. I guess I just trusted Casey too much.

"We'd flown up to Lake Tahoe to attend a party at Harrah's. Stu went to get our car, Dean went to get his, and the French Connection [Renee] went to get Casey's. So Casey and I were left together in the terminal waiting for them. Just then a voice came over the paging system asking if anyone had lost a Saint Bernard. I was tired and didn't think much about it when I saw Casey walk over to the counter. I just figured he was going over to chat with someone while we were waiting for the cars.

"But the next moment I saw a man bringing this Saint Bernard out on a leash and handing him over to Casey. I walked over as Casey was shaking the man's hand and thanking him. I asked Casey what he was doing, and he said he'd told them it was his dog. He began rolling around on the floor, playing with this huge dog who was so glad to see anybody after probably being locked up for hours. He kept calling the dog Bernerd as he played with him.

"I told him, 'Casey, don't do this. He probably only lives a few blocks from here.' But Casey said, 'Wait till you see the expressions on everybody's faces when they pull up out front and see this dog.' It really was the biggest Saint Bernard I'd ever seen. It looked like a baby horse.

"By now, people inside the building were starting to have doubts about 'Bernerd' belonging to Casey. They had their eye on him, so he's really loving the dog, and the dog is licking his face. As it turned out, the dog was too big to fit into Casey's car, so Casey told Stu to put the dog in the back of our Lincoln and he'd follow us over to our house, and then he'd have Renee go and get his Cadillac. 'We'll pick him up, or we'll find out who he belongs to 'cause he does have a license tag on him,' Casey promised.

"Stu put the dog in the back seat of our Lincoln, but he was so big we had to roll down both back windows. His head stuck out one side of the car and his tail stuck out the other. We got on the freeway at Burbank, and headed for Woodland Hills. Casey was following us, and I kept watching him because I knew he was going to pull something. Sure enough, I saw him take another lane and head for his house in Beverly Hills while we kept going toward our house in Woodland Hills with the dog.

"We got home and I tried to call Casey, but he wouldn't answer his phone. I tried to call him for days, but he wouldn't answer. In the meantime, I'm forced to keep our dogs locked up in the garage. I'm cleaning up after them while Bernerd is eating me out of house and home. Casey had an answering machine, and finally I left a message saying that if he didn't call me back, I'd never speak to him again.

"I told him I hated him and everything else I could think of just to make him call me. We had the dumb dog for four days before Casey finally called. He was laughing, but I was telling him, 'Casey, this is not funny anymore!'

"He said he'd be over in an hour. I'm waiting and waiting, and finally this car pulls up and parks way out at the far end of our driveway. This man got out and he had on a funny hat and the wildest looking sports coat you've ever seen. He had this great big umbrella he was using as a cane, feeling his way up the driveway like a blind man. I couldn't figure out who it was. It looked like this guy was blind. When he got up to the house and I finally saw who it was, Casey thought that it was a riot, but I wasn't laughing.

"I told him, 'Casey, I've had it! You've got to find out who owns this dog.' And he told me, 'Calm down, calm down. I've got his tag right here in my pocket.' He'd pulled it off at the airport when he was rolling around on the floor. When I found out that he had that tag the whole time, it made me even madder.

"Then he said, 'Maybe we'll get a reward for finding the dog,' which he and Stu thought really funny. Then he got the owner's number from information, and I could hear Casey telling him that he'd found the dog.

He told the guy that he'd been taking real good care of him, and the man was saying things like, 'Oh, the kids have missed him so much! We didn't know where he was. We're just so happy you called. Thank you so much! It's been so long, how's he doing?'

"Then Casey said, 'He's fine except for the vet bill.' The man said, 'What vet bill?' So Casey said, 'Well, he got into a little fight and was kind of cut up a little, and we have a vet bill.... And by the way, how much do your kids love this dog?' Obviously the guy said, 'Well, they're crazy about him.' So Casey said, 'How much would you pay to get him back?' At that point, I just took the phone away from him and told the poor man where we lived which, by the way, was forty miles away from where the dog had been lost. The owner just couldn't figure out how 'Bernerd' got from Burbank to Woodland Hills. Casey thought it was the funniest thing in the whole world, but I didn't speak to him for a full month after that."

When asked about a real estate deal that involved her and Casey, Lorrie roared with laughter, then composed herself and began, "We were living on a tree farm when we found this beautiful house just south of Ventura. We made an offer through the listing agent, but the owner didn't accept it, so I asked the real estate lady to stop by so we could restructure our offer.

"Casey had come over for dinner that evening, and we were having a drink and telling him about the house. I told him that I really didn't know what to do, because the owner was being so hardnosed about the offer. So Casey volunteered, 'Why don't you let me help you with this? I'll pretend to be your real estate attorney.'

"I said emphatically, 'No, Casey! This is the house of my dreams and I don't want this messed up. Just stay out of it. Just sit there and listen, because I kind of know what I have in mind to say.'

"The owner was a real wine connoisseur, which didn't mean anything to me at the time, but it did to Stu. Stu wanted him to throw all his good wine into the deal.

"Pretty soon the real estate lady showed up, and I asked her if she'd like a drink with us and she said yes, that she'd have a martini. So I went into the other room and fixed her drink.

"When I came back into the living room with it, Casey was sitting there with this big black book with pieces of paper sticking out from it. While I was out of the room, Stu had introduced Casey as our real estate attorney. I wasn't aware of it, so I gave her the martini and said, 'Do you have any ideas on how we should structure this counter offer?' Right then Casey popped up and said, 'I do!'

"I kind of looked at him thinking, 'I asked you to stay out of this. What are you doing?' I didn't say anything, though, and she started talking to him instead of me. I finally got the drift that she thought Casey was our representative, so I excused myself from the room. I told one of our daughters to go back in there and ask Casey to come into the kitchen and help me out.

"He came in just as my daughters were feeding our animals. The girls were preparing the dogs' dishes with these little bits of dry dog food. They looked almost like sweet snacks with powdered sugar on them.

"While this project was going on, I was trying to find out from Casey what he'd told the real estate woman. While I was busy trying to get him to understand and to stop fooling around, Casey had gotten out a silver tray and was arranging some of the dog food on it. The next thing I knew, he walked into the living room with the tray full of dog food. He went straight over to the real estate lady and she grabbed a handful and started eating. I couldn't believe it! She was sitting there drinking a martini and eating dog food.

"Of course, Casey was pretending like he was eating it, and Stu had a handful on his napkin, and they were all just having a wonderful time.

"In the meantime, I'm losing my house because she's talking to Casey and doesn't even want to talk to me anymore. He was dictating the terms of this unbelievable counteroffer. It was way lower than the offer we'd made originally, plus the guy had to throw in four cases of his best wine.

"The next thing I knew she asked me if she could use my phone. She called her broker and told him, 'You've got to come over here. I've got the damndest counteroffer and you've got to hear this.' In about twenty minutes the broker showed up. The broker and the real estate lady decided they should go over to the seller's house and present him this offer.

"A half hour or so later they returned and told us that the seller accepted the offer. I called the owner and asked him if it was true that he'd really accepted it, and he was just thrilled to death with the deal.

"Anyway, they proceeded to have more martinis, more dog food, and Casey ate five of my best crystal glasses, and a good time was had by all. Especially me, because I got my house."

LOVE LOST…AND FOUND

Sharkey Begovich, a stocky, rather powerful-looking man, led a colorful life and was well established in the casino business. From the moment Stu introduced them, Casey and Sharkey became friends. From a financial point of view, the gambling environment was not the best place for Casey to spend his time, but he did have some happy times there.

"When I first met Casey," Sharkey told me, "he was still drinking, and it was really hard to control him. He gambled away whatever he could get his hands on.

"Almost any gambling addict is that way. They get stuck, and yet they're always hoping that Lady Luck is going to shine on them. I was with Casey on many, many gambling escapades. If you haven't been around a gambling addict, you're very lucky, because they'll do without food or the necessities of life just to place another bet.

"I fought him on it, though, because every time I gave him money or anything of value, it was gone the minute he got it. I only had four of his belt buckles. I gave them back to him, but he told me he got ripped off for a whole bunch of them somewhere.

"I've seen him offer to sell that one he wore all the time, the 1955 All-Around Champion, but he never did sell it, and the main reason was that people didn't want to take it away from him. I was almost like that myself once about gambling, but I finally saw the light and backed off. There were some funny things that happened with Casey, though. He was always up to something."

Stu Carnall had talked about one of these humorous occasions -- the time he took Casey out to Wally's Hot Springs, just outside Gardnerville. "You get down in that ol' hot, mineral water and soak," he told Casey, "and it'll just cook all that old bad stuff right out of your system. You'll feel like a new man."

It was in the middle of winter, and Stu described Casey sitting out there in the snow in his own little round hot tub. "You couldn't feel the cold because you got pretty warm in that hot springs water. After awhile, I went back inside the little dressing room there. While I was dressing, I spotted Casey's clothes sitting on a bench, and I remembered that time in Reno when Casey had stolen mine. So I grabbed his and just left his hat and boots, like he did to me, and got into the car and left.

"I went on over to Sharkey's, and after a while Casey showed up. He climbed out of a stranger's car there in front of Sharkey's with nothing on but his hat, boots, and a towel. He walked in and sat down at a blackjack table and signaled for the cashier to bring him a thousand. He stayed there all day, in nothing but that towel. I'd finally gotten even with him!"

***

Casey left for Belgium on March 21, 1977, for the second time in his life. He was hired to act as a consultant on the construction of an American Western street to be built in a Disneyland-type theme park in Lichtaart, Bobbejaanland. Belgium country and western singers, Bobbejaan and Josee Schoepen owned the park.

Unfortunately, Casey was badly injured while he was there when a horse turned over on him. In addition to this, more misfortune headed his way -- Casey and Renee's relationship had crumbled to the point that Renee'd made the decision to leave Casey while he was on this trip.

As to what caused the breakup, after a big sigh Renee finally answered. "Let's say that Casey was getting unstable. I think his health was declining. He was drinking much too much, and there were a lot of people hanging around him that I didn't think were good for him. Not good enough for him, really, and I didn't like that. That's what happened. I started back to work in L.A., and we just drifted apart."

Renee said, "I told Steve Ford right after Casey left for Brussels that I wouldn't be there to pick him up at the airport when he got back. Casey didn't have a car, and I left him my automobile so he could get around. He was driving me crazy, because his drinking was just too much for me.

"Yet he was such a nice guy. He deserved the best. His problem was that he was such a good-hearted guy, he just didn't know how to say no to people. That's why so many people took advantage of him. It didn't matter to Casey whether people were up or down. He still was loyal to his friends. He tried to help everybody."

When Renee began dating her husband, Frank Gonsalves, she would run into Casey from time to time at the racetrack. Frank was a successful dairyman from Artesia, California, who owned thoroughbred horses and kept a box at Del Mar. In fact, Frank and Casey had known each other years before. Casey teased Renee by saying to her, "What an insult! You left me for a dairy farmer!"

The following year after Renee left, Casey began dating Sandra Clark. Sandy, as she was known, worked at the Estates in the tennis and golf shop. At the same time Sandy and Casey were dating, Casey became involved in a new venture called Team Rodeo, an attempt to present rodeo to the public. Various cities around the country would have their own rodeo teams, and they would compete against one another in much the same manner that other professional athletes do. The players, coaches, and managers would all be salaried, as they are in other team sports. Ultimately, it was an unsuccessful endeavor. However, it did mesh with Casey's idea that rodeo needed to be presented as a sport, and not as a spectacle, if it was ever to be a financial success for the participants.

Ron Foreman was vice-president of operations for the Los Angeles Rough Riders, which was the team that Casey coached, and Ron shared some of his memories of the venture. "There were two brothers who were the driving force behind it," he began, "and a fellow by the name of Mike Shapiro ended up in charge of it. He put it together and franchised it to the team owners."

Casey called on Steve Ford to join the L.A. Rough Riders, and Steve also shared some memories on this subject. "Team Rodeo was a concept they came up with to make rodeo a team event, like football. They put guys on set salaries and contracts. Each team would then be equated with a city, so there would be home town rooting, as there is with football, baseball, and basketball.

"The other concept was to take the timed events and make them more exciting. They ran them in heats of two side-by-side competitors, somewhat like a dragstrip. They used two roping chutes at the end of the arena, with a guy from the L.A. team in one, and a guy from the Salt Lake team in the other. And they literally had drag-strip lights above the roping chutes. You'd see them flash: red-red-red, yellow, green! And they'd both take off at the same moment.

"It was a great idea. They'd gotten Casey involved as coach and manager of the L.A. team. He kept talking to me about it on the phone. And I said, 'Well, Casey, that's great, but I don't know if it's going to go,' and so forth. But he kept pumping it up, till finally they held a draft. They drafted PRCA members and college kids. Each team got to pick kids. They had the teams in L.A., Tulsa, San Antonio, Salt Lake City, and Denver. There were a total of six teams to start with, and each kid signed for a schedule of games.

"They had standings, just like a football team would. They provided all transportation and so forth. Casey talked to me and talked to me, and finally got me to sign up with the L.A. team. I was to do two things: one, to be a media representative for them, and two, team rope for them. Every one of us really loved the idea but, it was kind of champagne appetite, soda pop salaries. The guys who owned the teams just didn't have enough money to stick with it for a good three years, which it needed to make it go. The first year was successful, in the sense that we held the rodeos in all the different sites and had good attendance, but a lot of the seats were giveaways. They held a championship game at the end of the year, like an all-star game, where the top five contestants -- like the top bull riders and the top bronc riders -- competed. The event was televised, and I co-hosted it with Merv Griffin. Merv actually took an hour and a half of his show and did the All-Star Rodeo from Las Vegas.

"Everybody lost money, although most of us got paid. Toward the end, Casey and I didn't get paid because they ran out of money. I don't know how much Casey lost, but I know I was out about twenty thousand dollars. It started off the next year, but after about a month the whole thing folded. They just had too many bills, and the bill collectors were after them.

"The PRCA blacklisted, then threatened to take the cards away from the PRCA members who participated. There were some top hands, too; Bobby Del Vecchio was on the Tulsa team, and Charlie Sampson was on the Utah team. A lot of these guys who were with us went on to become world champions. Well, once the whole thing fell apart, all of the guys got their PRCA cards back. All the cowboys wanted was to be able to be on the teams and also to be able to enter the regular PRCA rodeos. But the PRCA wouldn't let them do it.

"One night in Salt Lake City, one of our bronc riders coming down from Canada somehow couldn't show, so we were short a man. Casey was drinkin' quite a bit back then, and I think he'd even been drinkin' before the rodeo. And he just said, 'Aw, hell! I'll just ride him!' He was listed as a player/coach, so they said we could substitute him in the bronc riding. Here he was, thirty pounds overweight, drinking, and he hadn't been on a bucking horse in probably ten years.

"He borrowed some guy's saddle, and he got some spurs and another guy's chaps. The saddle didn't quite fit him, and everything was not quite right, but damn, he was going to ride anyway. Well, he takes his hat off and spits in it, then pulls his hat back down on his head and calls for the gate. Now, the gate opens, and for the first couple of jumps, no one knows who's going to get the best of it. Everybody's holding their breath, but about the third jump out, Casey reaches and starts spurring that bronc like it was fifteen years earlier. I mean, it was just beautiful! He spurred the hell out of that horse.

"He made the buzzer, and it was a good ride. It surprised him, too, I think, but he got feeling so good that he waved the pickup men away, and started fanning this horse with his hat. Well, he was going to jump off like he used to do in the old days, and he jerked the flank strap off. But when he went to bail off, his horse ducked to the right on him. It just stuck him in the ground like a post. I thought he'd really hurt himself. We rubbed liniment on him for about three days -- but he rode the hair off that horse.

"It was a lot of fun traveling with Casey, and we had some real good times. Once, in Denver, a couple of the guys had gotten into some trouble in the bar downstairs in our hotel. I'll never forget how the Denver police came up and yanked us all out of our hotel rooms about three in the morning. Everybody was standing around in the hallway in their underwear.

"They wanted to identify us, 'cause they were told the trouble downstairs was with some cowboys. Casey talked to them saying, 'Come back in the morning and bring the person who's gonna identify us. He can look at our people, and if it's one of them, you can take him.'

"I truly don't know what had happened in the bar. There'd been a fight or something." Steve laughed as he said, "But the next morning we'd packed up and left the hotel by six. We were on the plane and out of there from the Denver airport by seven.

"In about 1978, after my dad was out of office, I took Casey home with me for Thanksgiving. My folks had never met him personally. They knew about him and had seen pictures and had heard all my stories and everything, but they'd not yet met him. I think that they might have been a little suspect in their initial feelings toward him. They knew he drank a little, as all the stories I brought home seemed to be, as Casey later phrased it, 'alcohol related.'

"Just to give you a little background, Mom had already been through her bout with alcohol and had started the Betty Ford Center. By that time she probably didn't have too much patience for people who got themselves into a lot of trouble by drinking.

"We were having dinner, and there was just Mom and Dad, Casey and Sandy, and me. Casey'd been tipping a little wine and was being sort of quiet. Pretty soon we started talking about the assassination attempts on Dad's life. Casey hadn't said hardly anything all evening, but about that time he looked up from his wine glass and said to my Dad, 'Mr. President, I don't know why anybody would want to shoot you. You never did anything!'

"Dad and I really broke up laughing, but Mother, who sat at the other end of the table, didn't crack a smile. She was ready to check him into the Betty Ford Center. It was one of the most classic lines to ever come out of Casey's mouth, though, and it tells you what kind of guy he'd been all his life. He could get away with saying things that might be really offensive if anyone else had said them. He had charm and charisma. Casey could take what would otherwise be a tense situation and completely disarm it."

Casey and Sandy were married on November 17, 1979, in an outdoor wedding at the San Diego Country Estates. Friends came from all over to attend the ceremony -- more than seven hundred fifty well wishers. Casey's best man was Roy Rogers. Steve Ford and Rex Allen were groomsmen. Sandra's daughter Erica was the maid of honor, her twelve-year-old son was the ring bearer, and Casey's four-year-old granddaughter was the flower girl. After the marriage ceremony, the Sons of the Pioneers performed, as did Rex Allen and Roy Rogers. The throng of guests included celebrities such as Ben Johnson, Jack Ford, Olaf Wieghorst, and David Humphries Miller. Two famous Western artists came, as well as producers, directors, actors, stunt men, and others from the picture business. A host of other well-known attendees, including cowboys from rodeo and ranches, horse trainers, gamblers, and many folks from the race horse business also attended. Casey's family members were in attendance, including his daughter Beth.

The crisp November morning began with a small threat of rain that went away to make perfect weather for a grand wedding and reception. A serving line had been set up under a giant old oak tree which had been gaily decorated in yellow ribbons. Needless to say, it was a memorable and joyous occasion.

Casey called a week or so after the wedding saying, "Damn! We were so lucky! That big oak fell apart the very next mornin'. It would've killed a bunch of us, no doubt, if it'd fallen during the deal."

The tree was estimated to be over four hundred years old. Casey concluded by saying, "I don't mean that it fell over -- that sucker broke apart and fell into pieces! I wonder if it's an omen?"

One would think that it might have been an omen, as the marriage, like the tree, fell apart in a very short time.

Casey had little to say about it other than, "She started wantin' me to change the day after we were married."

HIS OWN COUNSEL

Bad luck had come Casey's way back on March 12, 1976, when he was the Director of Western Activities at the San Diego Country Estates. One of his guest customers had fallen from a horse and been injured at a planned event. The woman filed suit against the Estates, but she had also named Casey in the suit. She claimed that Casey had mistreated the horse, whose name was Barbedwire, by allowing it to be used in rodeo events. She also claimed that Casey had failed to warn her of the horse's inclination to run.

The woman, who'd broken thirteen bones in the fall, further claimed that the horse had been bridled by only a loop around the nose. She claimed that because there was no bit, she didn't have adequate control over the animal.

Casey's real problems arose when the insurance company for the Estates told him that they considered him an independent contractor and, as such, would have to provide his own defense. This was a huge emotional and financial load that lasted over a period of several years.

The attorney for the Estates, Paul Kennerson, pointed out that the woman had previously ridden Barbedwire several times without incident and should have been aware of the horse's habits. A defense expert witness, orthopedic surgeon Chester K. Barta, also disputed the woman's claims.

Steve Ford testified for Casey, saying he had ridden the horse three or four times. He also said, "I never felt the horse was vicious or dangerous." Laurie Sommermeyer and Charles A. Taylor termed the horse "spirited" and "extra-hyper." Taylor said, "Everybody knew about Barbedwire and was advised."

"You knew when you rode him that you should be careful?" Kennerson asked.

"Yes," Taylor replied.

Casey testified before the jury and Superior Court Judge Ben W. Hamrick that he had never mistreated an animal. He was not in a financial position to hire an attorney, so he represented himself. Without benefit of an attorney and with only an eighth-grade education, he defended himself in Superior Court. When the final verdict came in, Casey Tibbs won his case.

The whole trial episode had been tremendously stressful for Casey, and he often sought relief in alcohol. Later, he said he didn't realize at the time that he was developing such a problem with it. Nevertheless, there were still friends, old and new, who were supportive of him in many ways.

He met Dean Redfield at the Del Mar Racetrack in late 1980. Dean, an older gentleman, lived in a nice home in Escondido, and the two became good friends. When Casey and Sandy separated in October of 1981, Dean invited Casey to come and live with him.

Dean and Casey shared many common interests. Both men loved to barbecue and entertain, both relished the horse races, and they liked to laugh and have fun. Their living arrangement worked out well for several years. Dean was quite a few years older than Casey and enjoyed a good laugh. Casey provided him with plenty of those, and a few anxious moments, as well.

During this time I mentioned to Casey my need to locate pasture for my herd of horses. We were riding along together on the Portola Ride when the subject came up. I told him Amy and I were really overloaded with horses, and it'd become a huge burden to feed them.

Casey immediately responded and offered to help by finding some pastureland. "I've got a lease on the El Cap, and I'm not using it," he told me. "Bring Amy down, and we'll go down in there and look it over. If it looks okay, you can just bring the horses you want to pasture and kick them in there. I'll ride down and look them over once in a while, and they should be fine."

A few days later, Amy and I drove down to meet Casey. We'd not been to Ramona in quite awhile, and we badly underestimated how long the trip would take. We were to meet him in the clubhouse at the Estates Country Club, where he would be waiting for us at the bar.

We walked into the lounge nearly an hour late. He looked up from his drink, shot us a reproachful glance, then angrily shouted at us, "You're late! And I get real mad when people are late!" And with that he ate his glass. I guess he must have been pleased to have waited, as it gave him an opportunity to -- as he so often put it -- "get into our heads a little." Well, as it turned out, the El Cap was a heaven for horses with its river, lake, oaks, waterfalls, and pastures, so we "kicked them in." We had about twenty mares and a few geldings, and this first generous offer drew Casey, Amy, and me closer together as friends.

I'd met Casey in the fifties before I'd joined the Sons of the Pioneers, while I was working in the motion picture business. This was a period when Westerns were booming, and it was on the sets of the various TV shows or feature films that we first became friends.

Casey was a huge celebrity by then, although he still had one more championship to win. He knew that I'd ridden a few bulls and bareback horses at Eldon Yoast's rodeos in California. My rodeoing was no great thing, but Casey always treated me like a champion. Somehow, I missed being "victimized" back then. He'd introduce me and say things like, "Rusty rides bulls," or "Rusty's a pretty good rodeo cowboy." Those compliments invariably made me feel good, and I'm sure Casey knew it.

***

Having been friends with Casey for so many years, it's understandable to me how Casey could have concluded that he didn't have a drinking problem. Much of the time his drinking was just great fun and went part and parcel with celebrating.

George Peck recalled, "Dean Redfield's daughter got married while Casey was still living at Dean's during his drinkin' days. I picked Casey up in my old Plymouth convertible, and we drove down together to the Ruben E. Lee restaurant in San Diego for the reception. We partied and had a real good time. When we started home, Casey decided he'd take a nap, and he went off to sleep. When we got up there around Mira Loma, it started to rain pretty hard. We still had the top down on the car, and the rain woke Casey up. He started climbing out of that convertible while we were movin'! I grabbed him by his belt and was tryin' to drive and pull him back in at the same time. Just then he hollered, 'You damn fool! I told you, you shouldn't drive. You've driven us off into the ocean and you know I can't swim!'"

On another such happy occasion, Casey and I went as guests of Rancheros Visitadores, on the Janeway Ranch in the hills above Santa Barbara, California. There were twelve or fifteen different encampments there, each with its own name, such as Adolopho, Picadores, the 4-Q, Bustardores, Rodeo, etc.

Casey and I decided that we should visit each and every one of the camps, since so many of our friends were there and we both wanted to see as many of them as possible. I took my guitar and sang a few songs at each camp, then introduced Casey to the group. There were always new riders who'd not met him, and consistently a big, loud welcome and greeting at the mention of his name. At nearly every camp we were offered a drink. We didn't want to insult our hosts by not having a drink with them when one was offered.

We really were on our best behavior, even though it had become a bit difficult for me to sing and play by the time we finally got to the last camp. It wasn't until we'd accomplished our mission of visiting every camp and were finally headed back to our own that we "lost it." Our camp was a long way off. I don't know how my guitar ever survived the trek, as it was just on a strap over my shoulder. But I do remember that it was very dark, and we never saw a single picket line until we'd fallen over it. Standing back up was no easy task in the pitch dark amid the saddles, bales of hay, and rigging bags, but we stumbled and fell our way back to our camp.

Casey had come without his bedroll, and no matter how much I insisted, he would not take part of mine. I assured him that I had an overkill of bedroll and could easily spare some, but he wouldn't hear of it.

"No, no, I'll just build the fire up real good and sleep on a bale of hay," he told me. Campfires on those trail rides were always enormous things with huge piles of oak logs stacked nearby, so there was always plenty of wood. About 4:30 that morning, I heard Casey cussing. I looked up to see him nearly fall into the fire. "My damn legs are asleep," he said. The next morning I saw that one sleeve was nearly burned off his Lee jacket.

"Casey, did you get any sleep at all?" I asked.

He looked at me with his sheepish grin and said, "My head didn't sleep at all, but my legs slept real good!"

His Own Counsel

***

At least that night when Casey and I had been wandering from camp to camp and "overtraining," there'd been no danger of hurting anyone, or of getting a DUI. Afoot way out there in the middle of those beautiful hills on the Janeway Ranch, we posed no threat to anyone but ourselves.

Back home in Escondido, however, this was not the case. Casey continued to drink and drive until he totaled his car. He went to court and somehow they failed to take away his license.

Gilbert Aguirre was the ranch foreman for all the cattle operations on Rancho Mission Viejo and The Riata Cattle Company. Gil was a good friend of Casey's, and he loaned him a shiny new Cadillac. But Casey totaled that one also about a week later.

Stan Immenschuh, who first met Casey in the forties, was a calf roper and team roper, and their trails crossed occasionally. Later, when Stan had become a racehorse trainer, their friendship started to grow. Stan said, "He used to bet on my horses quite a bit if he thought they had a chance, and we really got to know each other then. We were both drinkin' a bit in those days. I went off to New Mexico and Texas and trained in the late sixties and early seventies, and I was still drinkin' then. When I came back and quit training in '74, Casey was already livin' at the Estates.

"It was funny, because I went through the Alcohol Recovery Treatment Program at the Veteran's Hospital in La Jolla, near San Diego. I'd spent thirty days there, and I had just got out the first part of the week, on a Monday or Tuesday. That following weekend they had Congressman Duncan Hunter's barbecue at my sister-in-law's place.

"I'd parked my car in the field where we always parked, and just then Casey came drivin' in. He'd been up to Denver doin' something for the PRCA and had just gotten back in time for the barbecue. I think he'd had a few on the plane, 'cause he was feelin' pretty good.

"We had to walk over to get on the shuttle that took folks up to the big house on the hill where the barbecue was held. Somebody'd told Casey about me takin' the treatment, and he started congratulatin' me, tellin' me how good I was doin'. 'Boy!' he said, 'that's just the best thing that ever could have happened, for you to do that.'" Stan laughed as he said, "He was still drinkin', and I remember thinkin', 'You might oughta take a little dose of that yourself, Casey.' That was in July, and by the end of that year, he'd quit."

Casey finally realized he had a drinking problem after he faced some serious problems with the law. He called Steve Ford and told him, "I want to get into your mother's center. Can you help get me in?" Steve immediately began arranging to get Casey a bed in the Betty Ford Center for Recovering Alcoholics.

At that point he began attending Alcoholics Anonymous. Casey had been to A.A. many years before, but as he phrased it, "I never *got it* back then. I thought it was a way to sell books or something."

A week or so after he started with the program, he related that they called on him to stand up and share with them how he was doing. "I'm doin' great," he told them. "I only have a little glass of wine now and then."

Casey confided that he really did think they would congratulate him. But that wasn't the answer they wanted to hear, and they let him know it in clear terms. "I'd heard them say that some people could drink a little bit, and I thought they meant me, but I'd misunderstood. They straightened me out on that pretty fast, though," he said.

At this point the old champion spirit rose again in Casey, and he began to sail with the A.A. program. Casey said, "I went into A.A. to save my ass, but I found out that my ass was connected to my soul."

In mid-December of 1983, Casey started attending as many A.A. meetings as he could. Often he went to two or three meetings a day. For further support, he bought a tape player and listened to tapes of A.A. guest speakers. He took his participation in A.A. very seriously, but Casey had to have fun with everything in his life, including A.A. He felt he was doing so well with A.A. that he didn't need to go to a recovery center, so he called Steve Ford again and canceled going to The Betty Ford Center.

Early on, he explained to me that part of the A.A. program involved admitting to the other members that your alcoholism had hurt other people. "I still haven't copped out on myself yet," he admitted, "but I had them laughing the other day."

"You did?" I asked. "How'd you do that?"

"Well," he told me, "this one ol' boy got up and he didn't want to cop out on himself either, and he sounded a little mad. He said, 'I don't think I've been

212

such a bad guy,' and he started telling about all these charities that he'd donated to and so forth *and*, the guy concluded, 'I've given fourteen pints of blood at the blood bank.' Then he sat back down.

"So when it was my turn, I got up and I said, 'I kinda have to agree with what this other guy said. I don't think I've been so bad either. I haven't given any blood at the blood bank, but I *have* been donating at the sperm bank. I don't think I'm up to fourteen pints yet, but I'm workin' on it!' They laughed so hard, we like to never got the meeting goin' again."

***

When he was just a young teenager, Casey met Jo Jo Whitefeather for the first time. She was five months younger than Casey, sitting on the tailgate of her dad's pickup truck, which was parked right behind the bucking chutes at the Cheyenne Frontier Days Rodeo. Jo Jo recalled, "My dad, J.C. Bell, had some business there with friends, and I was just sitting there with two long black braids hanging down to my waist, dangling my feet off the back of that pickup.

"Casey was getting ready to ride his bronc when he looked over and saw me. He was up next, but he came over and looked at me. I just kept dangling my feet, and he grabbed a hold of those two black braids, and he said, 'Honey, don't you move, 'cause just as quick as I get off this horse, I'll be right back!'

"But my dad happened to see him, and he came over when Casey went to get on his bronc, and he said, 'Come on, come go with me.' And I said, 'No, I'm gonna wait here for awhile.' But he said, 'Now listen, I know that kid. He's wilder than hell, and I'm just not going to let you go with him!'

"So, unfortunately, I was not there when Casey got back. I didn't see Casey again for years, even though my family was all rodeo people, too. I'd read about him, and I'd seen his pictures in the papers and magazines, but it wasn't until 1983 that I saw him again at the Cheyenne Frontier Days. I'd started off the dance floor and just turned around when Casey put his arms around me. He said, 'We're dancing, lady.' So later, we reminisced on the years and all the people we both knew, then he took me to dinner the next night out at Little America.

"He took me to South Dakota to meet all his family, and we stayed there with his sister Katie for about three weeks. We went out to Mission Ridge and prowled around his family's old homestead. Now I have a basement full of stuff we hauled back from there. We loaded the car trunk full of stuff, like old horse collars and everything.

"I loved his family, and he took me all around, and I met his brother Shortlog and went over to Murphy's son's place and stayed there for quite awhile. Then we went on to Spearfish and met Ardie. They were just the greatest people on earth.

"During this time he invited me to come out to California and live out there, but my father, who was extremely close to me, became critically ill. Even for a year before that, it was very hard for me to leave him. But when my father became critical, I was by his bedside for at least fourteen hours a day until he died. So I was tied up. But I will tell you this, I have never in my life loved anyone like I loved Casey.

"His family told me once they thought that I was the one who got him to go to A.A., but I told them, 'No, Casey did that all by himself.' All I did was go to A.A. with him sometimes. I cannot tell you how many meetings we went to, and I just sat with him. We'd go at noon, at night, Fort Worth to Houston to Las Vegas or wherever we were, 'cause I traveled a whole lot with him. But he would also go to meetings on his own. He was a very, very, strong person."

Casey had to appear in court before Judge Judy Suzanne Knauf in the spring of 1984. Although he showed proof that he'd been steadily going to A.A. since mid-December of 1983, she still ordered him to apply for admittance to The Fellowship Center of Escondido for sixty days.

Casey also had been ordered to report back to the court upon completion of his sentence. As his day to appear in court approached, he prepared himself for what he was going to tell the judge. "I'm gonna lay it on her," he told me. "I'm gonna tell her how much they've helped me, and how I'm just doin' so good. And how I'm attendin' extra meetings, and that her idea to send me there really worked good."

After his day in court I asked Casey how it'd gone. Casey replied, "It went pretty good...I guess. The judge said, 'That's wonderful news. I'm really pleased to know how much it's helping. And since it's doing you so much good, here's another thirty days. That ought to help even more.'

"Damn! I talked so good, I got myself an extra thirty days!"

A WORLD OF FRIENDS

Charlie Daniels and Casey Tibbs became lifelong friends from the first moment they met. As in the case of Casey's other friends, Willie Nelson and Sharkey, it was Stu Carnall who first introduced them.

Charlie told me, "Stu brought Casey out to one of our shows at San Diego State University years ago. I'd been wanting to meet him 'cause I'd been aware of Casey Tibbs for an awful long time. I never will forget the first time I ever met him. Casey took his hat off and gave it to me with his backstage pass on it. I've still got it hanging there at the house."

When Casey was struggling financially and with some of his deepest problems with alcohol, Charlie was a true friend to him. Sometimes celebrities are asked for many things besides their time. They're frequently asked for items for charity auctions. Sometimes they just do not have anything to give.

Casey said that Charlie would always give him items to donate to the celebrity auctions whenever he was having a hard time of it. This was a big help to Casey. Plus, Charlie gave Casey's morale a boost, frequently asking Casey to join him on the road whenever he could.

Throughout his career, Casey attended numerous charity events, which kept him flying all over the country, helping to raise money in any way he could. He was generous to a fault. At one such event, Carol Johnson, known to all her friends as Annie Carol, wife of actor Ben Johnson, told her favorite story on Casey. Her wonderful laugh pealed at the memory.

"We were at this big celebrity auction in Texas raisin' money for charity. I hadn't seen Ben for a couple of hours when I happened to see Casey leanin' on the bar set up at the end of this big tent. Casey was still drinkin' back then.

"Ben had donated a pair of his old boots to the auction, and I heard them auctioning something, and I thought I'd heard Ben's name mentioned, but the price was going for around twelve hundred dollars. I wanted to say hello to Casey anyway, so I wandered over there and I said, 'Casey, I haven't seen Ben for awhile, but they're auctioning something off for twelve hundred dollars. Do you suppose that could be Ben's boots?' And Casey replied, 'Only if he's in 'em!'"

***

George Peck was a multitalented friend of Casey's. Casey often introduced him as "my private butcher." George was living with his son Greg out on one of the oldest ranches in California. Casey and Dean Redfield were still great friends, but part of their regular ritual had been to have a few drinks every evening. Casey thought it would be best if he changed his environment so that he wouldn't be tempted to drink. George Peck invited Casey to come out to the ranch and live with him.

George remembered, "Casey came out to stay with me and my son in September of 1984, and he stayed with us a little over a year. I want to say this, by gum, he slept on the floor in his bedroll the entire time he was with us. He wouldn't let me give him a bed, but he did enjoy it there. I remember that the three of us spent one Christmas there together, and it was one of the best Christmases we ever had.

"Once when Casey's girlfriend Cary came out to visit him, Casey went and rented a room out at the Quail's Inn, in San Marcos. His girlfriend was quite a wealthy society lady. I went and picked them up at the hotel and drove them down to San Juan Capistrano to see about using some of that country for a shooting location for the TV series, *The Yellow Rose*.

"Coming back, Casey told Cary, 'We're gonna stop and get some wine and cheese and go for a ride on my yacht.' And I'm drivin', but I'm thinkin' -- what yacht? So anyway, we pull into their hotel there, which is

216

right on Lake San Marcos. Casey went down to the lake and rented one of them little paddle boats.

"He handed me a ship captain's cap, and I paddled this little boat around while they drank wine and ate cheese and fed the ducks. We must've had a thousand ducks around that boat. I sure thought that it was funny, and Cary just loved it."

***

At the conclusion of the lawsuit against Casey and the Estates, where Casey defended himself and emerged victorious, he was approached by one of the attorneys who told him, "You've got a sound case against the insurance company. If I were you, I'd hire a good attorney and file a suit against them."

Superior Court Judge Ben Hamrick, during the original damages trial in '81, had even stated that the insurance firm's refusal to provide Casey with legal defense verged on "a charade."

Casey hired San Diego attorney Brian Monaghan, who told the jury before Chief U.S. District Court Judge Howard B. Turrentine, that Great American Insurance Company's refusal to defend Casey was "absolutely outrageous."

He said that Casey, with only an eighth-grade education, facing top attorneys for Great American Insurance Company, was confronted with a "terrifying" experience. Casey maintained that by being forced to act as his own lawyer, he'd spent a substantial amount of time defending himself, which resulted in the loss of motion picture work and income.

Monaghan said Casey was under such emotional stress that he fell into heavy drinking. Casey's friend, Burt Kennedy, who directed many fine films, was called as a witness. Questioned by Monaghan, Kennedy said that once a person is on Hollywood's blacklist, it's tough to get back in the employment picture. Burt said, "Tibbs, according to Hollywood gossip, was in trouble. We heard that he was drinking, raising hell, and that he had some problems."

When Casey's lawsuit against the Insurance Company for The San Diego Estates ended, he was awarded $600,000: $200,000 in compensatory damages, and $400,000 in punitive damages.

As soon as he got the first part of the money, Casey bought a condominium right next to the Equestrian Center in the Estates, with a beautiful view of the rocky hills, vast lawns, and ancient oaks. He also bought a beautiful, nearly new, yellow Cadillac from his friend Steve Long.

Now that Casey had a good deal of money again and his alcoholism was under control, things looked pretty good. Well known for his charitable ways, however, he became a soft touch for old acquaintances with hard luck stories. He loaned money freely, knowing he'd never get it back.

Knowing how reckless Casey had been with his money in the past, and realizing that he again had a considerable amount of money in his possession, Casey's friends offered advice, suggesting that he talk to an accountant about how to best protect the money he'd received from the lawsuit. But Casey opted to be his own counsel on the matter, and he seemed determined to destroy the money as fast as he could.

As smoothly as Casey's life seemed to go after receiving his big settlement from the lawsuit, he very quickly lost thirty thousand dollars in a venture he went into with a stock contractor from South Dakota. Casey bought some rodeo livestock, then arranged to pasture his rodeo bulls and bucking horses in Pamo Valley, just outside Ramona.

When Casey put his rodeo livestock from South Dakota in the pasture he used locally, however, they ate something that affected their nervous systems. The local horses had somehow been avoiding the substance, but it was highly toxic to the new stock.

Casey fought vainly to save them. He built a high steel chute in an effort to control them while he administered large doses of Thiamine, the recommended treatment. But these animals were so wild due to the illness, even approaching them caused them so much stress they destroyed the chute. All efforts to treat them seemed to be doing more harm than good and, unfortunately, many of them died, bulls and horses alike. Worse yet, some of those that lived remained spastic.

Bracken fern was suspected at first, but it was never known for sure which plant was the culprit. One veterinarian thought it might have been a plant called fiddle-neck, so named because of the scroll shape of its yellow flowers. It does grow throughout Southern California, and there was plenty of it that year in Pamo valley. None of the California-raised animals were affected, however, and it remains a mystery why Casey's animals were.

***

Bobby Christensen Jr. first introduced Claire Stewart to Casey at the 1975 National Finals in Oklahoma City. "Casey was so handsome, he was intimidating," Claire recalled. "He asked me out, but I wouldn't go out with him because I really didn't know him. A year or so later I was in Reno, and I met a lady who told me that she was from Ramona. So I asked her, 'Do you know Casey Tibbs?' and she said yes, that she'd gone to his wedding. She told me how Roy Rogers had been his best man, and that Steve Ford was a groomsman, and that the marriage had only lasted about six weeks.

"Just as a joke, I gave her my card and said, 'Why don't you give this to Casey the next time you see him?' I'd written on it, 'Let's get married. I want to meet Roy Rogers.'

"About two years later, just as I was getting ready to leave on a trip, Casey called me collect, but I refused the call. He called back, and of course he didn't remember me. I was just leaving on vacation, so we just wrote and talked to each other on the phone. Then later I went down for a visit and we started going out.

"I finally moved down there, and we were together for three years. I'm honored to be included in his life story, because he really changed my life for the better. I was in a bad situation and the move helped me out a lot, plus I met so many wonderful people through Casey.

"Everybody in the world wanted to know Casey Tibbs. They all wanted him at their weddings…or at their funerals. And he got so many calls from people who had a friend in the hospital, and they'd ask Casey to call their friend and try to make him feel better. And he would always do it.

"He told me he knew all the presidents all the way back to Herbert Hoover. He'd been invited to the White House five times. He was modest, really. He never told anybody about these things. I would drag them out of him. He told me he once had dinner up in Calgary, Canada, with Prince Charles.

"When I moved down, we didn't know each other well enough to think of marriage, so we had a rental contract that we drew up ourselves. Any time people would come over, he'd haul that contract out and show it to them and have them sign it as witnesses.

"The contract divided up the chores, but say if the gardener ran away, we'd split the gardening. I was to have full use and access to the stove, ironing board, washer, dryer, brooms, mops, etc. It was really pretty funny."

Del Mar Racetrack was in proximity, and it drew Casey like a magnet. With his money from the settlement, he went regularly and bet heavily. It was not unusual for him to bet as much as two thousand dollars at a time. His losses mounted until he'd lost nearly everything he'd won in the lawsuit. Then his troubles began with the IRS.

Claire Stewart said that Casey became quite depressed. She said, "Sometimes at the track he'd lose so much that he'd seem nearly suicidal. He lost all that money! But I still cared about him. I told him, 'Men are a dime a dozen, but you are one in a million.'"

TRAIL RIDES AND MORE

Orange County, California, has an annual historic trail ride called *El Viaje de Portola,* which is Spanish for "The Trek of Portola." It has come to be referred to affectionately as "The Portola." It's strictly a stag affair and has its serious side. There's a blessing at the mission in San Juan Capistrano honoring the memories of the great *vaquero,* early pioneers, and explorers. The ride passes through some of the most beautiful ranch country one could ever want to see. Some of the ride leads over the very trail that Gaspar de Portola rode when he took the first Spanish expedition into Alta California. Some of the campsites are on the exact spots where Portola camped, escorting Father Junipero Serra to establish the California missions.

A brotherhood evolves out of the good times the ride generates that is hard to describe. It's days of hard riding, good food, roping, music, and entertainment that often melt into the glow of a late-night or early-morning campfire. At those times the most special moments occur. Great stories, songs, and poems emerge, sometimes from where you least expect them.

Casey treasured his membership in this great ride, and he especially loved The Portola for the many good friendships that evolved from it. The Portola Ride is loaded with real-life heroes from every kind of background. All of its members are high achievers in one sense or another. Our hosts each year are Rancho Mission Viejo, the Moiso, and the O'Neil families. In its early years, the ride alternated between Rancho Mission

Viejo and the Irvine Ranch, who were our hosts. The *patrones* of this great ride are many: Gilbert Aguirre, Buck Bean, Ernie Bryant, John Curci, Bud Curtis, Tad Devine, Tony Forster, Brad Gates, Dale Johnson, Harley May and Tony Moiso our host, as well as, Robin Moore, Lauro Neri, Ken Oliphant, Bill Riffle, Bill Shattuck, Fulton Shaw, Ken Steelman, Larry Vaughn, Bill Votaw, Charley Wheeler, Bill White, Dudley Wright, and Bernardo Yorba, descendent of Sgt. Jose Antonio Yorba who rode with Gaspar de Portola and Junipero Serra in 1769.

Participants include businessmen, storeowners, land developers, ranchers, horseshoers, doctors, veterinarians, cowboys, accountants, and lawyers. Sports figures, such as Marlon McKeever, Jeff Severson, Joe Capp, and Kirk Bleven also participate. Other names who lend a hand in the fun are Baxter Black, Kim Oviatte, Jimmy Morris, Billy Hogue, and Terrell Spence. Buck Bean, one of the *patrones* who works for the Rancho Mission Viejo, is also one of the major contributors to the success of the ride.

Casey usually rode his horse Scooter on The Portola. He had nicknamed him Hobo, because Casey always hitched a ride for him with somebody coming up from San Diego, primarily because Casey had gotten so many of those DUIs back in his drinking days.

Free of responsibility for a few days, good horses, beautiful country, and good friends mix well with good booze. However, the word was out on The Portola that Casey was on the wagon for keeps. He'd been carrying around some of those big chewable vitamin C tablets, and every now and then he'd take one out and chew it. I had to laugh when I saw Casey ride up beside Tony Moiso, our host, and offer him one saying, "Would you care for an Anabuse?"

Another annual trail ride held in Southern California is the Tortuga Ride. We camped up in the hills in the back part of Camp Pendleton Marine Base, near Oceanside, California. I passed the directions along to Casey. "Just tell him to ask at the gate at Las Pulgas," they told me. "Hell, there's going to be two hundred riders with almost that many pickups and horse trailers. They'll tell him how to find us. It's easy."

When darkness came, I had been singing at the campfire for awhile and I finally said to my friends Richard Zodnick, Cap Crowl, and Joey Comia,

222

"I'm getting worried about Casey. It's not like him to say he'll be here and not show up."

But Casey had called Amy after several hours of looking for the camp and told her, "If Rusty calls checkin' on me, I'm okay, but I just couldn't find them."

A few evenings later, Casey took Amy and our daughter Jenny and me to dinner in Mission Viejo at Bobby McGees. Over dinner he told us, "They sent me up one way first, and I drove for miles and miles. And every time I asked somebody else, they sent me off on some other wild goose chase. I finally wound up over at the base stables and no one there had ever heard of the ride. But then one little kid recognized me and asked me if I'd send him a picture and I remembered that I had some in the trunk of my car, so I signed a whole bunch of pictures for them. Two hundred civilians with horses, trucks, and trailers on that base, and nobody had a clue where they were.

"But you're never gonna believe what happened to me on my way home. As I was drivin' back through Oceanside, I remembered this lady friend that I hadn't seen in quite awhile, so I called her up. She was free for the evenin' so we went out and had a nice dinner, then I got us a room in a motel that sits right down on the beach.

"Well, she knew me and she knew the rules -- no air conditioning. Breathing air conditioning air makes me sick. So in the middle of the night the room had gotten stuffy, so she just slides open the glass door along the ocean side.

"I wake up about 4:00 in the morning when I hear her sayin', 'Sir! Sir! Those are his things, sir!' I raise up and look and there's this huge, dark shape of a guy silhouetted against the gray sky outside the glass door. He's just ducking out our door, and I can see he's got my stuff bundled up in his arms. And I know there goes my World Champion All-Around Buckle! I also had close to two thousand dollars on me, and a whole bunch of credit cards that I'd just gotten.

"Well, damn! I'm out of bed like a shot, and I never sleep in anything, so I'm strip naked. I can't run when I'm in my boots with my poor old knees like they are, but barefooted, I can barely walk. So I'm just a bellowin' and yellin', 'Hey! You rotten son of a buck! Hey!' And I break out the door, and I'm right on his heels, but I dang near knock down this old lady who's walkin' her two poodles. And her eyes are big as saucers. But I'm right after him again and just bellowin' like crazy.

"Well, he runs between these two buildings, and now I'm chasin' him down along the front side of the motel. I'm runnin' the best I can but the damn gravel is killin' me, so I'm sorta half runnin' and half hoppin'. There's this low wall on my left, and it's a gray, foggy morning, and now all of a sudden I don't see him ahead of me anymore. So I was just goin' to vault this wall when this big black guy raises up from the other side. He tosses me my stuff and he says, 'Here's your things. I got him down over here, mister. I'll hold him while you call the police!'

"Right away I run right out to a lighted phone booth on Pacific Coast Highway, and I'm tryin' to dig dimes outta my pants, which ain't easy 'cause I'm holdin' everything in my arms. And trucks and cars are goin' by honkin' their horns at me.

"I finally got the cops on the phone. And the cop said, 'Are you the naked guy in the phone booth? We've had three calls on you already.'

"I should've realized that the guy who gave me back my stuff was the same guy who took it, but I was so glad to get it all back that I didn't. Everything was there, though: money, credit cards, even her purse -- everything."

***

Casey called me one morning to tell me that Bob Wheeler, his friend and racehorse trainer, had been in a serious accident and was in the hospital. "Bring your guitar and we'll go down together and cheer him up. He's in a pretty bad way," he told me.

When we arrived outside Bob's room, we could see him through the window. His bed was elevated, and he had a bar overhead to lift himself up with. He was covered with casts and bandages, and there was a big steel pin sticking through a cast on his knee. His face was badly bruised and swollen, and he'd lost some teeth.

We crouched down out of sight and Casey whispered, "Sing *Blood on the Saddle* but don't let him see you!" I strummed the first chord, and sang, "There's blood on the saddle, blood all around, and a great big puddle of blood on the ground." As soon as I started to sing, Bob grabbed the overhead bar and tried to lift himself up to look. He would raise his head up a ways, and then collapse back into the bed, laughing. Pretty soon he'd try again, but between the pain and the laughing, he'd fall back again. When he finally saw us, he looked at Casey and said, "I might have known you had something to do with this."

Another friend of Casey's in the Ramona area was a young cowboy named Danny Johns. Danny was quite an amazing person. He worked hard, rode and roped with the best of them, yet he had one leg missing, right up to the hip. With an artificial limb, he worked cattle and horses and never seemed to want any help. Casey really admired Danny's spunk and ability.

Danny was a rather quiet, nice, young guy. Once when Casey's nephew came up to visit, Casey arranged for the two of them to pick up a colt for him in Lancaster. Casey's nephew Tony was also a really nice, quiet, young man.

The trip from Ramona to Lancaster is more than two hundred miles. So before he introduced them to each other, Casey took the trouble to take each one aside and tell them a little about the other guy. He wanted them to feel at ease with each other on such a long drive.

"He's a great guy," Casey told Danny, "but he's kinda sensitive. He feels sorta left out because he's hard of hearing. But if you'll just really speak up so he can hear you and tell him a few Western stories, he'll just love it. Then he won't feel left out." He told each the same story. Neither of the boys is hearing impaired in the least.

A friend of Casey's pulled up behind the truck and trailer at a stop sign just as Danny and Tony were leaving Ramona to get the horse. When he told Casey that he could hear them shouting at each other from clear back inside his truck, Casey went to the floor laughing.

Later in the morning he called the ranch manager out in Lancaster and asked him, "Did those boys have any trouble loadin' that colt?"

"I think they must have," the manager told him, "'cause they were loadin' him into their rig way at the back of the place, but I could hear 'em yellin' clean up here at the house." Casey howled as he told the last of it.

***

About this time, Casey had been working with Jason Hagen, putting together a concept called the Los Pecos Trail Rides. Special covered wagons were built that could be easily moved, yet held king-sized beds and came equipped with battery-powered lamps.

In October of 1988, the first ride was held in the Pamo Valley, just outside Ramona, the beautiful valley surrounded by rugged mountains where Casey and I had been keeping our horses. The ride itself wound through the valley and up the rugged slopes to the very top of the Wahiti, which is a whole series of grass meadows separated by trees and rock outcroppings. Casey had even renamed the Wahiti "Mystery Mountain" because of its unique, almost magical charm. The great food, music, and dancing was followed by songs and stories around the campfire. Quite a few celebrities went on the ride, and they seemed to really enjoy themselves. The highlight of the event took place on Sunday morning by a crackling campfire with the christening and dedication of Carlyle Taylor, the daughter of Annie Lockhart Taylor and Adam Taylor.

Casey and actress Kay Lenz were the godparents. I had my guitar handy, and I sang Bob Nolan's song, *Mystery of His Way*. It was definitely a unique setting for the ceremony, and Carlyle seemed content in her mother's arms, nursing her bottle. As I was singing, one of her tiny cowboy boots fell off, and Adam retrieved it and placed it back on her foot. She gave Adam a look that seemed to say, "That's my dad. He always looks after me." She was a lucky little girl, for God had blessed her with parents like Adam and Annie, and godparents like Casey Tibbs and Kay Lenz.

GOOD NEWS...AND BAD NEWS

When The ProRodeo Hall of Fame first opened its doors, it was called the Hall of Champions. It sits on a picturesque hillside in Colorado Springs, Colorado. It's a must for anyone traveling or vacationing in the area to stop and spend some time there. The displays are great, as are the films on rodeo that are run in their comfortable theater. It's also home for the offices of the Professional Rodeo Cowboys Association, and Procom, the Professional Rodeo Cowboys telephone network.

Mike Warner was the director of the ProRodeo Hall of Fame when asked to share a few thoughts on Casey. He replied, "Casey Tibbs exemplifies the image of a true American hero. He set the standard in saddle bronc riding. His superb skill at riding the most challenging horses with apparent ease left many in awe, especially his peers.

"During the first two years that I was at The Hall of Fame, then called The Hall of Champions, I heard a lot about Casey. It seemed every other person who toured the Hall would ask me about him. They'd seen him at rodeos and wanted to know how he was. Many of them would tell us stories about him, and most were quite amusing.

"I wanted Casey to get actively involved with the Hall, but I didn't think this great American legend would take the time. Little did I know he was just waiting to be asked. Casey just didn't want to throw his weight around, or to be an imposition. After he knew we needed some help from him, our relationship grew so that as time went on Casey phoned hundreds of times. He wrote me many letters suggesting ideas for improving the Hall and for raising funds. Finally, I asked him to serve as the national fund-raising director of the Hall.

"He did an outstanding job for us, and he kept himself busy calling his friends and seeking support for the ProRodeo Hall. Casey took time out of his busy schedule to appear at many events we hosted, both here and at other locations."

In addition to his work for the Hall, Casey's life had become an almost endless chain of charity events. I am involved with a good many also, and numerous times Casey and I attended the same events. We frequently traveled together on numerous trips. Casey and I started work on this book as early as the first part of 1984. Both of us had strings of young horses in training, and in between the horses and the charities, we found it difficult to fit in writing time. But as Casey so often reminded me, *"If you work for nothing, you'll never be out of work!"*

***

"I never knew how much fun I was missing out on, until I sobered up," Casey once remarked. He'd taken to ribbing his friends who were still drinking. Whenever something went wrong, such as when someone missed his steer at a roping, Casey would chime in, *"That was definitely alcohol related!"* It wasn't that he thought he should impose his newfound sobriety on the rest of the world -- it was just more devilment and his old sense of humor finding yet another outlet.

Casey took his victory over alcoholism very seriously. He was adamant about having this part of his life story told. "If it'll help anybody else, I think we should talk about it," he told me. "I had a lot of help from the A.A. program and the Fellowship."

An enormous sense of pride in his achievement swept through the thousands of us who called ourselves Casey's friends. Many call his victory over alcohol his greatest win. As stated earlier, Casey didn't believe he had a problem with alcohol. It'd been a part of his lifestyle for so long, it seemed natural to him to continue in the mode that had always worked for him so well in the past.

He had, however, become a danger to himself and others by drinking and driving. Alcohol had adversely affected his life in many other ways, too, without him realizing it. The loss of his relationship with Renee is one example. Having some of his old friends pull back from him as his drinking became excessive is another.

Director Robert Totten, known as "T" to his friends, directed many Western films, including twelve years of the TV series, *Gunsmoke.* He met Casey at the track through their mutual friend Ray Bell. Knowing that Casey thought a great deal of T and his wife Mikki, I asked T if he would share a few memories of Casey.

"I loved Casey's humor," he began, "and I enjoyed bumping into him at the racetrack and various banquets, such as the Golden Boot Awards and so forth. But I would feel most honored if you would have me included in your book as a brother in recovery with Casey. He and I were both friends of Bill Wilson, and Bill was a good friend to a lot of great people. Aisle Nine at Hollywood Park is where the Jack-a-Dandy bar is, right on the finish line. When I ran into Casey there, his favorite thing to say to me was, 'Well partner, we're in the wrong club. This ain't the Bill Wilson Club, but it's sure good to see you!'"

***

Western artist Edd Hayes had done a remarkable bronze from a famous photograph of Casey riding on a bronc named Necktie. The statue had been modeled from the photo taken in 1958 during a rodeo at Burwell, Nebraska. Edd titled the bronze, *Cap 'n' Necktie.* Cap is the nickname that stuck to Casey from the time when he was doing his act with his black horse, Midnight. The cowboys had all teased him, calling him Captain Midnight.

The ProRodeo Hall of Fame had been planning to place a bronze monument in front of the Hall. The board decided as far back as August of 1987 that the giant bronze was to be an enlarged version of Edd Hayes' superb *Cap 'n' Necktie.* Casey was thrilled by the honor. In addition to this, many other impressive things were beginning to happen for Casey at this time.

In December of 1987, Casey was honored at the First Living Legend Dinner and Roast held at the Sahara Hotel in Las Vegas, Nevada. The program was set during National Finals Week, and the room was sold out. Knowing that he would be roasted, Casey had gotten in shape for the event by putting himself on a careful diet. He looked really sharp in his black suit and boots, and wearing his best silver-belly hat. Trimmed down to his old riding weight, everyone commented about how good he looked.

It was a gala occasion, full of laughs as Casey's friends roasted him royally. It made everyone feel great to see a sober but happy Casey looking so good and enjoying life.

A few months later, Casey was thrilled when he won the annual Ben Johnson Event at the Lazy E. Arena in Guthrie, Oklahoma. Casey's pro partner was world champion steer roper Kenny Call. Casey seemed as proud of that roping buckle as of any championship buckle he had ever won.

He put the buckle on immediately and teased all the other ropers. He told the great champion roper Don McLaughlin, who'd not been in the competition, "I wish you'd have been in it. I'd have beat you, too!" It was his first champion roping buckle, and he loved it.

***

Casey first met Suzanne Creps at the Peppermill in Reno. Suzanne was a hard-working, conscientious parent, who'd been doing her best to raise her beautiful daughters.

Life had not been easy for Suzanne. On Memorial Day in 1983, she'd lost her lovely seventeen-year-old daughter Jennifer in an automobile accident. But there was a great strength of character in Suzanne that can be seen only in those people who place a high value on their own personal integrity. She'd worked hard to provide stability and love for her two remaining daughters, Gina and Jessica.

Casey was working as celebrity host at the Peppermill during various Western events; he'd been doing this for several years. He'd also celebrity hosted at other times at the Shy Clown in Reno, and the Maxim Hotel in

Good News...and Bad News

Las Vegas. Whenever he hosted at the Peppermill, his friend Eddie Nordquist would come to see him.

Suzanne recalled, "As the years went by, at different times Casey would come in and I would observe him and harbor my own private thoughts. I remember once he came in and the place was completely quiet. There wasn't a soul in there. I knew he was a rodeo celebrity, but I didn't know that much about his life. He looked kind of forlorn and lost that day, and I remember being worried about him. I look back now and realize that I cared about him -- even though I didn't really know him."

With all the pranks Casey had played on Eddie Nordquist, Eddie had become used to keeping a sharp eye on Casey. Eddie was always looking for ways to get even, too. "Casey would beat on me with his hat, there at the bar, or step on my sore feet, 'cause I've got arthritis. Whenever he'd get too ornery, I'd say that I was going to the bathroom and then sneak out the back door and leave. Casey soon caught onto that. Then he would take my glasses off before I left the bar so that I couldn't slip away." When Casey began asking Suzanne to go out with him, Eddie saw his chance to get even.

"I told her, 'Keep away from him! If you marry Casey Tibbs, you'll be having a night job all the rest of your life just to keep him going.'"

About two weeks before their first date, Suzanne, who seldom watched television, was flipping the channels when something caught her eye. She came upon the Ben Johnson Pro Celebrity Rodeo from the Lazy E. Arena in Guthrie, Oklahoma. She tuned in just as Casey was about to rope with his pro partner, Kenny Call. She watched with interest as the two of them won the event. Afterward, Pam Minnick interviewed Casey.

Suzanne recalled, "I happened to mention to Eddie that I'd seen it, and he told Casey, 'Oh, Suzie saw you on television the other day and she thinks that's the greatest thing. Show her the buckle you won.'

"I guess he thought he was going to put the moves on me, 'cause he'd say, 'Why don't you stop by the room and I'll show you the buckle?'

"I told him, 'First of all, I would never do that. Second, it's a company rule that casino personnel are not allowed in the hotel area, and I would never break that rule. It wouldn't look very good.' But I did say, 'Someday I'll see your buckle, Casey.' This went on for a couple of days. Finally, he walked in with the buckle and slid it down the bar to me. He said, 'Well, since you won't come up and see it, I thought I'd bring it down to you.' I looked at it for a couple of minutes then gave it back to him and said, 'That's very beautiful, Casey.'

"The next night, Stu Carnall came over to talk to me. He said, 'Casey wants to know if you'll go along with us to the rodeo tonight.' I told him I had another commitment.

"A friend of mine said to me, 'You know, Suzanne, I think you really want to go to the rodeo.' The little stinker went right over to Casey and said, 'If you work real quick, this girl will go to that rodeo with you.' Casey came over and asked, 'Would you really?' So I told him yes, but he'd better not wait, that I'd have to go home and change my work clothes. He said, 'No, no! You go home and change and we'll wait for you.'

"When I got back to the casino and parked my car, Casey was waiting with the big Peppermill limousine, which I assumed was filled with customers. I jumped in, and it was empty. Then Casey climbed in and said, 'It's finally going to be just you and me tonight.'

"And that was it. We kissed before we ever got out of the parking lot. The chemistry was instantaneous. Our love was meant to be. It was destiny, and it was meant to happen exactly when it did. Casey immediately wanted to get married, and he began asking my girls how they'd feel about him as a father. It was a terrifying time for me at first.

"The whole thing really scared me. Here I'd spent all these years ignoring this man because his lifestyle was so wild and crazy. He was also very careful to tell me that he had his alcoholism in check, and that he was hoping to get his gambling under control pretty quick, too."

Eddie Nordquist said of Casey and Suzanne's relationship, "I never saw him so shook up over a woman before. He was never a chaser...much. I saw plenty of women come around after him, and women were always interested in him. But he was more of a joker than he was a chaser. I drove him out to the airport and he told me that he was in love with Suzanne. 'There's the one girl I really love,' he said. 'I wish I'd have met her years ago.'"

***

National Finals Week was always the highlight of the year for Casey. Having been virtually the Father of the National Finals, he had special interest in it; he was invariably a "host" at one of the casinos. The last few years it'd been the Maxim in Vegas, and he took his job seriously.

National Finals Week in December of 1988 should have been especially great for Casey. It had only been a year since the First Living Legend Award Dinner in Vegas where he'd been the honoree. The giant bronze of him to be placed in front of the ProRodeo Hall of Fame was already in the works, his new Ben Johnson Champion Roping Buckle was on his belt, and his lovely Suzanne was there beside him.

Suzanne had flown to Vegas from Reno to be with him during the Finals, but unfortunately, Casey came down with what he thought was the flu. He got very sick at the start of the Finals, and they were both disappointed that he was ill. They had a horrible week, which Suzanne ever after referred to as "the date from hell."

Casey tried and tried to shake it, but he just couldn't seem to get better. After the Finals, Suzanne went down to Ramona to spend New Year's with Casey. Suzanne said, "When I went down there the last of December, he was pretty sick. He hadn't been doing at all well. I was with him New Year's Eve and for the following week, and that's when I talked him into going down to Scripps and having a real good checkup. He'd been to see a doctor there in Ramona, but I wanted him to have more tests."

When Casey went to Scripps in January, he thought his flu might have turned into pneumonia. Pat Mulloy, an old friend from South Dakota, drove Casey and Suzanne down to La Jolla. He stayed there with them until Casey's physical was completed and then Pat drove them back home. On February 2, 1989, when Casey went in to get the results of his tests, Pat again drove him. Suzanne had gone back to work in Reno by this time.

Pat was present when the doctor announced the results of the tests. "We were in this little cubbyhole, you know," Pat recalled, "a typical little doctor's cubbyhole. The doc told us that Casey had cancer. He had a spot on his lungs, but he drew diagrams showing where it was in his bones too, and he told Casey what the cancer would do. He said they could do chemotherapy or they could do radiation, or they could do a combination of both. But he said, 'We can't cure it. We can only slow it up some and ease the pain.'

"He said that there really was no cure they could offer, because they couldn't determine where it had gotten started. He told Casey that the type of cancer he had usually started in the pancreas, but the tests didn't show much deterioration there."

Pat continued, "I asked the doctor then, 'What are we talking about, time wise?' Casey was sitting up on the table buttoning up his shirt, and he said, 'I suppose about ten years.' But the doc said, 'Oh, no-no-no....'"

"So I said, 'What are we talking about then…three or four years?' And the doc said, 'I doubt it.'

"And that's about all that was said, except that the doc told him he had to eat and keep his strength up. He wanted to know if Casey wanted to set up an appointment for radiation, and Casey said no. The doctor wrote him a prescription for pain pills and we left."

That day Casey called Amy and me with the bad news, yet he still couldn't help finding some humor in it. "I've got some bad news and some good news," he told us. "The bad news is the results of my tests weren't too good -- the doctor says I have cancer."

We were, of course, stunned and full of questions, and Casey said the outlook was not too good. "What's the good news?" I finally asked him.

He chuckled and said, "The doctor wants to buy my boots." Amy and I wanted to please him, and we both knew that he wanted us to laugh, but neither of us could.

"I'm goin' to whip it," he told us.

I asked him if I should tell anyone. "You might as well," he said, "because it'll get out anyway. People will only get their feelings hurt if some of 'em know and some of 'em don't. But I'm goin' to beat it."

When the annual roundup and branding took place that spring on Rancho Mission Viejo in Orange County, California, Casey was there. The O'Neil, Moiso, and Avery families once again hosted the event. Traditionally, neighbors and friends pitched in to help with the separating, branding, ear marking, castrating, and later on, vaccination of the herd. Unlike the old days when neighbors helped each other with all the hard work, today friends were invited to watch and be entertained.

234

Good News...and Bad News

Great mariachi music lent a feeling of excitement to the happy fiesta. A vibrating sound filled the air that could be felt as well as heard, caused by the bawling of hundreds of cows and calves that had been separated until the necessary work had been completed. Even the distant call of bellowing bulls could be heard at times, protesting their exclusion from the roundup.

A few young bronc riders usually held an exhibition of bronc riding skills, as well as trick roping and all the other specialty acts adding to the entertainment. There was always plenty of food, cocktails, and ice-cold beer and soft drinks on hand. When the cattle were finally turned back out and the cows and calves found each other and rejoined the bulls on the lush green hills, the festivities continued with music and dancing on into the night.

The announcer, Bob Feist, introduced Casey and asked him to say a few words to the crowd. As Casey walked over to the microphone, his pain could easily be seen. He thanked everyone for their applause and said he was glad to be there. Then he added, "Some of you may have heard that I've been sick with the big 'C.' I just want to say that you shouldn't worry about it, 'cause I'm gonna whip it."

***

Even though the Board at the Hall of Fame had approved the erection of Edd Hayes' statue of Casey back in 1987, the money for the project had been slow in coming, and time kept rolling by.

"It'd been two years since we decided to do the monumental bronze of Casey," Mike Warner recalled. "At that time I was busy trying to raise money just to keep the museum going, and I really couldn't focus my attention on the bronze sculpture. We rolled along and rolled along and talked about it, and then we got the call from Charlie Daniels and David Corlew.

"It was just a week after Casey's cancer was diagnosed," Mike recalled. "David Corlew told me, 'Casey has cancer, and we know that you've been wanting to get this bronze done. Charlie and I were wondering if we could help get it done.'

"I told him the only thing lacking was money and time -- that was about it. David said, 'Well, we can sure help with the money part of it.' From then on, we had ongoing conversations with Casey and Charlie about doing a concert to help raise money for it. Charlie didn't want to do a concert because he felt it was too risky."

Charlie Daniels remembered, "We were very much at odds as to how to get it financed because it was expensive. What we proposed was to have a testimonial dinner. We happened to have a day off in Los Angeles, so we put this thing together. I say we, but David Corlew did more on this thing than anybody else."

Steve Ford also put his efforts into the project, as did many others. The dinner cost two hundred and fifty dollars a plate and was held at the Beverly Hills Hilton on April 12, 1989. The event was a huge success. Casey's friends came from all over the country. The place was so packed it was difficult to turn around, even in the lobby. Items were donated for an auction that took place during the evening. Stock contractor Harry Vold was the auctioneer.

The bidding became so enthusiastic and generous, an announcement was made less than halfway into the auction that they'd already raised enough money to cover the costs of the bronze. That didn't slow down the bidding at all.

When Casey's boots sold for an enormous amount, it prompted Casey to turn to me with that twinkle in his eye and say, "My doctor's here. I wonder what he thinks of that -- he only offered me five hundred!"

Casey, of course, was pleased by the success of the dinner, and thrilled that the erection of the enormous bronze tribute was a certainty. Later that spring, when Mike Warner called Casey to tell him when the date of the unveiling would be, Casey told him in a disappointed tone, "You'll have to do it without me. That's the same day as the Ben Johnson Pro Celebrity Rodeo in Los Angeles. I'm on the committee for that charity program, and I promised our chairman, Ann Lockhart, that I'd be there."

Mike told Casey, "We can't have the dedication without you, Casey. We'll have to change our date." Dedication of Casey's bronze, named *The Champ,* finally arrived on a beautiful Colorado day, August 10, 1989. A possibility of rain loomed, as there often is that time of year in Colorado

236

Springs, but the silver clouds that now and then moved in front of the sun were backlit and only added an extra dimension of beauty to the event.

Only the pedestal of the giant work was visible, as the rest was covered with brown canvas. Even the contour of the statue could not be detected, for under the canvas and surrounding the bronze were hundreds of helium-filled balloons.

When the brass band completed their opening overture, Mike Warner welcomed everyone. He began the ceremony by expressing fitting thanks and a personal tribute to Casey, followed by a short history of the project.

Lewis Cryer, president of the ProRodeo Hall of Fame, was introduced, and he dedicated the statue with moving and appropriate remarks. He said in part, "I hereby dedicate *The Champ* to one of the greatest members of the Professional Rodeo Cowboys Association, nine-time world champion Casey Tibbs. It shall serve to remind this and future generations of the sacrifices endured and the challenges faced and conquered, and victories achieved by Casey during his lifelong pursuit to develop rodeo into the highly competitive sport that it is today, and *The Champ* serves as a tribute to all rodeo cowboys!"

Each of the other ceremony participants was introduced in turn, and a series of brief speeches followed, which were mostly tributes to Casey. I also sang *South Dakota Cowboy,* a song I composed about Casey.

Then Edd Hayes revealed a secret. He'd made a bronze heart and had welded it inside the chest of the bronze image of Casey. On the heart is inscribed the words, "Ride, Cowboy Ride."

At this point, Mike announced, "It's time for us to see what we've all been waiting to see." The air buzzed with excitement as a huge crane began to slowly draw off the brown canvas while the band played the thrilling *Fanfare for the Common Man,* by Aaron Copland.

People gasped as more and ever more of the magnificent statue was revealed. The colored balloons leaking out from under the rising canvas hovered around like bees waiting to enter a busy hive at the peak of the honey flow. The musicians were great to begin with, but that day they were inspired. The beautiful clear tones of the trumpets thrilled us all and seemed to be calling out... Here it is... Here it is... Here it is now.... A long moment passed as everyone stared in awe before they began to applaud and cheer.

The bronze is a remarkable piece that captures a noble bronc and a great cowboy at the perfect instant and freezes them there for all time. It is the epitome of saddle bronc riding to be admired forever. Tears brimmed over throughout the crowd in the eyes of young girls and old grizzled cowboys alike.

The great pain of Casey's cancer that could easily be seen in his face seemed to drain away, replaced by a look of pride, humility, and pure joy.

Miss Rodeo America escorted Casey to the podium. He looked into the sea of familiar faces and began to name friends that he saw there, until he realized he could not name them all. He acknowledged his family that had come from all over, as well as his daughter Beth and granddaughter Kristen.

Looking up at the statue, he said, "I must say that this wasn't my idea, but I think it was a hell of a good idea! I want to thank Charlie Daniels for saying, 'Let's get it done! Why wait!'" He spoke briefly about his dream of a new wing that would honor the great cowboys who knocked at the door but never won a championship, "...like the Teshers, Jim Like, Joe Chase...." Then he paused again, knowing that he could never name them all either.

"There is one cowboy here I'd like to introduce. Gerald Roberts, because Gerald and his brother Ken were a big help to me in my early days in rodeo. We traveled together a lot and had a lot of good times. Gerald Roberts -- former world champion cowboy," Casey said with pride and affection.

Casey then motioned for Suzanne to join him as he said, "I'd like to introduce my lady friend, my lover, my doctor, and my nurse, Suzanne Creps. Thank you, Suzanne." As Suzanne approached, Casey put his arm around her. He said, "This beautiful lady has done a lot to keep me walkin' in the last few weeks," and he gave her a kiss on the cheek.

It was a special day for Casey, and it was wonderful for the rest of us to see him honored in this way. He suffered through tremendous pain from what he had begun calling the little "c" just to be standing there that day.

But there was a look of great strength in his eyes -- a look of pride as he gazed up at the immense bronze statue and said to Edd Hayes, "Thanks for makin' me look good." And then that look of mischief danced in his eyes again, as he turned and said...**"Hell, I *was* good!"**

Photo of Casey Tibbs taken in front of the thirty-five foot bronze depicting Casey Tibbs on Necktie in front of the ProRodeo Hall of Fame, Colorado Springs, CO. (*Courtesy of the ProRodeo Hall of Fame)*

HELL, I *WAS* GOOD!

Although his last year was one spent in excruciating pain, Casey lived through it with dignity and humor. Since conventional medicine offered him nothing, he began taking an "Indian cancer cure," which Casey called "South Dakota Mud." He told Amy and me that his lungs had cleared soon after he started taking it, and his X-rays taken a month or so later confirmed the improvement. His medical report stated, "The tumor in his left lung shows a decrease in size as if it had been subjected to radiation." Since he had not been radiated, we were all hopeful.

Amy and I called him regularly to check on him, but when we'd ask if he'd eaten, his reply was usually, "Not much." Once he told us he'd eaten only a cookie.

It was over a two hundred mile round trip for us to get from our place to Casey's and back, with much of it over a treacherous winding mountain grade. Because of the distance, we pleaded with him to come and stay with us so we could help him, but he wouldn't. His daughter also asked him to come and live with her in Auburn, California, but Casey refused her also. The same offer was extended by his sister, Katie, in Fort Pierre. His good friends, Carol and Ben Johnson in Arizona, had arranged entry for him in a wonderful clinic near them and offered their home as well, but Casey refused all offers.

He finally told us, "The woman I love is going to move down here and take care of me." He wanted to live in his peaceful home in Ramona, with its huge oaks and park-like grounds outside his windows, and with the woman he loved.

He told Amy and me that he wasn't able to eat much, partially due to his inability to wait in checkout lines at the market. His pain while standing would become unbearable and he'd have to leave. In his frustration at his own weakness and pain, he said he just wanted to shout at some of the women who would pull out hands full of coupons. He'd have to walk out of the store empty handed because he could stand the pain no longer.

Because of this, and Casey's inability to cook and care for himself properly, Suzanne Creps dropped her life in Reno and moved down to be with him full time. For Casey and for those of us who were worrying about him day and night, she was a godsend and a real angel of mercy.

Suzanne had planned to work part time, knowing that they would need her income. Because she needed flexible hours, she invested several thousand dollars of her savings in a water purifier franchise, intending to sell purifiers while caring for Casey.

She saw almost immediately that she was facing an impossible task. Shopping for him and cooking his meals, then watching to see that he ate and took his vitamins, was time consuming. Casey frequently didn't want to eat, and she had to fuss at him to keep him fed. Getting his business affairs in order was a huge job, as he'd let all his bookkeeping slide. The IRS was on his case and his taxes were mounting. Answering his phone calls and mail was a big order. He also received an avalanche of cards and letters which he enjoyed, but many needed responses.

In addition to all this, he was far weaker than she'd perceived through their phone conversations. It wasn't until she saw him that she realized the full extent to which his condition had deteriorated. She was afraid to leave him alone to run errands, much less to leave him alone long enough to make a sales presentation. So, of course, she never sold even one purifier.

Before too long, Casey's old friend Stan Immenschuh stepped in to assist them. Stan had been a hospital corpsman in the Navy attached to the Marines in Okinawa, and after the war he was stationed in China. With his medical experience, he became a great asset to them. Being a loyal and helpful friend, he stood by Casey and Suzanne right to the end.

Whenever Suzanne had to run errands, Stan would come over to the condo and look after Casey in her absence. Stan's employers, Norris and Joann Patton, also knew and loved Casey, and they made it possible for Stan to take this time away from his job. Casey was out of money, but he was rich in friends.

Hell I Was Good!

Casey had stopped taking the "South Dakota Mud" and tried another type of alternative remedy he'd heard about. He later said he regretted switching around. So many friends and fans sent Casey information about alternative remedies and cures that he felt completely overwhelmed. He asked Suzanne to screen his calls and check out each proposal for him, as he just wasn't up to it.

At times he was in such pain that it was impossible for him to even visit on the phone, and he would excuse himself and hang up abruptly. At other times the pain would ease a bit, and he would dream up some sort of mischief.

We took him an audio tape that someone had given our daughter Jenny that she thought Casey would enjoy. It was a series of prank phone calls that were hilarious, and Casey loved the tape. He played it repeatedly for himself and for his guests.

He loved to call Billy Hogue and tell him that he and Suzanne were splitting up. It was Billy that had moved all her things into the condo, and he'd told Casey that the job had darn near killed him. So Casey called him frequently to tell him he should come over and move her back out.

He also called his old ranching friends, anonymously, and would inquire if they wanted to join the Society to Preserve the Mustang. He knew full well that they were up to their ears in mustangs that were eating them out of the cattle business. The louder they squalled the better he liked it.

He forced Suzanne to call Eddie Nordquist and pose as a dispatcher from the Reno Sheriff's Department. Suzanne's job was to convince Eddie that the sheriff's department was sending over a particularly obnoxious friend of Eddie's. She told him they were going to remand him over into Eddie's custody till he came up for trial. This man was a troublesome, bad-natured alcoholic. Eddie nearly cried, begging the dispatcher [Suzanne] not to bring this guy over to his home. Of course, Casey was listening in and loving every minute of it.

Casey had to elevate one leg, and he would frequently lie with one leg propped on the back of the couch or on the arm of his easy chair. Suzanne massaged his legs, and he liked to have his feet rubbed, but his pain increased day by day. He faced this with courage that is hard to imagine, and his sense of humor never left him.

Once as Amy sat on the edge of his bed rubbing his feet as he'd requested, the phone rang. Casey began chatting with an old friend, but Amy jumped up off his bed as she heard him say, "Oh, I'm just lying here in bed with Amy Richards!"

Casey Tibbs

Suzanne's job of nursing Casey was made extremely difficult by the demanding schedule Casey kept for himself. When asked to attend a function, Casey would insist, "I can suffer just as well there as here," and they would go. Casey just couldn't disappoint his friends or fans, so he went many places, many times when he should have been home in bed.

He attended the Golden Boot Awards in Los Angeles on August 5, 1989, where he was awarded the Golden Boot, presented to him by Ben Johnson. He returned immediately to San Diego for the annual Duncan Hunter Barbecue.

Only a few days after his agonizing trip to the unveiling in Colorado Springs, he attended the Ben Johnson Pro Celebrity Rodeo, held in the Los Angeles Equestrian Center. The event was a fund raiser for handicapped kids, and Casey insisted on being there to help.

Shortly after the Ben Johnson Rodeo, Casey decided to try a clinic in Oklahoma that used nutritional therapy for cancer. He was pretty weak by this time, and he was completely out of funds. Suzanne had used up all of her savings as well.

Amy revealed to some of Casey's friends just how bad his financial situation was. Their response: "You let us know what he needs... anything!" Tony Moiso and Gilbert Aguirre provided air transportation for Casey and Suzanne to the clinic in Oklahoma. We spoke to Suzanne and Casey nearly every evening while they were there, which was close to a month, and he seemed to be gaining strength. He told us, "I'm eighty percent better than I was."

Then a group in Reno put on a Casey Tibbs Reunion without consulting Casey. Again, he didn't want to disappoint those folks who would travel so far to see him, so he left the clinic never to return. He flew to the reunion, then went directly back to Ramona afterward. Suzanne could never get him to go back to the clinic where she felt he had improved so much.

A group of his friends in Orange County put on a special dinner honoring him. Casey didn't know that all the proceeds were to go toward his mounting expenses. We held our breath and were relieved when he accepted their gift of love and support. He was really touched when they finally told him, "Use this any way you want, Casey. You can put it on a horse at the track if you like!" But he didn't gamble with any of it. That money made all the difference to him. It made it possible for the hot water heater to be turned back on in his condo, for one thing.

That was just one of many money-saving measures Casey and Suzanne had been enduring.

Some of Casey's friends couldn't bear to call him for fear they would break down and cry, but we always encouraged them to call anyway. Sometimes he couldn't talk for long, but it always gave him a lift when friends and family called. Casey had that old twinkle in his eye when he told us that his old friend Charlie Beals had called. He said that when Charlie began to cry, he told him, "I don't know what you're bawlin' about -- I'm the one who's sick!"

Just as the money from his special dinner in Orange County was nearly gone, help came again by way of Gary and Evelyn Gist who owned and operated the Gist Buckle Company. They put together an event at the Sahara Hotel in Las Vegas. It was to honor Casey, and again, all the proceeds went to him. They planned it for December to coincide with the National Finals Rodeo of 1989. The event was a great deal of work, and the Gists did a beautiful job on it. Many young rodeo contestants came to the event to honor Casey, and as they met him, it was a very emotional scene.

In those last days of his life, the money that event brought him lifted much weight from his shoulders. It kept food on his table, paid his utilities, the house payments, and paid for his medication. It also enabled Suzanne to hire a tax accountant to fight Casey's mounting IRS problem, which looked like it might cost him his home. The money that was raised at the Gist event carried Suzanne and Casey right up to the time of his death. The last of it helped pay the expenses of taking him home for burial next to his parents in South Dakota.

During that last National Finals Rodeo Week of 1989, Casey went to Vegas and attended the Finals in a wheelchair, though he hated to be seen that way. He invited us to join Suzanne and him in Benny Binion's box during the rodeo. A steady stream of cowboys came by to pay their respects to Casey. Many of them were rodeo legends themselves. All were stunned and visibly shaken as they left the box, having seen their old friend in such a weakened condition. Jim Shoulders was so saddened that the tears streamed down his face.

It was a bittersweet moment for me, sitting beside my friend, watching and enjoying with him what was most obviously his last rodeo. It was also the only time I heard Casey complain. He had his leg up on the rail, keeping it elevated as he usually did, and he was rubbing it vigorously. He was actually digging his fingers deep into the muscle in a fruitless effort to gain some relief from the pain. I felt completely helpless. I said, "I'm sure sorry, Casey. I wish I could help you."

"Yeah, I know," he answered, "but there's nothin' you can do. I feel like my ass is in a vise and I can't get away from it."

Realizing how bad I was feeling for him, he tried to break the black spell by saying, "I wonder whatever happened to the 'golden years'?"

I felt even worse, so he said, "Oh well, it could be worse, Rusty. We've got the best seats in the house and we're about to see the greatest rodeo in the world!" Just then the orchestra began to play the National Anthem. I stood up and removed my hat when Casey tapped me. I turned around and he was holding his arms up towards me. "Help me up," he said.

I leaned down and said, "Casey, it's okay, everyone understands, just stay seated."

He gave me a disgusted look and said, "Are you gonna help me up, or am I gonna have to do this by myself?"

I reached down and lifted him to his feet. He looked ashen, but he held on to the rail and took off his hat. It was a tough moment, but I was proud of him.

Benny Binion wanted Casey to stay on there in Vegas with him. He told me he was prepared to see to it that Casey had care till the end, but Casey declined. He wanted to get back home as soon as possible.

Home at last in Ramona, his pain mounted day by day. Amy mentioned to him that she'd read where marijuana was sometimes used very effectively to control the pain of cancer. He shot her a look and his instantaneous response, "Say no to drugs!"

Christmas approached and the battle raged on. Victories were few and far between. Suzanne confided in us that it was becoming nearly impossible to get him up out of bed, as he was just too uncomfortable anywhere else. We learned of a chair that Casey enjoyed sitting in at the drug store in Ramona. It was comfortable and motorized so it could stand him on his feet when he needed to get up. The chair was quite expensive, and not being in a very good financial position ourselves, we called a few mutual friends. A small group of us went in together on it and gave it to him for Christmas. We put a big lavender bow on it and included a card from all of us. We were all delighted to be able to do anything for him that might bring him even a moment of pleasure.

He was too ill to get up the day we brought it to him, but he used the chair regularly after that. It allowed him to be out in the living room, and he did love it. We passed the word around that he wanted a Western-style Christmas tree, and his friends started sending small Western items to hang on it. Suzanne began decorating the tree, and Casey loved to sit in his chair supervising and giving directions.

Both Suzanne and he were really enjoying their last Christmas together. She hung miniature bits, spurs, saddles, bareback bronc riggings, bull ropes, and all manner of other unusual Western miniature items on the tree. Soon it was completely laden with them. It was beautiful, and the most unique Christmas tree imaginable.

Casey loved to sit in his chair in the living room with a fire burning in the fireplace as he stared into its flames or gazed at his Christmas tree. Many friends and family phoned him. Jim Shoulders called him in December, the day before the funeral for Benny Binion, and they enjoyed a long visit together.

He continued to talk about getting well, and Suzanne and he never acknowledged that there was any other possibility. To an outsider seeing him for the first time, his deteriorated condition was only too apparent. But Casey and Suzanne were in a "living mode," and they were not considering anything else. A visitor with Hospice training finally laid it on the line to Casey and Suzanne. She told Casey, "You're living on borrowed time. It's a miracle you're not dead already. Get your affairs in order!" Both Casey and Suzanne were devastated by the announcement. Gone was the joy they'd been feeling, and it thoroughly wrecked their holiday. Shocked by the grim reality, Casey began to speak of where he wanted his possessions to be placed. He taped his instructions on a tiny personal tape recorder, but he was without a will or trust.

Immediately after Christmas, Amy called Buck Bean at Rancho Mission Viejo. Buck alerted Tony Moiso and Gilbert Aguirre to Casey's need. Again they saw a chance to help, and they arranged for an Orange County attorney friend, Ken Steelman, to set up a living trust for him.

Fortunately, some of Casey's family were there at the time. Katie Hannum, Doc Tibbs and his lovely wife Nyla, and Beth and Kristen were there over the holiday, too. His family urged him to return home with them to South Dakota, but Casey would not consider it. He would stay in his quiet home with Suzanne. He wanted to marry Suzanne, but he was afraid the IRS would hold her responsible for his debt to them. Even though they both wanted to marry, they did not.

At Casey's request, Suzanne paid every bill that he owed, with the exception of his enormous IRS bill. That was just not possible. It was much too large. However, through much effort, Suzanne did succeed in getting it reduced by nearly half.

Life went on at the condo. His friends were busy building a ramp to enable him to leave the condo in his wheelchair in an emergency, and they visited with him, of course. Other friends made the trip down to see him. But there were also visits from a different sort of friend that Casey enjoyed. During the last two months of his illness, a coyote came through his yard every evening and stood silently gazing toward him for several minutes. Casey's interest in the coyote never seemed to bother it a bit. Casey and Suzanne began to watch for him, and he never failed to appear. Suzanne remarked to us that it was strange to her that though she looked for him, she never saw the coyote again after Casey died.

Casey kept a hummingbird feeder just outside his window, and he loved to watch the tiny birds come to feed. He'd watch the level of the fluid in the feeder, and he made sure Suzanne didn't forget to fill it. Four hummingbirds came most often, and he could recognize them. He named them Green Man, Skinny, Red Throat, and Fat Boy.

Suzanne's intense loving care never weakened, but she was weakening physically. She was losing weight and was getting very little sleep. Their friends finally persuaded her to hire a housekeeper to come once a week. Casey's constant pain had shortened his patience as well as his temper. When he wanted something, he wanted it right now, and he took to bellowing "SU—ZY" at frequent intervals. The new cleaning lady was scared to death of him. She told Suzanne that she didn't want to clean his room at all. Suzanne convinced her that she should just wait and clean it last. "Just dust and wipe down the furniture, but whatever you do, don't stand in front of the television. His favorite show is on right now. Just wait until after you're done with the rest of the room, then stand to one side of the set. Lightly wipe off the TV, then quickly do the screen last," Suzanne told her.

Well, while the poor lady was dusting the screen, she bumped the TV and the screen went blank. She threw her hands into the air, apologizing as fast as she could, then tried to turn the set back on. "Oh—Oh—Oh! I'm so sorry, Mr. Tibbs!" she wailed.

Finally she got the set back on, but as she reached to finish the job, it went off again. Twice more! The last time, she turned to face him, very puzzled. "Are you doing something to the TV?" she asked him. His eyes danced with mischief as he smiled at her and silently tapped the remote control against his cheek.

Casey had plans to spend Super Bowl Sunday watching the game and sharing a special meal with the Mulloys. It had become an annual event they'd shared over the last four or five years. That Sunday dawned clear and bright, but Suzanne was exhausted, as Casey had wakened her in the night calling out, "Help me up! I'm leaving. I've got to go to Mexico!" A week or so earlier Suzanne and Casey had discussed whether he should enter a clinic near the border close to San Diego. The clinic used the same type of therapy as the clinic in Oklahoma City. Perhaps Casey dreamed about it, but he insisted, "Get up! I've got to go!"

Suzanne convinced him to wait till morning, as she was too tired to move. In the morning he was very affectionate, hugging her and not cooperating in getting his clothes on.

"Hurry, Casey," she urged him. "The Mulloys will be here soon. You've got to get dressed!" By now, just getting him bathed and dressed took nearly two hours, and then Suzanne had to work to clear his lungs.

Casey's friend, Dr. Brown, was a physician in the Ramona area. In better days he'd sometimes joined Casey and Willie Tellam on roundups and brandings. Now he frequently dropped by to check on Casey's condition. He'd taught Suzanne a procedure to help loosen the congestion from Casey's lungs, allowing him to cough and clear them.

Suzanne was an apt student and an excellent caregiver. Dr. Brown explained that this procedure was essential, and he taught her a suctioning procedure to use when it became necessary. It was well past midday when Suzanne at last got Casey bathed, dressed, and out into the living room and into his chair. He began having great difficulty breathing, and Suzanne was helping to clear him.

That's when the Mulloys arrived. It always took considerable effort to get his lungs to clear. It was hard on Casey and difficult for Suzanne, but he always felt so much better when it finally happened. This time it wasn't working, and Suzanne worked desperately to help him, with Pat Mulloy assisting her.

Casey was struggling, and Suzanne was frantic, but it wasn't happening. "Cough, Casey, you've got to cough, or you're going to die on Super Bowl Sunday!" Suzanne recalled that she fairly shouted it at him. And he did try, but he could not clear his air passages. Slowly it became apparent that he wasn't going to be able to do it this time, and he was going to die.

Finally, Suzanne took his hand in her hands and said, "Casey, it will be okay. It's okay for you to go." She felt him relax, and a peaceful look came into his face. "Go toward the light," she told him, "and watch for the cowboy hats."

With a knowing glance, Casey looked at Suzanne and said, "OK." And he was gone.

Casey Tibbs died on January 28, 1990, at 1:10 P.M. It was just five and a half months after the unveiling of his bronze statue at the ProRodeo Hall of Fame in Colorado. He was preceded in death by his parents, his sister Regina (Murphy) Holloway, and three brothers: John (Johnny) Tibbs, Thomas (Tommy) Tibbs, and Frank (Shortlog) Tibbs. Casey was survived by his sisters Velma (Dolly) Muir, Katherine (Katie) Hannum, Ardie Cook, and brothers Ancel Tibbs, Thad (Doc) Tibbs, his daughter Beth Donley, granddaughter Kristen Donley, and his fiance, Suzanne Creps, as well as several wonderful nieces and nephews.

Casey's service was held at 2:00 on Friday Feb. 2, 1990, at the Fred Grand Arena where so many Casey Tibbs Roundup Rodeos had been held. The weather was beautiful, and over twenty-five hundred people came to remember, honor, and pay their last respects to Casey. Considering the remoteness of the location and that it was a work day, this huge turnout was indeed a tribute to the kind of person we were honoring.

A stage in the center of the arena was beautifully decorated with a mass profusion of floral displays, and life-sized photos of Casey appeared among the flowers. Cowboys and celebrities made up our equestrian honor guard. They formed a line down the arena on horseback and faced the grandstands. Each rider wore a cowboy hat and a purple scarf tied around his neck. I would be riding my horse and leading Casey's horse Scooter into the arena. I'd spoken to each one of the guard personally before the service, and I'd asked that each of them remove their hat just as Scooter passed before them.

Charlie Daniels had written a wonderful poem, and as my horse entered the arena, Red Steagall began to read it. I led Casey's horse into the arena with Casey's boots turned backward in the stirrups, his chaps draped over the seat, his familiar-shaped black hat and purple satin scarf hung from the saddle horn. As Scooter passed by the first honor guardsman and the man removed his hat, twenty-five hundred people stood up, and every hat there came off. It was an emotionally charged moment. Not only was I scheduled to speak first, I also had to sing, and I didn't think I was going to make it. I knew I needed help. Then, just as Red finished the poem, Scooter arrived in front of the stage among the flowers.

That wonderful, gentle, broke horse started to buck! Don't ask me why. He just did. For one short moment I got tickled and considered letting Scooter go on with it and wipe out the flowers and just have fun, because I knew that Casey would have loved it.

But then the young lady was there to take the horses, and my better judgment took over. I gave him a little bump on the nose to make him quit. But it gave me a lift, and it helped me through a tough time.

When Red Steagall said at the beginning of the service, "Although this is a solemn occasion, it is also a celebration of Casey's life and the things that he meant to all of us," the whole gathering burst into applause. Nearly two dozen people took part in the actual storytelling, which was often punctuated with laughter. Many of them came from distant states, as did many in the audience.

World Champions Larry Mahan, Harley May, Eddy Akridge, and Deb Copenhaver took part in the ceremony. Other speakers included Steve Ford, Alex Cord, David Corlew, Mike Warner, Louis Cryer, Bob Hunter, Rick Le Fevour, Lois Glenn, and myself. Suzanne gave her thoughts through Anne Lockhart's voice, including the following beautiful words:

In the last few moments

God gave us the serenity and wisdom

to know that it was time for you to go,

and to accept the thing we could not change.

But Casey, we learned so many things this cancer could not do…

Cancer is so limited...

It cannot cripple love,

It cannot shatter hope,

It cannot corrode faith,

It cannot eat away peace,

It cannot destroy confidence,

It cannot kill friendship,

It cannot shut out memories,

Casey Tibbs

It cannot silence courage,
It cannot invade the soul,
It cannot reduce eternal life,
It cannot quench the spirit.
We will be forever grateful for the time we shared...
Thank you for helping us learn the meaning of Unconditional Love.

"Cancer can't kill love!"

Bob Hughes, Suzanne's father, sang *You'll Never Walk Alone*. I sang *Casey Tibbs, South Dakota Cowboy,* and Eddy Akridge sang *Peace in the Valley*. Red Steagall had written a beautiful poem that he read, and I thank him for allowing us to reprint it here. He introduced it by saying, "These are my thoughts."

There wasn't much that we could do
When things were gettin' tough
Except to let you know that we were there.
Those of us whose lives were changed
Because you were our friend
Want you to know how much we really care.
A million reams of paper
Will be covered up with ink
As reporters tell the story of your rides.
And you will be remembered as the greatest of all time
And no one else will ever match your stride.
But those of us who knew you will
Remember other things.
To us you were a very special friend.
You brought us close together.
We stood on common ground
In prayerful vigil knowing it must end.
The love you gave to all of us
Can never be repaid
Unless we give that love to someone else.
And if we learned our lesson well

Hell I Was Good!

Then we must realize
That the greatest gift is giving of oneself.

When Rusty called this morning
And told me you were gone
I saddled up and rode off through the trees.

We sure will miss you, partner
But you're not hurting anymore
And knowing you're at peace puts me at ease.

Yes you lost the battle
But, my friend, you won the war.
The world's a better place 'cause you were here.
The torch you lit in everyone
Burns brighter every day.
We'll hold it high, give Casey Tibbs a cheer.

Toward the end you still
Would ride in rodeo parades
Where throngs of cheering fans would line the street.
You were so uncomfortable
But you would smile and say,
"I'm givin' back what those folks gave to me."
Casey, you're the greatest
In a hundred different ways.
Your spirit was undaunted 'till the end.
And wherever cowboys gather
And remember golden times
We'll drink a toast and think of you, old friend.

Gil Aguirre hosted the reception held at Moe and June Pratt's. We had a campfire, and we sang and talked and thought of Casey...and we laughed....

The next day, Suzanne took Casey home to Fort Pierre, South Dakota, for his funeral and burial. Steve Ford, David Corlew, and Connie Long accompanied her on the trip.

Again there was a huge turnout for the service in Fort Pierre. People came from all over to join Casey Tibbs' wonderful family to say good-bye and to honor him for the last time. His funeral was February 5, 1990, at 2:00 P.M. He was buried next to his mother in Scotty Philips Cemetery in Fort Pierre, South Dakota.

Etched in his black headstone is the same image from *The Champ* bronze of Casey riding Necktie, and the words inscribed: **"Hell, I *was* good!"**

Further Information on Casey Tibbs

For those readers who are interested in knowing more about this remarkable man, there are several locations which house numerous trophies of Casey's and personal memorabilia: A wealth of these treasures is being preserved by The Casey Tibbs Foundation.

The Casey Tibbs Foundation
Dayle Angyal (Tibbs)
P.O. Box 911 Fort Pierre,
SD 57532
www.**caseytibbs**.com

The newly opened **Casey Tibbs South Dakota Rodeo Center**
Donations to the Center may be made to:
The Casey Tibbs South Dakota Rodeo Center
PO Box 37
Fort Pierre, SD 57532
605-494-1094
Email: info@caseytibbs.com

The ProRodeo Hall of Fame in Colorado Springs, Colorado, also has a wonderful display on Casey, in addition to the larger than life size bronze of him on Necktie in front of the building.

Casey fully supported this institution during his lifetime. He consistently pressed for recognition to go to all the hard-knocking ProRodeo cowboys, even if they had never won a Championship. For information, or to send contributions in Casey's memory to support the Hall of Fame and their work, contact: www.**prorodeo**.com

The ProRodeo Hall of Fame and Museum of the American Cowboy
101 ProRodeo Drive
Colorado Springs, CO 80919

The National Cowboy Hall of Fame and Western Heritage Museum Oklahoma City, Oklahoma, has a Casey Tibbs display. Casey was inducted into their Hall of Fame many years ago. They may be contacted for information, or contributions in Casey's memory can be sent to:

The National Cowboy Hall of Fame and Western Heritage Museum
1700 Northeast 63rd Street
Oklahoma City, OK 73111

RUSTY RICHARDS WEBSITE:
www.rustyrichards.com

Rusty's **American Cowboy** CD is available at www.cdbaby.com This CD contains the song *Casey Tibbs South Dakota Cowboy*. The CD has been named one of the 25 top Western albums of all time by the Western Music Magazine.

About the Author

Rusty Richards calls himself a cowboy who sings, and he has experienced the cowboy life in almost every way possible. He began breaking horses when he was twelve, worked on ranches, and at age sixteen had his own TV show called *Song Trails with Rusty Richards*. After three years in the Marines he entered Eldon Yoast Rodeos around California, riding bulls and broncs.

Rusty worked in films as an extra and did stunt work. Through his work in films Rusty met Casey Tibbs, and they immediately became friends. While in the marines, Rusty had read about Casey. "I thought he was fantastic," Rusty said, "and I would have given anything just to have gotten a peek at him through a knothole in a fence. Little did I know that one day he would become my closest friend, and I would write his biography."

When the TV Westerns began to fade, Rusty received a call from a friend who told him The Sons of the Pioneers was looking for a tenor, and that Rusty had been recommended. Rusty joined the group and his career with them spanned twenty-one years.

While with the Sons of the Pioneers, the group was inducted into the Cowboy Hall of Fame in Oklahoma City, and the group's star was placed in the Hollywood Walk of Fame. The Smithsonian Institution declared the group a "National Treasure," and the Academy of Country Music awarded them "The Best Touring Band."

Rusty has received two Pioneer Awards in Arizona, is a Member of the Colorado Country Music Hall of Fame and a Member of the Aksarben Hall of Fame in Omaha, Nebraska. The National Western Film Festival in Ogden, Utah, presented Rusty with The Golden Lariat Award, and the California Country Music Association gave him the Pioneer Award. The National Festival of the West awarded him the Cowboy Spirit Award, and the Western Film Festival in Sonora, California, presented Rusty with The Ben Johnson Award. In 2004 Rusty was inducted into the Western Music Hall of Fame.

Other Titles by Moonlight Mesa Associates, Inc.

Western Titles:

Stoney Greywolf Bowers, *Reflections from the Wilderness*,

ISBN 9780977459360

Jere D. James, *Saving Tom Black*, ISBN 978090977459353*

Jere D. James, *Apache*, ISBN 9780977459377*

Jere D. James, *Canyon of Death*, (Forthcoming 2011)

J.R. Sanders, *The Littlest Wrangler*, ISBN 9780977459384

J.R. Sanders, *Some Gave All* (Forthcoming 2011)

Anthology: *Award-Winning Tales from the Corral*. (2012)

Suspense:

R.L. Coffield, *Northern Escape*, ISBN 9780977459346*

R.L. Coffield, *Murder in Thomas Bay*. (2011)

R.L. Coffield, *Death in the Desert*, ISBN 9780977459339*

Other:

*Life Was a Cabaret: A Tale of Two Fools, A Boat, and a Big-A** Ocean*,

ISBN 9780977459308*

www.moonlightmesaassociates.com

*Available in Kindle edition